Carolyn Hilarski, PhD
John S. Wodarski, PhD
Marvin D. Feit, PhD
Editors

Handbook of Social Work
in Child and Adolescent
Sexual Abuse

Pre-publication
REVIEWS,
COMMENTARIES,
EVALUATIONS . . .

"This book provides a vivid glimpse of the state of child and adolescent sexual abuse practice and risk-factor research. It is conceptually rich. Each topic can be consulted independently or reading the book sequentially works well for a course. This is a great resource for clinical child psychology students, social workers, and counseling educators. The book has much to offer all of us."

Barbara Thomlison, PhD
Professor of Social Work,
Institute for Children & Families at Risk,
Florida International University

"Instructive. This book contains chapters written by leading experts in child and adolescent sexual abuse and is particularly useful because it takes into account that sexual abuse is an international problem by including chapters not only from important authors in the U.S., but also Canada, Great Britain, and Australia. It is an important addition to the sexual abuse literature."

Kathleen Coulborn Faller, PhD, ACSW
Marion Elizabeth Blue Professor,
School of Social Work; Director,
Family Assessment Clinic,
The University of Michigan

NOTES FOR PROFESSIONAL LIBRARIANS
AND LIBRARY USERS

This is an original book title published by The Haworth Press, Taylor & Francis Group. Unless otherwise noted in specific chapters with attribution, materials in this book have not been previously published elsewhere in any format or language.

CONSERVATION AND PRESERVATION NOTES

All books published by The Haworth Press are printed on certified pH neutral, acid-free book grade paper. This paper meets the minimum requirements of American National Standard for Information Sciences-Permanence of Paper for Printed Material, ANSI Z39.48-1984.

DIGITAL OBJECT IDENTIFIER (DOI) LINKING

The Haworth Press is participating in reference linking for elements of our original books. (For more information on reference linking initiatives, please consult the CrossRef Web site at www.crossref.org.) When citing an element of this book such as a chapter, include the element's Digital Object Identifier (DOI) as the last item of the reference. A Digital Object Identifier is a persistent, authoritative, and unique identifier that a publisher assigns to each element of a book. Because of its persistence, DOIs will enable The Haworth Press and other publishers to link to the element referenced, and the link will not break over time. This will be a great resource in scholarly research.

Handbook of Social Work in Child and Adolescent Sexual Abuse

THE HAWORTH PRESS
Titles of Related Interest

Handbook of Social Work in Child and Adolescent Sexual Abuse

Carolyn Hilarski, PhD
John S. Wodarski, PhD
Marvin D. Feit, PhD
Editors

The Haworth Press
Taylor & Francis Group
New York • London

For more information on this book or to order, visit
http://www.haworthpress.com/store/product.asp?sku=5804

or call 1-800-HAWORTH (800-429-6784) in the United States and Canada
or (607) 722-5857 outside the United States and Canada

or contact orders@HaworthPress.com

Published by

The Haworth Press, Taylor & Francis Group, 270 Madison Avenue, New York, NY 10016.

PUBLISHER'S NOTE
The development, preparation, and publication of this work has been undertaken with great care. However, the Publisher, employees, editors, and agents of The Haworth Press are not responsible for any errors contained herein or for consequences that may ensue from use of materials or information contained in this work. The Haworth Press is committed to the dissemination of ideas and information according to the highest standards of intellectual freedom and the free exchange of ideas. Statements made and opinions expressed in this publication do not necessarily reflect the views of the Publisher, Directors, management, or staff of The Haworth Press, or an endorsement by them.

Cover design by Jennifer M. Gaska.

Library of Congress Cataloging-in-Publication Data

Handbook of social work in child and adolescent sexual abuse / Carolyn Hilarski, John Wodarski, Marvin Feit, editors.
p. cm.
ISBN: 978-0-7890-3201-0 (hard : alk. paper)
ISBN: 978-0-7890-3202-7 (soft : alk. paper)
1. Child sexual abuse. 2. Sexually abused children—Rehabilitation. 3. Sexually abused teenagers—Rehabilitation. 4. Social work with children—Handbooks, manuals, etc. 5. Social work with teenagers—Handbooks, manuals, etc. I. Hilarski, Carolyn. II. Wodarski, John S. III. Feit, Marvin D.

HV6570.H36 2007
362.76'53—dc22

2007028837

To Chris Hilarski

CONTENTS

ABOUT THE EDITORS

Carolyn Hilarski, PhD, MSW, LCSW, ACSW, is Associate Professor at SUNY Buffalo State in the Department of Social Work. With more than a decade of experience in practice, she has worked on many grant-funded research programs and currently serves on several editorial boards. Dr. Hilarski is the author of over two dozen manuscripts and books, most recently *Addiction, Assessment, and Treatment with Adolescents, Adults, and Families.*

John S. Wodarski, PhD, MSSW, is the author of numerous texts and journal publications and is Editor-in-Chief of *Stress, Trauma, and Crisis: An International Journal* and of the Social Work Series (Haworth). Besides being the recipient of over 100 foundation awards, Dr. Wodarski is a leading researcher in child and adolescent health behavior. He is Professor of Social Work at the University of Tennessee.

Marvin D. Feit, PhD, is Dean and Professor of the Norfolk State University Ethelyn R. Strong School of Social Work. In addition to being the author or co-author of many books and articles, Dr. Feit is also the co-editor of the *Journal of Social Service Research* and the founding editor of the *Journal of Health and Social Policy* (Haworth), the *Journal of Human Behavior in the Social Environment* (Haworth), and the *Journal of Evidence-Based Social Work Practice.*

Handbook of Social Work in Child and Adolescent Sexual Abuse
© 2008 by The Haworth Press, Taylor & Francis Group. All rights reserved.
doi:10.1300/5804_a

CONTRIBUTORS

Ramona Alaggia, PhD, Associate Dean and Associate Professor, University of Toronto School of Social Work, Toronto, Ontario, Canada.

Elizabeth Baksh, MSW, Social Worker, University of Central Florida, Department of Psychology, Orlando, Florida.

Fallon Cook, BSc, Research Fellow, Brain Science Institute, Swinburne University of Technology, Hawthorn, Victoria, Australia.

Grant James Devilly, PhD, Professorial Fellow, Brain Science Institute, Swinburne University of Technology, Hawthorn, Victoria, Australia.

David Dia, MSW, Assistant Professor, University of Tennessee College of Social Work, Memphis, Tennessee.

Reesa Donnelly, MS, Doctoral Student, University of Central Florida, Department of Psychology, Orlando, Florida.

Jennifer J. Freyd, PhD, Professor of Psychology, Psychology Department, University of Oregon, Eugene, Oregon.

Theresa A. Gannon, PhD, Lecturer in Forensic Psychology, Department of Psychology, Keynes College, University of Kent, Canterbury, United Kingdom.

Elizabeth Gilchrist, Professor in Forensic Psychology, Psychology Department, Keynes College, University of Kent, Canterbury, United Kingdom.

Rachel Evelyn Goldsmith, PhD, Postdoctoral Fellow, Mount Sinai School of Medicine, New York, New York.

Handbook of Social Work in Child and Adolescent Sexual Abuse
© 2008 by The Haworth Press, Taylor & Francis Group. All rights reserved.
doi:10.1300/5804_b

xiii

Donna Harrington, PhD, Professor and Doctoral Program Director, University of Maryland School of Social Work, Baltimore, Maryland.

Elizabeth Hisle-Gorman, MSW, Doctoral Candidate, University of Maryland School of Social Work, Baltimore, Maryland.

Theresa Knott, MSW, RSW, Lecturer, York University School of Social Work, Toronto, Ontario, Canada.

Debra Nelson-Gardell, PhD, Associate Professor and Chair of MSW Program, University of Alabama School of Social Work, Tuscaloosa, Alabama.

Barry Nurcombe, PhD, Senior Lecturer in Psychiatry, University of Queensland, St. Lucia, Queensland, Australia.

Kimberly Renk, PhD, Associate Professor, Department of Psychology, University of Central Florida, Orlando, Florida.

Angela Roddenberry, MS, Social Worker, Department of Psychology, University of Central Florida, Orlando, Florida.

Sharon Shin Shin Tang, MS, Doctoral Candidate, Clinical Psychology, Department of Psychology, University of Oregon, Eugene, Oregon.

Tracey Varker, PGradDip, Research Fellow, Brain Science Institute, Swinburne University of Technology, Hawthorn, Victoria, Australia.

Kimberly A. Wade, PhD, Assistant Professor in Psychology, Department of Psychology, University of Warwick, Coventry, United Kingdom.

Marie Bee Hui Yap, BA, BSc, Research Fellow, Brain Science Institute, Swinburne University of Technology, Hawthorn, Victoria, Australia.

Chapter 1

Historical Overview

Carolyn Hilarski

INTRODUCTION

Almost 40 years ago, when Henry Kempe and colleagues first described the "battered child syndrome," no clinician or researchers would have predicted how common the abuse of children actually is today, nor would they have predicted that the spectrum of maltreatment would come to include neglect [and] sexual abuse.

(Leventhal, 2000, p. 268)

The abuse of children is a phenomenon that spans the breadth of human existence (Kalichman, 1999). Throughout this time, infants were considered feeble, immoral, mentally incapable, and connected to sickness and wickedness almost universally (Colon, 2001). As such, they were and continue to be sold, exploited, neglected, murdered, mutilated, raped, and prostituted in spite of laws meant to curb this behavior (Robinson, 1995).

EARLY CIVILIZATION

This chapter explores the story of child maltreatment across millenniums and cultures with the anticipation that their chronicle will influence the reality of the future of our offspring.

Historians cite Mesopotamia as the birthplace of civilization (Van Loon, 1999). The Sumerian peoples of southern Mesopotamia settled

Handbook of Social Work in Child and Adolescent Sexual Abuse
© 2008 by The Haworth Press, Taylor & Francis Group. All rights reserved.
doi:10.1300/5804_01

in that area around 5000 BC (Polock, 2004). They used pictograms and later the cuneiform (wedge shaped) alphabet (3000 BC)—honed even further by the conquering Semites (Akkadians, Babylonians, Assyrians, 2000 BC) who adopted the Sumerian culture—to document political, religious, personal, and financial affairs (Crawford, 2004). King Lipit-Ishtar (1934-1924 BC), and later King Hammurabi (1792-1750 BC) of Babylon employed this language to elaborate on the first written laws or codes of behavior meant to defend the feeble and/or infirmed lower classes (Colon, 2001). At this time, the judicial system worked more as a mediator leaving the litigants to carry out any punishment. Unlike today, the accused was required to show proof of innocence. In ambiguous circumstances, a trial by *ordeal* was necessary. It was believed the Gods would declare the verdict by allowing the accused to live or die while, for example, being bound and thrown into a freezing river or forced to swim forty yards across an icy current[1] (Bottero, 2001).

Males owned their children, wives, animals, slaves, and all named properties. A child who did not respect his or her father was predisposed to any sort of punishment from dismemberment to death. In this circumstance, a child might lose his tongue for lying or an eye for an evil look (Sulzberger, 1915). If a man went into debt, he might settle it with his own slave labor along with his children and wives, or he could sell his children or wife into slavery or servitude to repay the debt. However Hammurabi's Code paragraph 117 limited the child or wife's enslavement to no more than three years (Weber, 1988).

Before the law codes, females were sold into marriage and sometimes to more than one man. Later, arranged dowry or contracted marriages were common (Dixon, 1992). The female child remained with her biological family until the arranged time for relocation to her husband's home where she resided until her death (Weber, 1988). The female, upon her marriage, came with assorted possessions depending upon the wealth of her family. She owned these and all other bestowed gifts throughout her life. A female wishing to divorce her husband would need to rally all of her personal resources and use any covert means such as feigning madness or denying her husband intimacy to persuade him to release her. She could sue for divorce according to Hammurabi's Code (Tinsley, 2006). However, she was required to prove deserving of such a request. If, after investigation, the husband was found guilty of, for example, abandoning his family, he was obliged according to code 137 to liberate his wife with all of her possessions in addition to giving the wife the custody of their children (Colon, 2001). However, if *she* was found guilty of, for example, waywardness or maliciousness, or her accused husband was not convicted, she would be killed (Tinsley, 2006), although the husband was granted the right to spare her if he wished (Bottero, 2001).

Hammurabi's Code also attempted to protect legitimate, illegitimate, abandoned, and unborn children from harm or losing their inheritance. For example, children abandoned to dung heaps had to be registered as part of the family so they would inherit (if they lived) their share of the father's wealth upon his death. In the event of a parent or parents' death, several codes supported the rearrangement of the family roles and wealth to ensure the maintenance and stability of the unit (Colon, 2001).

Around 550 BC, Cyrus the Great of Persia conquered Mesopotamia. The Aramaean alphabet replaced the 3,000-year-old cuneiform language (Nissen, Damerow, & Englund, 1993). Education was no longer valued, and children, women, and slaves lost their meager independence and rights under the new law of the land (Fuentes, 2004).

ANCIENT GREECE

Exploitation

It was considered a medical necessity for Greek females to engage in intercourse once menarche began (Demand, 2004). The reason for this was straightforward and related to the child's well-being. The menstrual blood had no way of leaving the body with the "orifice of egress" (hymen or maidenhead) unbroken. As a result, the menstrual blood (considered a toxic fluid) accumulated near the heart threatening the health of the virgin. Females experiencing such symptoms as bloating (understood as the filling up of lethal blood) or madness (from toxicity) might be cured with marriage and intercourse as long as the virginal state was short lived once puberty began. Thus, it was the male's duty, as the bearer of health and sanity, to have sex with the female child and the younger the better (Garland, 1986).

Bringing children into the world was no small matter in ancient Greece. Giving birth was a dangerous task and commonly took the life of the mother or child or both. This was due in part to unclean environments. However, a significant factor was the mother's age (barely pubescent). If a child was born to a child-mother without incident, a special offering was made to Artemis to celebrate the miraculous event (Garland, 1986).

The Greeks may have celebrated the miracle of birth, however, once the child was born, its chances of remaining in the family were slim. Children were commonly thrown away for the slightest of reasons (Colon, 2001). Killing the child outright (infanticide) was considered immoral (Symonds, 2005) unless the infant appeared "sickly" (Donohue, Hersen, & Ammerman, 1995). However, abandoning or "exposing" an unwanted child on a street corner was acceptable, especially if the child was female, injured at birth, or had a birth defect (Boswell, 1984). The reasons for this behavior were varied. Female children were limited in the jobs that they could do, and they needed a considerable dowry to marry. As such, it was rare for a poor or common family to raise a female child and a rich family to raise no more than one (Garland, 1986). Moreover, the purpose for raising a child was to carry on the family name, property, and genetic code—a job only the healthiest child might accomplish. It was thought foolish to waste one's time raising a defective or weak individual (Wiedemann, 1989).

In Sparta, it was customary to present all male children to the Council of Spartan Elders, which decided whether the male infant was suitable to be raised. If the child was lacking in any way, the decision to *expose* was proclaimed. The reality was that *all* children were considered a burden to their relatives and one male heir per family was deemed adequate. If a male child lived beyond the age of ten, its parents were less concerned about its mortality and more likely to relieve the family of another mouth to feed (Boswell, 1984).

Mothers had no parental privileges in ancient Greece. The individual who provided the seed possessed ownership of the children. Consequently, the child's destiny was decided by the father or his family, if the father was deceased, in concert with the state or local government, and needed to be made within the first ten days of the infant's life prior to the welcoming and naming ceremony (Garland, 1986). The child was considered nonexistent until he or she was given a name and registered. Therefore, killing or exposing an infant during this time was standard practice and bereft of moral indignation (Rawson, 1991).

A bond, often sexual, between an adult male and a young boy is referred to as pederasty. In ancient Greece, pederasty was a common behavior (Block, 2001). Indeed, according to Plato, it was acclaimed as an educational opportunity and right of passage for male citizenship (Percy, 1996). However, male adults having sex with male children had little to do with the child's formal education or becoming a better citizen and more with serving the adult pedophile's sexual needs (Verstraete, 2004). At the age of seven, free male children left their home and lived at school until the age of eighteen. This was often the ideal circumstance for a male child to be harmed or sexually abused (Block, 2001). Solon, the lawgiver (see Dixon, 1994), attempted to curb the sexual abuse of male children by proclaiming that no child would be schooled before sunrise or after sunset, however, the pedophiles prevailed (Colon, 2001).

Young females who lost their virginity, often against their will, would shame the honor of their family and, as a result, were commonly sold as slaves for prostitution (Colon, 2001).

THE ROMAN EMPIRE

Exploitation

The position of *paterfamilias* gave males complete control of their entire family's destiny (Dixon, 1992). An infant lived according to his or her potential value to the family. Youth disobedience at any time was cause for mutilation or murder (Colon, 2001). Women were not permitted to divorce, although the male could easily withdraw from the union. The paterfamilias was judge and jury of his domain and had the legal right to murder his wife for such a thing as drunkenness (Dixon, 1992).

Infants were generally inconsequential in Roman society. Poets, historians, and even physicians barely mention them. Indeed, it was inappropriate to mourn a young child's death or mark the infant's grave. The newborn or toddler's mortality rate was so high that it was hardly worth taking the time to attach or even formulate a word to describe this time of life. Moreover, one never knew when one might have to sell or expose a child owing to indigent circumstances (Martin, 2005). Children were raised, at great expense, to carry on the bloodline and to mind their parents in old age. If an individual was childless, patron slaves or kin-friends often assumed the role of progeny and accepted the cultural responsibilities that went with that position (Colon, 2001).

Roman literature cites many examples of the sexual abuse of males and females. To illustrate, it was, at least in theory, illegal according to Roman law to engage in coitus unless you were married, with a slave, or paying for the service (McGinn, 1998). Incest, sodomy, rape, and abduction were additional criminal acts and the age of the victim was of little consequence. If a child appeared complicit with an unlawful action (e.g., complied out of fear), he or she was not a victim but a collaborator and therefore given the same punishment as the perpetrator (Killias, 1991). The type of penalty faced by the adult had to do with the actual crime and not the fact that he or she was hurting and abusing a child. If the child happened to be perceived as a victim, then he or she might be protected as an adult. For example:

> We hear of one case where a mother is alleged to have conceived an unnatural passion for her son, thus driving him to suicide; she was exiled for ten years, to protect her [other] son. (Robinson, 1995, p. 56)

Abduction

The apprehending of a person for sexual purposes was a capital crime and severely punished in the Roman Empire (Robinson, 1995). All participating parties were punished.

> If willing agreement is discovered in the [abducted] girl, she shall be punished with the same severity as her ravisher, since impunity must not be granted even to those girls who are ravished against their will, when they could have kept themselves chaste at home up to the time of marriage, and when if the doors were broken by the audacity of the ravisher, the girls could have obtained the aid of neighbors by their cries, and could have

defended themselves by all their efforts. But, we impose a lighter penalty on those [unwilling] girls. (Robinson, 1995, p. 72)

The "ravishers," if convicted, were not allowed to appeal their death sentence. Moreover, their coconspirators (e.g., the victims) received the same sentence unless they were slaves (in which case they were commonly burned at the stake), or *other* caregivers (e.g., they might have molten lead poured down their throats), or parents (often banished). Persons *convicted* (rarely happened) of abducting slaves or a freed women were given much lighter sentences, often a small monetary compensation (Robinson, 2003).

Pederasty (Sodomy)

Most Romans viewed pederasty as a common and inconsequential sexual activity rather than couching it in an educational or spiritual venue as in the Greek era (Verstraete, 2004). It was not illegal and generally esteemed (Boswell, 1980).

Incest

It was legal for a Roman to marry a close relative[2] and illegal to wed a dissimilar class or ancestry. Children born of mixed lineage were illegitimate and not eligible to register as a Roman citizen. The Romans and Greeks went to great lengths to keep their bloodlines pure. The Greeks in particular ignored incest laws to preserve the Hellenic ancestry (Ottenheimer, 1996). An ancient wedding invitation illustrates this:

Herais invites you to the marriage of her children, at home, the 5th, starting at the ninth hour. (Colon, 2001, p. 95)[3]

Another example is a husband who is out of town on business and writing to his wife, whom he refers to as his *sister:*

Know that I am still in Alexandria. . . . I ask and beg you to take good care of our baby son, and as soon as I receive payment, I will send it to you. If you are delivered of child, if it is a boy keep it, if a girl discard it. (Colon, 2001, p. 95)[4]

This letter further reveals the attitude regarding female children and exposure.

Enslavement

The slaves of Rome were not all captives of war or children of slaves. Many were Roman citizens. Parents unable to support their children often sold them into slavery, left them exposed for others to use at will, or traded them as payment for outstanding debts (Dixon, 1992).

Abandoned male infants were excellent candidates for castration and for the life of a eunuch slave. Exclusive Roman homes purchased these children at great cost. Their worth as sodomy play toys was considerable (Boswell, 1980). It was illegal to engage in homoerotic sex with a free man; thus, a male castrated slave was a fine solution for a master attracted to buggery (Daniel, 1994). According to the famous physician Paulus Aegineta, castration should be completed by placing a very young infant in a hot water bath to aid the testicles to descend and become quite soft at which time they would be squeezed until they disappeared (Colon, 2001).

Very young infants found exposed were often sold into slavery as sexual "pets" or used for begging after they were deliberately mutilated. So many children were exposed as infants and forgotten by their natural parents that it was common for fathers to "bed" their daughters or sodomize their biological sons (Boswell, 1998).

A marriage or a family relationship was not an option for a slave. Any child born to a female slave belonged to the slave's owner even after she was freed (Dixon, 1992).

THE MIDDLE AGES (500 TO 1400)

In the Medieval era, children were sold into slavery or prostitution on a universal and monumental scale to settle debts or for monetary gain. As infants, they were murdered, given to religious sects as payment for heavenly access, or employed as young as four years of age. Across Europe, two out of three children died before the age of six because of poor and laborious working or housing conditions, malnutrition, neglect, disease, or slaughter (Donohue et al., 1995). The infant mortality rate was so high in the Native American communities that the naming ritual was delayed until the age of ten (Trigger & Washburn, 1996). An Incan child had to wait until puberty to receive a permanent name. Celebrating a birth was commonly delayed for several days to years across most cultures[5] (Colon, 2001).

Servitude

Some children were forced to work in very hazardous environments. Their small size allowed them to perform jobs that an adult was incapable of doing, such as digging in small mine shafts or cleaning the walls of wells. The majority of children (of all classes and across many cultures) relieved their parents of their care by working on the family's farm or by becoming an apprentice. Both males and females left their homes for apprentice work, often around the age of seven, and were easy prey for sexual perpetrators. A ten-year-old girl working in her uncle's stable testified and the account read as follows:

> She called Jean Merlin, the farmhand, to help load up. But as soon as Merlin was in the stable, he asked [her] to kiss him, took her, lay her down, exposed himself to her, grabbed her thighs, and stuffed her mouth with straw so that she couldn't cry out. (Alexandre-Bidon, 1999, p. 80)

Abandonment/Infanticide

With rare exception, killing or deserting an infant was a common behavior across the globe (Breiner, 1990; Donohue et al., 1995). In Eskimo tribes, female infanticide was so customary that males wishing to marry often had to steal their female partners from neighboring villages (Douglas, 1966; Morell, 1995). Native American tribes consistently killed or abandoned malformed or twin infants—leaving them in badger holes or suffocating them (Ramsey, 1994). Pacific islanders strangled their unwanted female, twin, or deformed infants because of superstitious beliefs or for population control (Richard, 2005). In China, families were delegated to a certain number of offspring (four sons and three daughters). All other children were drowned or abandoned (Caldwell & Caldwell, 2005).

In some European regions, children were eaten. Severe climatic changes caused famine between 600 and 800 AD (Fagan, 2000). Medieval storytellers write:

> Many [hungry persons] would present eggs or pieces of fruit to children to lure them to isolated spots and then massacre and devour them. (Alexandre-Bidon, 1999, p. 35)

Indeed, the Western population declined during the early Middle Ages. Destitute families had few expectations that their "living" children would survive to a marriageable age. If, by a miracle, this happened, the offspring frequently did not legally marry. It was just too difficult to provide for a family. Clandestine marriages were common (Macy, 2000), and children born from these unions were considered illegitimate and often murdered. To reduce the number of children killed because of poverty or clandestine unions, the church sanctioned a certain type of abandonment by declaring thus:

> [All priests] announce publicly to their parishioners that if a woman must conceive and give birth following a clandestine union, she certainly must not kill [her child] . . . but rather carry the baby to the doors of the church and leave it there . . . [for the faithful to raise]. (Alexandre-Bidon, 1999, p. 18)

Violence

The Middle Ages in Europe was chaotic from migrating barbarians, famine, and foreign invaders. The Thuringians, a Germanic clan, and later the Merovingians (Contreni, 1996), a French tribe, were especially violent to male and female captured youth. If children in their possession were not killed outright, they were enslaved for prostitution purposes (Colon, 2001).

In the Meso-American culture, captured, orphaned, or noble children, from age three months to eight years, were prime targets for sacrifice. Hundreds to thousands of children each year were ceremonially dismembered and murdered by having their beating hearts torn from their bodies, thrown into mud pits, bludgeoned, throats cut, or entombed alive (Fleming, 1987). Incan females (around the age of ten) were chosen by the state to spend their lives as concubines to nobles or as priestesses, a situation in which sacrifice was a likely fate.

Disobedient children were met with severe forms of punishment, such as being left out all night, submerged in mud holes, or beaten with thorny switches across the soles of their feet (Colon, 2001).

The Timucua and Natchez tribes of southern North America ritually sacrificed their first born or other children in homage to their chief or other Gods (Stojanowski, 2005).

During the Medieval Inquisition (1200 AD), any deviant behavior (colic, petulance, mischievous, sickly, etc.) by children might elicit a condemnation of being "filled with evil spirits." It was believed that demons possessed infants who were conceived because of some broken religious taboo. Remedies for this affliction were parental abandonment, humiliation, imprisonment, torture, or death (Henningsen, 1996).

Enslavement

Slavery was alive and well in medieval Europe. As in Rome, child slaves were merchandise for the slave trade or were found as exposed infants and reared as slaves (Donohue et al., 1995). Italian slaves, in the late Middle Ages, were a diverse group purchased from Russia, Africa, Bulgaria, Albania, and England. Purchased slaves were often very young females meant for domestic labor, which included complying with the male family member's sexual needs that sometimes resulted in pregnancy. Although, a rural landowner might embrace an added slave to his numbers, a master wishing household services might not appreciate such a condition and wish to rid the home of this inconvenience. The following letter from a slave merchant to a slave owner illustrates such a circumstance:

[Dear Sir]

The slave you sent [to sell] is sick, or rather full of boils, so that we find none who would have her. Furthermore, she says she is with your child, two months gone or more, and therefore she will not be worth selling. We will sell or barter her as best we can, and send you the account. (Phillips, 1985, p. 99)

The Goths[6] were especially avid and cruel slave owners known for mutilating and castrating their child and adolescent possessions (Alexandre-Bidon, 1999).

In China, it was acceptable and indeed common to sell children into slavery, as one observer reported:

> Young slave girls are very cheap in China; and, indeed, all the Chinese will sell their sons as slaves equally with their daughters. (Colon, 2001, p. 263)[7]

Rituals

"Right of passage" or "beatification" ceremonies were universally common and often completed anytime before or at puberty. Rituals of adornment included tattooing, piercing, and head and feet wrapping or molding. Right of passage conventions included icy water baths, exposure to various insect stings, lengthy fasting and isolation, limb stretching, body cutting and skewering, castration, and carrying weights (Colon, 2001).

THE RESTORATION (1400 TO 1600)

The Renaissance brought cultural and scientific revolution for everyone but children (Tucker, 1974). Child maltreatment continued, by the rich and the poor, as in the medieval era. The high infant death rate was in part due to infanticide (Sandidge, 2005). Marriage was a complicated and expensive venture especially for the common person. The bride needed to provide a dowry and the groom had to negotiate a *bridal deposit* in addition to a *morning gift* (Yalom, 2004) in payment for his bride's virginity. Most important, marriage required access to land to ensure the family's survival. The church taught that marriage was for procreation, yet youth were considered a great burden, as Eustache des Champs asserts:

> Happy is he who has no children, for babies mean nothing but crying and stench; they give only trouble and anxiety. (Colon, 2001, p. 214)[8]

Children were often killed out of economic necessity, illegitimacy, and abusive discipline (Symonds, 2005).

> Katherine by a blow on the ear given by her mother did bleed at the nose very much, which did stay for an hour and more (John Dee, 1589). (Colon, 2001, p. 299)[9]

During this period, parents were beginning to abandon their unwanted children to churches or orphanages rather than leave them on the street. However, children continued to die at alarming rates from neglect and illness (Boswell, 1984). One glimpse of concern for children's plight was displayed with the first book addressing children's disease by Thomas Phaire in 1545 (Nutton, 2001).

Exploitation

Pederasty existed in Italy (especially in Florence) among the leading figures of the day (e.g., Leonardo da Vinci and Michelangelo) (Colon, 2001). The Catholic Church attempted to suppress this behavior, acclaimed as sodomy, through civil and religious venues. The convicted adults were often fined and the youth *coconspirators* (the legal age of "consent" was six to ten years old) were tortured or flogged. Some were burned at the stake (Dupont, 1993).

London's population burgeoned during the Reformation. Poverty had increased in the outlying hamlets and the poor streamed to the city—especially abandoned youth. The punishment for thievery was death and children from age seven (considered adults) caught thieving were hanged. To reduce the ever-increasing numbers of street vagrants and the accompanying crime, the Act of 1536 decreed that beggar youth (age five to fourteen) must be appointed to apprenticeships (Panter-Brick, 2000). Children who did not agree to this arrangement were publicly beaten. When the strength of street youth outnumbered the apprenticeship placements[10] or a child ran away because of abuse while in an apprenticeship, they were enslaved, branded, and chained for two years according to the Act of 1547[11] (Judges, 2002). However, street children and crime continued to rise across Europe (Colon, 2001).

Female children, living in the sixteenth to the eighteenth centuries, who became pregnant, suffered with a venereal disease, or were found in a sexual relationship with an adult were often tortured, imprisoned, or murdered for demonic possession. It was believed that the devil's power forced them to influence innocent adult men to commit sin. Hundreds of children, from the age of three, were exposed to all forms of abuse because they were deemed witches and needed to be purified (Kahr, 1991).

Abandonment

The Reformation laws (Council of Trent in northern Italy [1548-1563]) established the common rules of formal marriage. Namely, that marriage had to be registered in the parish church of birth and conducted by a priest in front of two witnesses after openly announcing the impending union for three consecutive weeks. Before this, individuals were considered married if they lived together in "free or common marriages." The bond between the couple was verbal "I marry you," which was sanctioned by canon law and presence. The new marriage law purportedly freed emancipated individuals to marry their beloved instead of a person their parents or an individual with authority chose for them (Sperling, 2004). However, the new Reformation marriage laws were slow to "take hold" among the common citizens. Consequently, their unions were considered illegal and their offspring illegitimate (Symonds, 2005). Infants born of adultery, rape, illegal unions, or from impoverished families were found almost daily in the sewers and streets across Europe. These children became the livelihood and/or sexual abuse victims of the pedophiles and sociopaths whether they were monks or lords (Merrick, 1998), orphanage attendants, slavers, or street beggars (Colon, 2001).

COLONIAL AMERICA (1600 TO 1700)

Colonial expansion in America brought imprisonment, physical torture, sexual abuse, and murder to children. "Good parents" corrected defiant youth; *spare the rod and spoil the child* was the child-rearing colloquialism. A child who did not lead his or her life with religion, work, and family as a motivating force was considered neglected and badly reared. Children under the age of six were expected to work long hours for little rewards (Jordan, 2004). The Stubborn Child Laws allowed parents to put a disobedient child to death for any sort of noncompliant behavior (Straus, Gelles, & Steinmetz, 2003). Public health officials today have estimated that in Colonial America as many as two-thirds of the children died before they reached the age of four. Deaths were due, in part, to disease, starvation, accidents, beatings, and torture (Reinier, 1996).

In the early 1600s, the number of delinquent and homeless English and Irish children was so high that the politicians declared[12] that all street children would be indentured to the American colonies (Snow & Anderson, 1993). This was profitable for the colonist as each "bound" child meant an allotment of fifty acres of land (Price, 1995). Tens of thousands of children were indentured from England and Scotland between 1600 and 1800. William Green, 1762, described his experience:

> We were put ashore in couples chained together and driven in lots like oxen [to be inspected by purchasers who] search us there as the dealers in horses do. (Colon, 2001, p. 333)[13]

Selling indentured children developed into such a big business that child kidnapping became a problem. The *contractors* of child cargo could fetch £25 per youth from the colonist. However, one purchaser argued:

> White servants are . . . [an] . . . inferior sort of people, who have either been sent over to Virginia or have transported themselves thither, have been, and are, the poorest, idlest and worst of Mankind, the refuse of Great Britain and Ireland . . . (Hugh Jones, 1724). (Colon, 2001, p. 333)[14]

The French, Portuguese, and Dutch also "sent out" their unwanted children to Louisiana, the West Indies, Algeria, Africa, East Indies, and New York (Colon, 2001). Children working as factory, field, or domestic indentured slaves experienced sexual victimization at the highest level—some moving into prostitution after the indenture assignment was completed (Simpson, 1987).

GLOBAL ISSUES (1700 TO 1900)

The Industrial Revolution turned the civilized world upside down. Yet conditions for children remained morbid. High death rates and abuse of all sorts were still common. European youth had only a 50 percent chance of living to their fifth birthday (Donohue et al., 1995).

Abandonment/Infanticide

Young girls from poor homes across Europe were commonly forced to work in households far away from their villages of birth. Desperate to find a suitable union and unprotected by family and community, young women often became pregnant. Abandoning their infant to a "work house" or orphanage, or, in desperation, killing the child, often seemed the only resolution when the courtship failed or the father of the child was unable to obtain land to support a family (Symonds, 2005).

> Many . . . [abandoned infants] belong to poor mothers . . . [or] widows who leave them . . . [to] find work . . . [others are] poor married women who, only seven or eight months after having one child, find themselves pregnant again and so expose the [newborn]. These infants are the worse for having been weaned at such an early age on soups of milk and wine and they become so weak that it is impossible to save them (Spain 1790: Pedro de la Vega). (Colon, 2001, pp. 324-325)[15]

Begging, mutilation, indentured slavery, or prostitution remained the common destinies of abandoned infants found alive. The sodomy and rape of young males (reported as young as six years) was so rampant in France (1700 and 1800s) that there were "pederast patrols" roaming the streets with hopes of reducing the numbers of victims. It was believed that male prostitutes engaged in their work because they had been violated at an earlier age. Legal agents tried to persuade the young sexual abuse victims they encountered to move on and stay away from the perpetrators, but they met with little success (Merrick, 1998, 2001).

Infants abandoned at orphanages had a one in four chance of living to the first year in France and to an even shorter period in Spain.[16] Overwhelming numbers[17] of abusive and neglectful wet nurses and *meneurs* (drivers responsible for transporting abandoned infants) who left their charges unfed and victims of the elements[18] in addition to general neglect, malnutrition, and disease were responsible for most deaths (Fuchs, 1984).

Exploitation

Poor or indentured children were forced to work twelve to fifteen hour days from the age of three as glove, rope, and shoemakers in addition to weavers and chimney sweeps (Reinier, 1996). Youth not performing as desired were beaten. Children who were stolen, rented, or indentured as chimney sweeps were tortured with burning, suffocation, or sharp prods to encourage their ascent to the tops of chimneys (Clamp, 1984). Both female and male children worked long hours in the ore mines transporting material much like children in the Roman era.

> [Children] . . . chained, belted, and harnessed like dogs [with] a go-cart, black, saturated with wet, and more than half naked, crawling upon their hands and feet, and dragging their loads behind them. (Colon, 2001, p. 364)[19]

There were no laws to protect youth; therefore, kidnapping was rampant. An adult could make a reasonable living renting or selling kidnapped children for work or sexual purposes.

Mutilation (e.g., blinding) of infants was still common for begging purposes (Schorsch, 1979). In Germany, this was referred to as "angel making."

> Children are mutilated intentionally and made sick, so that by their misery they will inspire pity on the arm of the female beggar and finally die . . . [The females] know no other way of earning a living, . . . [so] . . . they make angels. (Colon, 2001, p. 371)[20]

By the time the child reached the age of three, he or she was no longer useful for begging and once their teeth were sold for denture making they were indentured or killed (Schorsch, 1979).

In Europe and America, from the seventeenth century to well into the twentieth century, it was considered medicinal to have intercourse with a very young child and was quite a common practice. Sex with a virginal child or infant was thought to cure venereal disease (Crewdson, 1988; Simpson, 1987). The author John Glaister (1921) stated:

> It is a fact beyond dispute, owing to the prevalence of a widespread belief amongst persons of the lowest classes, that coitus with a healthy young person of the opposite sex will cure them

of gonorrhea, that gonorrheal infection is conveyed to young children—especially females—hence it is that rape upon young female children under twelve years of age is so prevalent. (Davidson, 2001, p. 64)

Rape investigations documented in the early twentieth century described ambiguous or erroneous assessments by physicians who often did not test the child for venereal disease or sexual victimization and testified that the child's vaginal discharge was not from sexual rape of a perpetrator with venereal disease—but from filth, masturbation, exposure to other children, soiled washing utensils, or contaminated clothes in the home. The suggested cure was to wash the child and apply medicated powder. In some cases, a child was raped by more than one perpetrator making conviction impossible even if there was verified testimony (Davidson, 2001).

Enslavement

African-American, Chinese, and European children were purchased as slaves to perform many tasks. Female child slaves had to be very cautious for rape was common (Fox-Genovese, 1988). All children continued to be purchased for the sexual pleasures of adults and other children (Hellerstein, Hume, & Offen, 1981; Phillips, 1985).

Rituals

A common initiation ritual across the African, Middle East, and Asian (Muslim) cultures was, and continues to be, genital mutilation. There are four forms of female circumcision performed when the female is between four and ten years. The sunna (type 1) removes the prepuce and some portion of the clitoris. Type 2 removes the clitoris and some of the labia minora. Infibulation (type 3) removes the clitoris, labia minora, and portions of the labia majora. The remaining labia majora is sewn or put together with thorns and the woman is bound for several weeks. Type 4 involves the following:

> Pricking, piercing or cutting the clitoris or labia; stretching or cauterization by burning the clitoris; cutting the vagina or surrounding tissue; scraping of tissue surrounding the vaginal orifice or cutting of the vagina; introducing corrosive substances or

herbs into the vagina to induce bleeding or for the purpose of tightening or narrowing it. (Wallis, 2005, p. 26)

Males were and continue to be circumcised around the same age as females (Colon, 2001).

COMMUNITY RESPONSE

Early civilization understood, on some level, that children who survived exposure or abandonment were abused. King Hammurabi (1750 BC) attempted to stop parents from exposing or enslaving their children with the law codes (Sarton, 1993). Early Christian era theologians and leaders (e.g., Augustine [354-430]) strived to stop infanticide and exposure by declaring this behavior murder and suggesting that males should abstain from bedding their wives if they were too poor or did not wish to have children; adding that it was well known that vile persons often took *exposed* children and abused them (Elsakkers, 2001). In 315 AD, Constantine outlawed exposure[21] and a century later, Valentinian III (423-455) forbade the sale of infants,[22] while the church declared that any woman guilty of exposing her infant would be excommunicated. Justinian's (527-565) legal codes confirmed that children could not be sold, enslaved, or abandoned as this was murder and punishable with death (Reid, 2004). Canon Law 17 (589 AD) implored the legal system to halt the widespread practice of infanticide (Alexandre-Bidon, 1999). Yet it persisted well into the nineteenth century (Dixon, 1992).

Laws regarding incest established in 1640 in New England and in the Orphan Courts in the 1700s attempted to help maltreated children (Pleck, 1987).

The possibility that children might actually suffer sexual abuse was formerly documented in 1860 by Tardieu, a French physician who published a manuscript to assist court cases involving adult/child sexual behavior (Araji, 1997). Up to this time and later, the sexual maltreatment of children was simply not acknowledged among the masses (Hetherton & Beardsall, 1998). The legal and popular consensus was that children involved in sexual relations with adults were considered coconspirators[23] or prostitutes owing to depraved moral character, poverty, or lack of education. These "bad" children were frequently imprisoned to preserve the integrity of the family. In cases of incest, the mother commonly favored the sexual abuse of her children over the loss of income from her husband. Only very young children (under six years) were viewed as "less guilty," but rarely as victims (Guarnieri, 1998).

In the late 1800s, a movement to stop the abuse of children began—focusing on "baby farming," infanticide, child labor, and humane treatment for delinquent youths (Williams, 1983). These supporters of *justice* challenged the entrenched belief that parenthood and family unity were more important than individual rights and were responsible for the Prevention of Cruelty Act in 1889 (Behimer, 1982). However, the explanation for most of the sexual abuse cases that came to the legal system was child oedipal hysteria. The accusing youths were considered pathological (e.g., mentally disturbed, malicious; van der Kolk, Weisaeth, & Hart, 1996). The belief was that a decent man would never harm his child in such a way (Masson, 1984). Indeed, incest was thought an uncommon behavior until the 1970s (Swanson & Biaggio, 1985). And, even when it was acknowledged, it was considered the child's fault (Henderson, 1975). In fact, children suffering with venereal disease were thought to be infected by close proximity to another child, a servant, a parent, or some other "carrier" or mechanism. Intercourse with an infant continued to be considered a cure for venereal disease into the 1940s and explainable as a medical treatment that gave the suffering adult perpetrator no pleasure (Smart, 2000).

In 1959, the United Nations pleaded with the people of the world to nurture their children with the *Rights of the Child* document (Colon, 2001). Several decades later, the U.S. Congress passed the Child Abuse Prevention and Treatment Act (CAPTA, 1974) to help provide services, appropriate treatment, and education regarding the *new understanding of child abuse* (Golden, 2000).

In the 1980s, the mainstream recognition that children were sexually abused by adults emerged (Neinstein, Goldenring, & Carpenter, 1984). The media played a huge role in this process by framing child sexual abuse as a public safety issue (Pillai, 2005).

In 1988, CAPTA broadened the definition of child abuse to include sexual abuse and exploitation. CAPTA has undergone several revisions since that time (Rein, 2005).

Throughout the 1980s, mental health services for sexual abuse victims and offenders improved significantly in the United States. Within a three-year period, several hundred programs began operations and by 1986 that number had doubled (Conte, 1990).

In the 1990s, the Child Abuse Prevention and Treatment Act (CAPTA) increased the reported child abuse cases dramatically. President Clinton responded by singing Megan's Law in 1996, which mandated states to register the names of child sex offenders and circulate information confirming their residence within a designated area. As of 1999, a registered sex offender is a classified individual, allowing his or her offender categorization to be publicly disclosed by law enforcement (Lees & Tewksbury, 2006).

Recent crime control policies infer that the public prefers a punitive response to dealing with sexual offenders. Legislation has been developed to enhance or extend their incarceration. Mandatory minimum sentences, habitual offender legislation, "three strikes and you're out," and "truth in sentencing" were designed to literally incapacitate the offender. Such policy changes reflect increased public frustration with both criminals and the criminal justice system (Greenberg, 1997).

CONCLUSION

For too many children in America, childhood is not a period of stability, safety, and normal development. Instead, these children are the victims of maltreatment at the hands of family members and caretakers.

(Golden, 2000, p. 1050)

At this moment, the abuse of children is a critical and pressing social concern after being hidden in the dark for centuries. Prevention of sexual violence against children is in its infancy—there is much to do before the light flickers.

NOTES

1. "In one ordeal the accused was required to take [a] hot iron in his hand; in another to walk blindfolded among red-hot ploughshares; in another to thrust his arm into boiling water, . . . in another to swallow the morsel of excretion; in the confidence that his guilt or innocence would be miraculously made known" (Spooner, 2004, p. 45).

2. Under Roman law, brother/sister marriages were legal until 212 AD (Otten-heimer, 1996).

3. As cited in Lewis, 1983, p. 43.

4. As cited in Lewis, 1983, p. 54.

5. The Incans celebrated a child's birth at age three.

6. The Goths were a barbarian tribe who ritualized war. Their history spanned 700 years. They possessed the land from northern Poland to the Atlantic Ocean (Heather, 1998, p. 2).

7. As cited in Latham, 1982, p. 192.

8. As cited in Huizinga, 1924, pp. 25-26.

9. As cited in Houlbrooke, 1988, p. 138.

10. It is difficult to find a willing employer for chronic street children.

11. Two years later, the Slave Act of 1547 was repealed. In 1572, severe punishment for vagrancy returned. The first offense: whipping and mutilations (ear boring—burning through the gristle of the right ear with a hot iron an inch in diameter) (Snow & Anderson, 1993, p. 11); the second offense: death as a felon (Judges, 2002, p. xxxvi).

12. The Vagrancy Act of 1597.

13. As cited in Coldham, 1992, p. 121.

14. As cited in Coldham, 1992, pp. 63-64.

15. As cited in Sherwood, 1998, p. 99.

16. 1790: 87 percent death rate.

17. In Paris, the foundling home Hotel-Dieu cared for 700 children in 1670 and 7,500 children by 1790.

18. These children were often transported in open baskets hanging from the side of a mule for up to a week.

19. As cited in Pinchbeck and Hewitt, 1969, p. 401.

20. As cited in Anderson and Zinsser, 1988, p. 246.

21. Carcopino, 2003.

22. Boswell, 1998.

23. Meaning they were legally able to consent to a sexual act.

REFERENCES

Alexandre-Bidon, D. (1999). *Children in the middle ages: Fifth-fifteenth centuries.* Notre Dame, IN: University of Notre Dame Press.

Anderson, B. S., & Zinsser, J. P. (1988). *A history of their own* (Vols. 1 & 2). New York: Harper & Row.

Araji, S. K. (1997). Identifying, labeling, and explaining children's sexually aggressive behaviors. In S. K. Araji (Ed.), *Sexually aggressive children: Coming to understand them* (pp. 1-46). Thousand Oaks, CA: Sage.

Behimer, G. K. (1982). *Child abuse and moral reform in England: 1870-1908.* Stanford, CA: Stanford University Press.

Block, E. (2001). Sex between men and boys in classical Greece: Was it education for citizenship or child abuse? *Journal of Men's Studies, 9*(2), 183-204.

Boswell, J. (1980). *Christianity, social tolerance and homosexuality: Gat people in Western Europe from the beginning of the Christian era to the fourteenth century.* Chicago: University of Chicago Press.

Boswell, J. (1998). *The kindness of strangers: The abandonment of children in Western Europe from late antiquity to the renaissance.* Chicago: University of Chicago Press.

Boswell, J. E. (1984). Expositio and Oblatio: The abandonment of children and the ancient and medieval family. *American Historical Review, 89*(F), 10-33.

Bottero, J. (2001). *Everyday life in ancient Mesopotamia.* Baltimore: Johns Hopkins University Press.

Breiner, S. J. (1990). *Slaughter of the innocents: Child abuse through the ages and today.* New York: Plenum Press.

Caldwell, J. C., & Caldwell, B. K. (2005). Family size control by infanticide in the great agrarian societies of Asia. *Journal of Comparative Family Studies, 36*(2), 205-226.

Carcopino, J. (2003). *Daily life in ancient Rome: The people and the city at the height of the empire* (E. O. Lorimer, Trans., 2nd ed.). London: Yale University Press.

Coldham, P. W. (1992). *Emigrants in chains.* Gloucester, UK: Alan Smith.

Colon, A. R. (2001). *A history of children: A socio-cultural survey across millennia.* Westport, CT: Greenwood Press.

Conte, J. R. (1990). The incest offender: An overview and introduction. In A. L. Horton, B. L. Johnson, L. M. Roundy, & D. Williams (Eds.), *The incest perpetrator: A family member no one wants to treat* (pp. 19-28). Thousand Oaks, CA: Sage.

Contreni, J. J. (1996). Constructing Merovingian history. *French Historical Studies, 19*(3), 755-758.

Crawford, H. E. W. (2004). *Sumer and the Sumerians.* New York: Cambridge University Press.

Crewdson, J. (1988). *By silence betrayed: Sexual abuse of children in America.* Boston: Little, Brown, & Company.

Daniel, M. (1994). Arab civilization and male love. In J. Goldberg (Ed.), *Reclaiming Sodom* (pp. 59-65). London: Routledge.

Davidson, R. (2001). This pernicious delusion: Law, medicine, and child sexual abuse in early twentieth century Scotland. *Journal of the History of Sexuality, 10*(1), 62-77.

Demand, N. (2004). *Birth, death, and motherhood in classical Greece.* Baltimore: Johns Hopkins University Press.

Dixon, P. (1994). The beginning of democracy. *Calliope, 5*(2), 5-11.

Dixon, S. (1992). *The Roman family.* Baltimore: John Hopkins University Press.

Donohue, B., Hersen, M., & Ammerman, R. T. (1995). Historical overview. In M. Hersen & A. Robert (Eds.), *Advanced abnormal child psychology* (pp. 3-19). Hillsdale, NJ: Erlbaum Associates.

Douglas, M. (1966). Population control in primitive groups. *British Journal of Sociology, 17*(3), 263-274.

Dupont, F. (1993). *Daily life in ancient Roma.* Cambridge, MA: Blackwell.

Elsakkers, M. (2001). Genre hopping: Aristotelian criteria for abortion in Germania. In K. E. Olsen, A. Harbus, & T. Hofstra (Eds.), *Germanic texts and Latin models: Medieval reconstructions* (pp. 73-92). Belgium: Peeters Publishers.

Fagan, B. M. (2000). *The little ice age: How climate made history, 1300-1850.* New York: Basic Books.

Fleming, S. (1987). Infant sacrifice at Pachacamac, Peru: Dignity in death. *Archaeology, 40*(2), 64-77.

Fox-Genovese, E. (1988). *Within the plantation household: Black and white women of the old south.* Chapel Hill, NC: The University of North Carolina Press.

Fuchs, R. (1984). *Abandoned children: Foundlings and child welfare in nineteenth-century France.* Albany, NY: State University of New York Press.

Fuentes, A. (2004). *A guide to the bible.* Dublin, UK: Four Courts Press.

Garland, R. (1986). Mother and child in the Greek world. *History Today, 36*(3), 40-47.

Glaister, J. (1921). *A text-book of medical jurisprudence and toxicology.* Edinburgh, UK: E. S. Livingstone.

Golden, O. (2000). The federal response to child abuse and neglect. *American Psychologist, 55*(9), 1050-1053.

Greenberg, M. L. (1997). Just deserts in an unjust society: Limitation on law as a method of social control. *New England Journal on Criminal and Civil Confinement, 23*(2), 333-346.

Guarnieri, P. (1998). Dangerous girls, family secrets, and incest law in Italy, 1861-1930. *International Journal of Law and Psychiatry, 21*(4), 369-383.

Heather, P. (1998). *The Goths.* Malden, MA: Blackwell.

Hellerstein, E. O., Hume, L. P., & Offen, K. M. (1981). *Victorian women: A documentary account of women's lives in nineteenth-century England, France, and the United States.* Stanford, CA: Stanford University Press.

Henderson, D. J. (1975). Incest. In A. M. Freedman, H. I. Kaplan, & B. J. Sadock (Eds.), *Comprehensive textbook of psychiatry* (2nd ed., pp. 1530-1539). Baltimore: Williams & Wilkins.

Henningsen, G. (1996). The child witch syndrome: Satanic child abuse of today and child witch trials of yesterday. *Journal of Forensic Psychiatry, 7*(3), 581-593.

Hetherton, J., & Beardsall, L. (1998). Decisions and attitudes concerning child sexual abuse: Does the gender of the perpetrator make a difference to child protection professionals? *Child Abuse & Neglect, 22*(12), 1265-1283.

Houlbrooke, R. (1988). *English family life, 1576-1716.* Oxford, UK: Blackwell.

Huizinga, J. (1924). *The waning of the middle ages.* London: Edward Arnold.

Jordan, A. (2004). Children at work. *Appleseeds, 6*(5), 20-22.

Judges, A. V. (2002). Key writings on subcultures, 1535-1727: Classics from the underworld. In A. V. Judges (Ed.), *The Elizabethan underworld: A collection of Tudor and early Stuart tracts and ballads* (Vol. 1, pp. xiii-xxxvii). New York: Routledge.

Kahr, B. (1991). The sexual molestation of children: Historical perspectives. *Journal of Psychohistory, 19*(2), 191-214.

Kalichman, S. C. (1999). Mandatory child abuse reporting laws: Origins and evolution. In S. C. Kalichman (Ed.), *Mandated reporting of suspected child abuse: Ethics, law, & policy* (2nd ed., pp. 11-42). Washington, DC: American Psychological Association.

Killias, M. (1991). The historic origins of penal statutes concerning sexual activities involving children and adolescents. In T. Sandfort, E. Brongersma, & A. V. Naerssen (Eds.), *Male intergenerational intimacy: Historical, socio-psychological, and legal perspectives* (pp. 41-46). Binghamton, NY: The Haworth Press.

Latham, R. (1982). *The travels of Marco Polo.* New York: Arabis Books.

Lees, M., & Tewksbury, R. (2006). Understanding policy and programmatic issues regarding sex offender registries. *Corrections Today, 68*(1), 54-57.

Leventhal, J. M. (2000). Sexual abuse of children: Continuing challenges for the new millennium. *Acta Paediatrica, 89*(3), 268-271.

Lewis, N. (1983). *Life in Egypt under Roman rule.* Oxford, UK: Clarendon Press.

Macy, G. (2000). The lady has rights, too. *National Catholic Reporter, 36*(41), 22.

Martin, G. (2005). *Juvenile justice: Process and systems.* Thousand Oaks, CA: Sage.

Masson, J. M. (1984). *The assault on truth: Freud's suppression of the seduction theory.* New York: Farrar, Straus, & Giroux.

McGinn, T. A. J. (1998). *Prostitution, sexuality, and the law in ancient Rome.* Oxford, UK: University Press.

Merrick, J. (1998). Commissioner Foucault, inspector Noel, and the "pederasts" of Paris, 1780-1783. *Journal of Social History, 32*(2), 287-308.

Merrick, J. (2001). The arrest of a sodomite, 1723. *Gay and Lesbian Review, 8*(5), 29-30.

Morell, V. (1995). Cold dark facts: The case of the missing Inuit baby girls. *Equinox, 81,* 22-24.

Neinstein, L. S., Goldenring, J., & Carpenter, S. (1984). Nonsexual transmission of sexually transmitted diseases: An infrequent occurrence. *Pediatrics, 74*(1), 67-76.

Nissen, H. J., Damerow, P., & Englund, R. K. (1993). *Archaic bookkeeping: Early writing and techniques of economic administration in the ancient near east* (P. Larsen, Trans.). Chicago: The University of Chicago Press.

Nutton, V. (2001). Thomas Phaer and the Boke of Chyldren. *Journal of the History of Science in Society, 92*(1), 165-167.

Ottenheimer, M. (1996). *Relatives: The American myth of cousin marriage.* Champaign, IL: University of Illinois Press.

Panter-Brick, C. (2000). Nobody's children? A reconsideration of child abandonment. In C. Panter-Brick & M. T. Smith (Eds.), *Abandoned children* (pp. 1-26). New York: Cambridge University Press.

Percy, W. A. (1996). *Pederasty and pedagogy in archaic Greece.* Chicago: University of Illinois Press.

Phillips, W. D. (1985). *Slavery from Roman times to the early transatlantic trade.* Minneapolis, MN: University of Minnesota Press.

Pillai, M. (2005). Forensic examination of suspected child victims of sexual abuse in the UK: A personal view. *Journal of Clinical and Forensic Medicine, 12* (2), 57-63.

Pinchbeck, I., & Hewitt, M. (1969). *Children in English society* (Vols. 1 & 2). London: Routledge and Kegan Paul.

Pleck, E. (1987). *Domestic tyranny: The making of American social policy against family violence from colonial times to the present*. New York: Oxford University Press.

Polock, S. (2004). *Ancient Mesopotamia*. New York: Cambridge University Press.

Price, E. T. (1995). *Dividing the land*. Chicago: University of Chicago Press.

Ramsey, C. (1994). Cannibalism and infant killing: A system of demonizing motifs in Indian captivity narratives. *Clio, 24*(1), 55-69.

Rawson, B. (1991). *Marriage, divorce, and children in ancient Rome*. New York: Oxford University Press.

Reid, C. J. (2004). *Power over the body, equality in the family: Rights and domestic relations in Medieval Canon Law*. Grand Rapids, MI: Wm. B. Eerdmans Publishing.

Rein, M. L. (2005). *Child abuse: Betraying a trust*. Detroit, MI: Thomson/Gale.

Reinier, J. S. (1996). *From virtue to character: American childhood, 1775-1850*. New York: Twayne Publishers.

Richard, P. (2005). Manuscript XVII. *Journal of Pacific History, 40*(1), 105-115.

Robinson, L. O. (2003). Sex offender management: The public policy challenges. *Annals of New York Academy of Science, 989,* 1-7.

Robinson, O. F. (1995). *The criminal law of ancient Rome*. Baltimore: Johns Hopkins University Press.

Sandidge, M. (2005). Changing contexts of infanticide in medieval English texts. In A. Classen (Ed.), *Childhood in the middle ages and the renaissance: The results of a paradigm shift in the history of mentality* (pp. 291-306). Berlin, Germany: Walter de Gruyter GmbH & Co.

Sarton, G. (1993). *Ancient science through the golden age of Greece*. Mineola, NY: Dover Publications.

Schorsch, A. (1979). *Images of childhood*. New York: Mayflower Books.

Sherwood, J. (1998). *Poverty in eighteenth-century Spain*. Toronto, Canada: University of Toronto Press.

Simpson, A. E. (1987). Vulnerability and the age of female consent: Legal innovation and its effect on prosecutions for rape in eighteenth-century London. In R. P. Maccubbin (Ed.), *'Tis nature's fault-unauthorized sexuality during the Enlightenment* (pp. 181-205). Cambridge, UK: Cambridge University Press.

Smart, C. (2000). Reconsidering the recent history of child sexual abuse, 1910-1960. *Journal of Social Policy, 29*(1), 55-71.

Snow, D. A., & Anderson, L. (1993). *Down on their luck: A study of homeless street people*. Berkeley, CA: University of California Press.

Sperling, J. (2004). Marriage at the time of the council of Trent (1560-1570): Clandestine marriages, kinship prohibitions, and dowry exchange in European comparison. *Journal of Early Modern History, 8*(1/2), 67-108.

Spooner, L. (2004). *An essay on the trial by jury*. Philadelphia: Fredonia Books.

Stojanowski, C. M. (2005). Spanish colonial effects on Native American mating structure and genetic variability in northern and central Florida: Evidence from Apalachee and western Timucua. *American Journal of Physical Anthropology, 128*(2), 273-286.

Straus, M. A., Gelles, R. J., & Steinmetz, S. K. (2003). Spare the rod? In M. Silberman (Ed.), *Violence and society: A reader* (pp. 136-145). Upper Saddle River, NJ: Prentice Hall.

Sulzberger, M. (1915). *The ancient Hebrew law of homicide*. Philadelphia: J.H. Greenstone.

Swanson, L., & Biaggio, M. K. (1985). Therapeutic perspectives on father-daughter incest. *American Journal of Psychiatry, 142*(6), 667-674.

Symonds, D. A. (2005). Reconstructing rural infanticide in eighteenth century Scotland. *Journal of Women's History, 10*(2), 63-85.

Tinsley, B. S. (2006). *Reconstructing western civilization: Irreverent essays on antiquity*. Cranbury, NJ: Associated University Press.

Trigger, B. G., & Washburn, W. E. (1996). *History of the native peoples of the Americas*. New York: Cambridge University Press.

van der Kolk, B. A., Weisaeth, L., & van der Hart (1996). History of trauma in psychiatry. In B. A. van der Kolk, A. C. McFarlane, & L. Weisaeth (Eds.), *Traumatic stress: The effects of overwhelming experience on mind, body, and society* (pp. 47-76). New York: Guilford Press.

Van Loon, H. W. (1999). *The story of mankind* (J. Merriman, Trans.). New York: W.W. Norton & Company.

Verstraete, B. (2004). New pedagogy on ancient pederasty. *Gay & Lesbian Review, 11*(3), 13-14.

Wallis, L. (2005). When rites are wrong. *Nursing Standards, 20*(4), 24-26.

Weber, M. (1988). *The agrarian sociology of ancient civilizations*. New York: Verso.

Wiedemann, T. (1989). *Adults and children in the Roman empire*. New Haven, CT: Yale University Press.

Williams, G. J. R. (1983). Child protection: A journey into history. *Journal of Clinical Child Psychology, 12*(3), 236-243.

Yalom, M. (2004). *Birth of the chess queen*. New York: HarperCollins.

Chapter 2

Child and Adolescent Sexual Abuse

Carolyn Hilarski

INTRODUCTION

In the past few decades, the complex issue of child sexual abuse (CSA) has received unparalleled consideration from all facets of society and this attention has enlightened researchers, policymakers, and the public to how little is actually known about the tragedy (Bolen, 2001). This chapter discusses the definition, prevalence, risk and protective factors, and life stage consequences of CSA victims with the purpose of clarifying the existing information regarding sexual violence against children.

DEFINITION

CSA is an equal opportunity experience. Victims and perpetrators are among both genders and most age groups (see Salter et al., 2003).

Defining CSA appears almost unattainable and, as such, arbitrary (Putnam, 2003). There is literally no standard characterization (Haugaard, 2000). Indeed, the legal language and research concepts used to identify its presence vary from region to region according to local culture (Star & Lani, 2002). To date, the common way to identify or operationalize CSA is to describe the specific sexual behaviors involved,[1] the age of the victim,[2] and the perpetrator's characteristics[3] (see Alaggia, 2004). A legislative definition via the Child Abuse

Handbook of Social Work in Child and Adolescent Sexual Abuse
© 2008 by The Haworth Press, Taylor & Francis Group. All rights reserved.
doi:10.1300/5804_02

29

Prevention and Treatment Act (CAPTA; January 1996)[4] is frequently cited and asserts that CSA is:

> the employment, use, persuasion, inducement, enticement, or coercion of any child to engage in, or assist any other person to engage in, any sexually explicit conduct or any simulation of such conduct for the purpose of producing any visual depiction of such conduct; or the rape, and in the cases of caretaker or other inter-familial relationships, statutory rape, molestation, prostitution, or other form of sexual exploitation of children or incest with children. (Wyatt, Carmona, Loeb, Ayala, & Chin, 2002, p. 199)

Is this definition sufficient? Are we sure about the parameters of the term *child*? A lack of clarity results in ambiguity, which assists perpetrators to continue their behavior.

Actually, defining CSA goes beyond policymakers, researchers, and practitioners, as they must rely on the participant reporting to substantiate a CSA circumstance. How does the *average individual* define sexual abuse? Often, the issue of consent is not considered. If the perpetrator couched the sexual behavior as a "game" or "loving expression" and there was no force or threat or if the suspected victim enjoyed the interaction it is generally difficult for victims and professionals alike to identify the circumstance as abusive (Wyatt, 1985; Wyatt et al., 2002). Labeling a CSA situation is associated with the victim's or observers' perceptions influenced by individual experience and family and community values and culture (e.g., biases). To illustrate, the medical community might recognize CSA as an observable genital wound or disease. The legal community might identify CSA as documented proof of sexual force or injury. Adult/child intercourse is the way most adults characterize CSA (Wurtele & Miller-Perrin, 1992), which might influence their child's perception[5] of abuse.

The sine qua non is that the definition of CSA is adjusted according to professional or community needs (Haugaard, 2000). Some states do not even bother to include or define the term in their criminal statutes (Melton, Petrila, Poythress, & Slobogin, 1997). However, a potential useful definition might describe CSA as "contacts or interactions [ranging from seemingly benign to invasive] between a youth and an adult [or person with power or authority] when the youth is being used for the sexual stimulation of the perpetrator or another person" (Wurtele & Miller-Perrin, 1992, p. 5).

PREVALENCE AND INCIDENCE

Historical records across the millennia describe unbridled child maltreatment (Colon, 2001; Lascaratos & Poulakou-Rebelakou, 2000). Yet, only recently has sexual abuse of children become a national concern and only since the late 1960s did it come to the attention of the mental health and child welfare professionals (Putnam, 2003).

How common a problem is CSA? There are two ways to answer this question—with incidence and/or prevalence data. *Incidence* data are obtained yearly by canvassing Child Protective Service (CPS) agencies and/or the legal system regarding new cases. Surveying a population and estimating the percentage that shares child victimization experiences is how *prevalence* data are acquired. As essential as this data is, both incidence and prevalence information are problematic and do not fully answer the challenging question—How many children are sexually abused each year?

Prevalence Data

There are numerous methodological issues with prevalence data (Goldman & Padayachi, 2000). First is the issue of operationalizing CSA (Haugaard, 2000). Some epidemiological research considers only those cases of abuse perpetrated by family members, whereas others include all cases. Some may exclude noncontact abuse (e.g., exposure, inappropriate comments, or requests for sex) (Briere & Runtz, 1988); yet, others include it (Russell, 1984). Still others exclude incidents in which the victim and the perpetrator are close in years (Finkelhor, 1979b), whereas others consider sexually abusive behavior ageless (Badgley et al., 1984). Additional issues include sampling, probability versus nonprobability, and measurement[6] (Goldman & Padayachi, 2000) (see Table 2.1 for study examples). Because of these various issues, CSA can realistically only be estimated (Paolucci, Genuis, & Violato, 2001).

TABLE 2.1. Prevalence Studies of Nonclinical Populations

Study	N	%	Victim Age	Population and Measure	Screening CSA Defined Questions
Finkelhor, 1979	796	19.2	<16	College students[a] Questionnaire	4 Precise—wanted or unwanted noncontact and contact[b]
Sedney and Brooks, 1984	301	16	Not given	College students[a] Questionnaire	General—contact and noncontact sexual activity
Briere and Runtz, 1988	278	15	<15	College students[a] Questionnaire	General—wanted or unwanted sexual contact[b]
Seidner and Calhoun, 1984	595	11	<18	College students[a] Questionnaire	2 General—contact/noncontact sexual activity w/older person[b]
Badgley et al., 1984	1,006	24	<18	Random sample (Canada) Questionnaire	4 Unwanted contact and noncontact
Russell, 1984	930	28	<14	Random sample—interview	14 Precise—exploitive wanted or unwanted contact and noncontact
Kinsey et al., 1953	4,444	24	<18	Volunteer—interviews	General—wanted or unwanted contact and noncontact

[a]Underrepresents the lower socioeconomic levels.

[b]With offenders 5 years older.

To illustrate the influence that methodological issues have on the variance of CSA prevalence data, Finkelhor (1994) examined more than twenty population studies regarding CSA and found that 7 to 36 percent of the females and 3 to 29 percent of the men reported CSA. Almost twenty years earlier, Finkelhor's (1979a) study showed that 20 percent of females and approximately 10 percent of males reported CSA. The estimates are literally "all over the map."

As imprecise as the current prevalence data may be, it remains helpful in revealing, at a minimum, some level of the extent of the problem in order to plan for services and track trends and possible outcomes (Leventhal, 2000).

Incidence Data

The primary issue with incidence data is that it describes only *reported* cases leaving concerned persons to wonder about the numbers of unreported victims (see Koss, 1998). To illustrate, law enforcement collects crime statistics according to the most serious offense[7] when multiple crimes occur during a single episode. Therefore, if a child is raped and murdered, murder is the reported crime for that occurrence (Mosher, Miethe, & Phillips, 2002; NIBRS, n.d.).

An added issue is that victims, irrespective of ethnicity, do not generally report their victimization[8] (Finkelhor, 1998). If they *do* report, generally, it is because the perpetrator was a stranger and the attack was particularly devastating (Wyatt, Loeb, Solis, Carmona, & Romero, 1999), thus leaving a subgroup of intrafamilial or molestation types of offenses undocumented.

Another concern is that professionals are hesitant to report suspected CSA (Mitchell & Rogers, 2003). Negligible evidence, the youth's age, the negative effects of reporting,[9] and the professional's relationship to the caregiver or family appear to influence this behavior (Van Haeringen, Dadds, & Armstrong, 1998). Consequently, only those children with substantive evidence of abuse are reported (Goldman & Padayachi, 2000).

Confirmation of sexual abuse involves considerable documentation that includes collateral validation, the gender and age of the victim and perpetrator, and the level of violence and chronicity of the abuse. This type of inquiry demands consistent and extensive funding, which can be a reporting issue for rural or poverty-ridden townships (Plummer,

2001). However, it should be noted that families with low socioeconomic status appear more likely to be counted in the CSA numbers
than those with higher incomes[10] influencing prevalence data and
misrepresenting subgroups of individuals (Zellman, 1992).

The current primary incidence studies are the National Incidence
Study of Child Abuse and Neglect (NIS-3; Sedlak & Broadhurst,
1996),[11] the Fifty-State Survey (Peddle & Wang, 2001), and the
National Child Abuse and Neglect Data System (NCANDS). Other
available incidence information comes from the FBI Bureau of Jus-
tice. It uses two measures to collect data: the Uniform Crime Reports
(UCR)[12] (FBI, n.d.) and the National Crime Victimization Survey
(NCVS)[13] (BJS, 2006) (see Table 2.2).

Developed by the Children's Bureau of the U.S. Department of
Health and Human Services in partnership with State Child Protective
service agencies to collect annual statistics regarding child abuse, the
data from the NCANDS offer reasonably efficient information on
child victimization (DHHS, 2004, 2006a). The 2003 report described
that approximately 906,000 children were substantiated victims of
child maltreatment across forty-nine states. Of these, 9.9 percent were
sexually abused (3 percent by primary caregivers; DHHS, 2003,
2006b). In 2004, 9.7 percent of the 872,000 substantiated cases
across forty-seven states were deemed sexual abuse victims (DHHS,
2004, 2006a) revealing a very slight decrease in child victim reports.

The NIS-3 (Sedlak & Broadhurst, 1996) continues to work on estimating the numbers of abused children in the United States by collecting data from sources other than the legal system (NIS-4, n.d.).
These resources include CPS workers, legal records, hospitals,
schools, day-care agencies, mental and public health workers, and social service agencies. Of the 1,553,800 children who were considered
"harmed"[14] in the 1993 study, 217,700 child victims of sexual abuse[15]
were established (Sedlak & Broadhurst, 1996). Field researchers believe this figure is low (Massat & Lundy, 1998).

A replacement for the seventy-year-old Uniform Crime Report
(UCR), which collects information on eight types of crime,[16] is the
National Incidence-Based Reporting System (NIBRS; 1991-1996).
This newer system describes forty-six types of crime within twenty-
two offense classes, understood as "group A offenses," and unlike the
UCR documents both male and female and completed and attempted

TABLE 2.2. Sources of Incidence Data for Child Sexual Abuse

Three Primary Sources

National Incidence Study of Child Abuse and Neglect (NIS-3)

Last completed in 1993 and reported in 1996 (Sedlak & Broadhurst, 1996)

Limitations | Biased toward perpetrators in a caretaking role; 42% of data from CPS (which handles cases in which a caretaker is mistreating a child); nonfamilial perpetrators sexually abuse children far more than caretakers do

Fifty-State Survey

Collected by Prevent Child Abuse America formerly the National Committee to Prevent Child Abuse (Wang & Daro, 1998; Peddle & Wang, 2001) from CPS, child fatalities, and state departments

Limitations | Data type and definition varies from state to state (e.g., standards for abuse vary by state; some states report only substantiated cases); no nonreporters included

National Child Abuse and Neglect Data System (NCANDS)

Annual report since 1990; gathers summary data (compilation of fifteen key aggregate indicators of state child abuse and neglect statistics and case data)

Limitations | Biased toward perpetrators in a caretaking role; gathers data from CPS only; no nonreporters; data may be overreported because of multiple reports on a single child (Jones, 2001)

Additional Sources

National Crime Data (FBI)

Two primary surveys:

The National Crime Victimization Survey (NCVS)

Started by the Bureau of Justice Statistics of the Office of Justice Programs (Department of Justice) in 1972 to complete the FBI's Uniform Crime Report

Limitations | Population ages twelve and older (younger children not counted); interviews; reported cases only (Kilpatrick, 2004)

The Uniform Crime Report (UCR)

Limitations | Reports only rape cases by age for certain states; data from legal systems across the nation

No differentiation between adult and child cases of assault and rape

Literally thousands of police agencies in the United States with no uniform practices for collecting information on sex crimes and there is no central data collection (Mosher, Miethe, & Phillips, 2002)

victimization (NIBRS, n.d.). The UCR and the NCVS currently categorize crime by two groups.[17] The NIBRS categorizes sexual assault by forcible rape, statutory rape, forcible sodomy, sexual assault, forcible fondling, and incest (Prentky & Burgess, 2000); in addition, the "hierarchy rule" does not apply (NIBRS, n.d.). NIBRS information gathered from twelve states between 1991 and 1996 revealed that two-thirds of all criminal reports of sexual abuse pertained to children under the age of eighteen; one-third were eleven years or younger; and 14 percent were younger than six years (BJS, 2000).

The Fifty-State Survey of Child Abuse and Neglect is data collected by the National Committee to Prevent Child Abuse from state CPS agencies. In 1999, sexually abused children comprised 10 percent of the estimated 3,244,000 youth reported to CPS across the nation (Peddle & Wang, 2001). This percentage reflected an increase from the 1997 survey, in which 7 percent of the youth were reported sexually offended, and a decrease from the 1986 survey, in which 16 percent of all reports involved sexual abuse (Wang & Daro, 1998).

The reduction in reported CSA victims in the past decade must be cautiously accepted (Leventhal, 2000). As a result of the upsurge of media attention and public interest on the topic of CSA in the 1980s, there was a marked increase in the number of reported and substantiated cases from the 1970s. In the 1990s, a decline in public interest[18] may have resulted in less attention to the signs of suspected abuse and fewer reports to child protective agencies. A portion of the decrease may be also due to the changing definition of what constitutes child abuse,[19] improved services, lengthier offender incarceration, and improved community monitoring.

In summary, there is no general agreement among researchers and professionals on the prevalence of child sexual abuse;[20] however, many verbalize that it is significant (Haj-Yahi & Tamish, 2001; Jones, Finkelhor, & Halter, 2006; Pillai, 2005; Putnam, 2003). Since the CSA *revelation in the 1970s,* reports of rape, for example, have declined dramatically (see BJS, 2005). However, this account is considered flawed and misleading (Stanley & Kovacs, 2004). Declining CSA reports may reflect, in part, factors other than an actual reduction in abuse. The lack of studies concerned with the incidence and circumstances of CSA only add to the estimating difficulty (Paolucci et al., 2001).

RISK AND PROTECTIVE FACTORS

CSA is a pervasive problem across the globe (Banyard, Williams, & Siegel, 2001; Haj-Yahi & Tamish, 2001; Wilcox, Richards, & O'Keeffe, 2004) with considerable long- and short-term consequences for the child victims and their family members (Banyard et al., 2001). Yet, a subgroup[21] of children, because of individual characteristics and environmental circumstances, appear to escape the negative outcomes understood to commonly co-occur with CSA (Lynskey & Fergusson, 1997). The next section discusses the risk and resilience factors associated with child maltreatment.

The Family

The concept of resilient families is a relatively recent idea. Resiliency, in this context, refers to a family's ability to regain a steady state after a perceived misfortune or to maintain a functional level of homeostasis during an understood crisis (Wolin & Wolin, 1995). The focus is on the family's capacity to use its strengths[22] to cope with life stages and/or hardships (Norman, 2000). Caregivers who are older, educated, with a predominate internal locus of control, reasonably high self-efficacy and self-esteem, an optimistic attribution style, mature defenses, efficient coping, an ability to empathize, rational expectations, and accurate understanding of child development are ideal protective factors for their children (Carr, 1999). The caregiver's strengths support and characterize the family system as flexible, connected, adaptive, with shared values, goals, priorities, expectations, and worldviews (McCubbin & McCubbin, 1993).

On the other hand, families struggling with poverty[23] and its associated problems pose an extreme risk for child maltreatment (Adams, 2005). These families tend to engage in harsh punishment, suffer chronic negative life events, experience early unplanned pregnancies, report a lack of education, have a history of depression or some other mental health issue, have a high level of system chaos, and the children in the family often have multiple alternate caregivers (Brown, Cohen, Johnson, & Salzinger, 1998). Frequently, one or both caregivers suffer with substance abuse[24] (Carson, Gertz, Donaldson, & Wonderlich, 1991) and many if not all of these behaviors are observed and reported generationally. CSA victims, as adults, will commonly find themselves in abusive relationships and will perpetrate or enable the abuse of their offspring (Barrett, Sykes, & Byrnes, 1996).

Attachment

An infant, approximately seven months, seeking perceived safety with a primary caregiver is understood as *attached* to that individual (Flanagan, 1999). Given that the brain evolves through the process of environmental interaction, human evolutionary factors are naturally influenced by the *attachment system* (Kandel, 1998). To illustrate, a subgroup of young children will show distressed behavior when separated from their primary caregivers (Bowlby, 1982b). The presenting anguish is reportedly due to the child's interpretation of the circumstance as "dangerous," which stimulates the inherent "flight or fight" response (Kandel, 1983). Unconscious early experiences (e.g., chronic fight or flight activation) may alter the way a child integrates information, stores memory, and ultimately behaves[25] (Kandel, 1998; Teicher, 2002), which influences the caregiver response. The reciprocal process of the infant/caregiver interaction shapes the child's attachment style[26] (Fraley, Brumbaugh, & Marks, 2005). Child maltreatment and certain attachment styles (e.g., insecure attachment) appear generational (Berk, 1989; Katsikas, Petretic-Jackson, & Knowles, 1996; Morrison, Frank, Holland, & Kates, 1999). The chronic state of anxiety associated with the insecure attachment style (Sroufe, 2005) along with apparent limited problem solving skills and supportive systems leave these individuals vulnerable to perceived stress and amenable to the maltreatment of others (Egeland, Jacobvitz, & Sroufe, 1988).

Securely attached individuals appear to possess an optimistic and trusting worldview. They interpret challenging life events as manageable and consider their personal attributes as generally positive (Shapiro & Levendosky, 1999). They maintain close relationships and function successfully in peer groups (Sroufe, Carlson, Levy, & Egeland, 1999). They acquire these resilient traits from interactions with their primary caregiver who is likely securely attached as well (Cassidy, 2003).

Social Support

Many factors influence a child's reaction to abuse (Briere & Elliott, 2003). However, youth who intentionally seek socially supportive relationships put into motion a powerful protective measure against the negative consequences of maltreatment. Children with supportive environments are able to withstand an amazing amount of stress (Ruggiero, Del Ben, Scotti, & Rabalais, 2003). It takes only one perceived caring individual to ameliorate the painful consequences of CSA in some individuals (Perkins & Jones, 2004).

Parentified Child

Adults, who acted as parents, to either their parents and/or their siblings, as children are described as *parentified children.* In a subgroup of families, expecting a child to take on the excessive and developmentally inappropriate responsibilities of an adult is a generational phenomenon (Alexander, 1992) and linked to sexual abuse. Parentified children suffer with *intimacy* disruptions in their caregiver *attachments,* which they perceive as linked to their behavior. If they desire a connection with their caregiver(s), they often must accept the role of "parent."[27] Not agreeing to this role can result in a "cut-off"[28] or some other negative circumstance (e.g., caregiver anger).[29] The following are the outcomes: personal and family boundaries are violated or blurred and the child is exploited; the child is often unable to meet the needs of the caregiver and therefore feels guilty and inept; identity development is impaired, and multiple issues of loss precipitate anger, resentment, depression, school issues, and social problems (Jurkovic, 1997).

Locus of Control

A child with an *internal locus of control* believes or expects that things happen because of something within the self. A youth with an *external locus of control* believes or expects that things happen because of events beyond his or her control or outside the self (Rotter, 1966). Research has shown a positive link between external locus of control and various types of psychopathology[30] including posttraumatic stress disorder (PTSD) (Daigneault, Tourigny, & Hebert, 2006). The suggested explanation for these associations is the individual's worldview that one is powerless and vulnerable to life circumstances and an unexpected calamity can occur at any time (Drugan, Basile, Ha, Healy, & Ferland, 1997; Seligman & Maier, 1967;

Seligman, Maier, & Geer, 1968). This type of schema generally triggers a fear response (Freeman & Beck, 2000). In fact, anxiety appears common among CSA victims in comparison with the general population. Prevalence rates for anxiety disorders among child CSA victims range from 20 to 48 percent (Deblinger, McLeer, Atkins, Ralphe, & Foa, 1989; McLeer, Deblinger, Atkins, Foa, & Ralphe, 1988).

An internal locus of control is a protective factor for CSA victims (Pearce & Pezzot-Pearce, 1997). Individuals with high levels of internal locus of control report positive beliefs about inner resources to overcome adversity (Luthar, 1991; Luthar & Blatt, 1993), have less depression, possess or enjoy adequate social supports, and have active problem solving initiatives (Banyard, 1999).

Generally, children are internally or externally oriented according to their caregiver's inclination. However, a child's position can be modified by other significant interactions and life experiences (Gemelli, 1996).

Additional Issues

Other protective factors that promote resiliency are spirituality and involvement in extracurricular activities (Perkins & Jones, 2004), good intellectual ability, an easygoing temperament (Doll & Lyon, 1998), and a positive worldview (Miller-Perrin & Perrin, 1999).

LIFE STAGE CONSEQUENCES

The child's response to sexual abuse relates, in part, to developmental (Erikson, 1968) and life stage plasticity[31] (MacDonald, 1987) at the time of the abuse. Issues to consider are the *developmental tasks* at the time of the abuse, the *perception* that the child holds of the circumstances of the abuse, and the *developmental abilities of the child to express thoughts and feelings* about the abuse (Finkelhor & Kendall-Tackett, 1997). Examples of altered *developmental tasks* abound. To briefly illustrate, an insecure attachment is sometimes the consequence of early childhood victimization by a caregiver (Carlson, Cicchetti, Barnett, & Braunwald, 1989). Chronic dissociation (used as a defense mechanism) can be a consequence of preschool victimization (Kirby, Chu, & Dill, 1993) and prepubertal sex abuse is thought to stimulate the endocrine system and prematurely initiate puberty in females (Putnam & Trickett, 1993).

A child's *perception* of an event mediates its impact (Rutter, 1990). To illustrate, a circumstance will appear more traumatic to a victim who believes that he or she was hopelessly in danger (Resnick, Kilpatrick, Dansky, Saunders, & Best, 1993). The ability to change thoughts or perceptions is not fixed. Perceptions evolve over time within the internal and external environment (Stein, Fonagy, Ferguson, & Wisman, 2000).

No matter what the developmental stage or how the victim perceives the abuse, the *expressive outcome* will be associated with the victim's level of development. For example, abused preschool children are likely to be disruptive whereas abused children who are slightly older may blame themselves and display depression.

CONCLUSION

CSA is a ubiquitous and potentially debilitating experience for a subgroup of youth. Prevention is the ideal resolution. Early recognition of risk and protective factors, timely identification and protection of CSA victims, and family intervention are appreciable goals for reducing the likely outcomes of violence against children.

NOTES

1. For example, genital exposure, voyeurism, showing pornography, penile penetration, oral sex, genital manipulation (Johnson, 2004).

2. In definitions of CSA, there is inconsistency regarding what constitutes being a "child" (e.g., under sixteen years) (Johnson, 2004).

3. The sexual activity often must occur with an older individual—frequently the difference in age must be five years and the relationship between the offender and the victim is described to differentiate between a *family* or *other* perpetrator (Johnson, 2004).

4. Senator Walter Mondale helped to pass the CAPTA Act in 1974 (PL 93-247) to increase awareness that child abuse was "real" and to encourage reporting and supportive services for CSA victims. The law was amended in 1996 (PL 104-235) to reduce the amount of time sexually abused children remained in foster care and increase services to victims and families (in 1996, 659,000 CSA victims were in foster care; Sealander, 2003).

5. Children's perceptions are influenced by their primary caregivers (NCPCA, 2004). If the primary caregiver perceives, for example, that it is a "loving" experience for his or her adolescent daughter to sit on his or her grandfather's lap, the child's uncomfortable feelings about this behavior might be disconcerting (why am I feeling frightened in a loving circumstance?). This can become convoluted for youth who are taught to "trust their feelings" in, as an example, a CSA prevention program.

6. How the data are collected—face to face interviews, self-administered questionnaires, or telephone surveys in addition to the number of screening questions—influences the prevalence outcome (see Goldman & Padayachi, 2000). Prevalence studies tend to be retrospective and suffer from limitations relating to memory, such as, repression (Wilsnack, Wonderlich, Kristjanson, Vogeltanz-Holm, & Wilsnack, 2002) or compliant secrecy to avoid punishment or separation from the family (Svedin, Back, & Soderback, 2002). Moreover, children may not be developmentally equipped to share victimizing experiences. They may not understand that a certain action is abusive especially from a female caretaker (Kelly, Wood, Gonzalez, MacDonald, & Waterman, 2002).

7. The "hierarchy rule" directs multiple offense cases (Mosher et al., 2002).

8. Arata (1998) found that only 6 percent of CSA victims reported to the legal authorities and substantiated court cases also revealed significant underreporting (Widom & Morris, 1997). Perceptions that the reporting process will be shameful, anxiety provoking, stigmatizing, or endanger/hurt *loved others* results in the victim maintaining silence (Morison & Greene, 1992).

9. Three professional concerns have been delineated—"bad for me" (too time consuming, may result in lawsuit, loss of income, discomfort with family); "I can do better than the system," and "not reportable" (not enough evidence, already reported elsewhere, suspected abuse not severe enough; Zellman, 1990).

10. Individuals with more money have more resources to conceal CSA (Lesniak, 1993).

11. This study was last conducted in 1993. Information was drawn from multiple sources where nonreporting or misguided accounting is common (Van Haeringen et al., 1998).

12. Has no specific category for CSA (FBI, n.d.). Collect data from the city, county, state, tribal, and federal legal systems (NIBRS, n.d.).

13. Information is provided by self-report interviews with children twelve years and older—missing younger youth. Also, parents serve as proxy interviewees, so, intrafamilial sexual abuse is not likely to be disclosed.

14. Experienced a maltreatment event (Sedlak & Broadhurst, 1996).

15. This reflects an increase of 83 percent from the NIS-2 (Sedlak & Broadhurst, 1986) study.

16. Understood as the "summary system: Part I offenses" (NIBRS, n.d.).

17. UCR: Forcible rape and sex offenses; NCVS: Rape and sexual assault (Prentky & Burgess, 2000).

18. Media reports involving false complaints of sexual abuse may have been nationally perceived as unfairly stigmatizing to the alleged abuser influencing policies and standards and the level of reporting.

19. Over time, the definition of CSA may have altered the substantiating and reporting of cases. To illustrate, in the later 1990s, children (two or three years apart in age) observed sexually fondling may have been considered engaging in sexual play; whereas, in the late 1980s this behavior may have been reported and substantiated as sexual abuse (Leventhal, 2000).

20. Some believe that we may never know the exact number (Finkelhor, Ormrod, Turner, & Hamby, 2005).

21. It is estimated that 25 to 33 percent of children will not develop deleterious outcomes associated with CSA (Lynskey & Fergusson, 1997).

22. An example of resiliency is when an automobile tire is hit with a bat it will return to its original shape because of its characteristic strengths (Norman, 2000).

23. In the Fifty-State Survey, more than half of the states reported poverty as a number one issue associated with child abuse (Wang & Daro, 1998).

24. Seventy percent of CSA victims reported substance abuse or dependency in a male caregiver and 22 percent in the female caregivers. Drugs reduce internal inhibitions and increase impulsiveness (Lesniak, 1993).

25. It is important to note that the brain and the mind are two different entities. In a cyclical pattern, each may influence the other (see Siegel, 2003). For example, if a youth understands (cognitions) that the world is dangerous and nonsupportive, the locus coeruleus (the brain's trauma center) is constantly on alert. This type of mind/brain activity can launch chronic disease (Allen, 1995).

26. The attachment style is considered stable, yet modifiable (Fraley et al., 2005). For an in-depth study of attachment theory, see Bowlby (1982a).

27. The child sacrifices his or her personal needs by acting as a nanny, "confidant," surrogate partner, supportive friend, and/or wage earner. The caregiver may use the child to satisfy possessive, dependent, aggressive, and sexual needs (Boszormenyi-Nagy & Krasner, 1986).

28. The family cognition is "You are either with us or against us." A cut-off is either overt or covert rejection.

29. Children may also take on the parent role to manipulate their environment (reduce abusive behavior or tension). Occasional success at manipulating the parent can alter the child's perception of the circumstance (I am in control) and encourage the child to continue to use manipulation when frustrated or anxious.

30. Panic, phobia (Casella & Motta, 1990), and depression (Sawyer, Tsao, Hansen, & Flood, 2006).

31. A sensitive or susceptible period when the organism is most vulnerable to environmental stimulation (MacDonald, 1987).

REFERENCES

Adams, B. L. (2005). Assessment of child abuse risk factors by advanced practice nurses. *Pediatric Nursing, 31*(6), 498-502.

Alaggia, R. (2004). Many ways of telling: Expanding conceptualizations of child sexual abuse disclosure. *Child Abuse & Neglect, 28*(11), 1213-1227.

Alexander, P. C. (1992). Application of attachment theory to the study of sexual abuse. *Journal of Consulting and Clinical Psychology, 60,* 185-195.

Allen, J. G. (1995). *Coping with trauma: A guide to self-understanding.* Washington, DC: American Psychiatric Press, Inc.

Arata, C. M. (1998). To tell or not to tell: Current functioning of child sexual abuse survivors who disclose their victimization. *Child Maltreatment, 3*(1), 63-72.

Badgley, R. F., Allard, H. A., McCormick, N., Proudfoot, P., Fortin, D., Ogilvie, D., et al. (1984). Sexual offenses against children and youth: Occurrence in the population. In R. F. Badgley et al. (Eds.), *Sexual offenses against children* (Vol. 1, pp. 175-193). Ottawa, Canada: Canadian Publishing Centre.

Banyard, V. L. (1999). Childhood maltreatment and the mental health of low-income women. *American Journal of Orthopsychiatry, 69*(2), 161-171.

Banyard, V. L., Williams, L. M., & Siegel, J. A. (2001). The long-term mental health consequences of child sexual abuse: An exploratory study of the impact of multiple traumas in a sample of women. *Journal of Traumatic Stress, 14*(4), 697-715.

Barrett, M. J., Sykes, C., & Byrnes, W. (1996). A systematic model for the treatment of intra-family child sexual abuse. *Journal of Psychotherapy and the Family, 2,* 67-82.

Berk, L. E. (1989). *Child development.* Boston: Allyn and Bacon.

BJS. (2000). *Sexual assault of young children as reported to law enforcement: Victim, incident, and offender characteristics.* Retrieved June 18, 2006 from www.ojp.usdoj.gov/bjs/.

BJS. (2005). *Rape rates continue to decline.* Retrieved June 18, 2006 from www.ojp.usdoj.gov/bjs/.

BJS. (2006). *Crime and victim statistics.* Retrieved June 19, 2006 from http://www.ojp.usdoj.gov/bjs/cvict.htm.

Bolen, R. M. (2001). *Child sexual abuse: Its scope and our failure.* New York: Kluwer Academic/Plenum Publishers.

Boszormenyi-Nagy, I., & Krasner, B. (1986). *Between give and take: A clinical guide to contextual therapy.* New York: Bruner/Mazel.

Bowlby, J. (1982a). *Attachment and loss* (2nd ed., Vol. 1). New York: Basic Books.

Bowlby, J. (1982b). Attachment and loss: Retrospect and prospect. *American Journal of Orthopsychiatry, 52*(4), 664-678.

Briere, J., & Elliott, D. M. (2003). Prevalence and psychological sequelae of self-reported childhood physical and sexual abuse in a general population sample of men and women. *Child Abuse & Neglect, 27*(10), 1205-1222.

Briere, J., & Runtz, M. (1988). Symptomatology associated with childhood sexual victimization in a nonclinical adult sample. *Child Abuse & Neglect, 12*(1), 51-59.

Brown, J., Cohen, P., Johnson, J. G., & Salzinger, S. (1998). A longitudinal analysis of risk factors for child maltreatment: Findings of a 17-year prospective study of officially recorded and self-reported child abuse and neglect. *Child Abuse & Neglect, 22*(11), 1065-1078.

Carlson, V., Cicchetti, D., Barnett, D., & Braunwald, K. (1989). Disorganized/disoriented attachment relationships in maltreated infants. *Developmental Psychopathology, 25,* 525-531.

Carr, A. (1999). *The handbook of child and adolescent clinical psychology: A contextual approach*. New York: Routledge.

Carson, D. K., Gertz, L. M., Donaldson, M. A., & Wonderlich, S. A. (1991). Intrafamilial sexual abuse: Family of origin and family of procreation characteristics of female adult victims. *The Journal of Psychology, 125,* 579-597.

Casella, L., & Motta, R. W. (1990). Comparison of characteristics of Vietnam veterans with and without posttraumatic stress disorder. *Psychological Reports, 67*(2), 595-605.

Cassidy, J. (2003). Continuity and change in the measurement of infant attachment: Comment on Fraley and Spieker (2003). *Developmental Psychology, 39*(3), 409-412; discussion 423-429.

Colon, A. R. (2001). *A history of children: A socio-cultural survey across millennia*. Westport, CT: Greenwood Press.

Daigneault, I., Tourigny, M., & Hebert, M. (2006). Self-attributions of blame in sexually abused adolescents: A mediational model. *Journal of Traumatic Stress, 19*(1), 153-157.

Deblinger, E., McLeer, S. V., Atkins, M. S., Ralphe, D., & Foa, E. (1989). Posttraumatic stress in sexually abused, physically abused, and nonabused children. *Child Abuse & Neglect, 13*(3), 403-408.

DHHS (2006a). *Chapter 3, victims; child maltreatment 2004*. Retrieved June 26, 2006, from http://www.acf.hhs.gov/programs/cb/pubs/cm04/chapterthree.htm#types.

DHHS (2006b). *Child maltreatment 2003: Summary of key findings*. Retrieved June 20, 2006, from http://www.childwelfare.gov/pubs/factsheets/canstats.cfm.

Doll, B., & Lyon, M. (1998). Risk and resilience: Implications for the delivery of mental health services in the schools. *School Psychology Review, 27*(3), 348-363.

Drugan, R. C., Basile, A. S., Ha, J. H., Healy, D., & Ferland, R. J. (1997). Analysis of the importance of controllable versus uncontrollable stress on subsequent behavioral and physiological functioning. *Brain Research Protocols, 2*(1), 69-74.

Egeland, B., Jacobvitz, D., & Sroufe, L. A. (1988). Breaking the cycle of abuse. *Child Development, 59*(4), 1080-1088.

Erikson, E. (1968). *Identity, youth and crisis*. New York: Norton.

FBI (n.d). *Uniform Crime Reports*. Retrieved June 19, 2006, from http://www.fbi.gov/ucr/ucr.htm.

Finkelhor, D. (1979a). *Sexually victimized children*. New York: Free Press.

Finkelhor, D. (1979b). What's wrong with sex between adults and children? Ethics and the problem of sexual abuse. *American Journal of Orthopsychiatry, 49*(4), 692-697.

Finkelhor, D. (1994). Current information on the scope and nature of child sexual abuse. *Future of Children, 4*(2), 31-53.

Finkelhor, D. (1998). Improving research, policy, and practice to understand child sexual abuse. *Journal of the American Medical Association, 280*(21), 1864-1865.

Finkelhor, D., & Kendall-Tackett, K. A. (1997). A developmental perspective on the childhood impact of crime, abuse, and violent victimization. In D. T. S. L Cichetti

(Ed.), *Rochester symposium on developmental psychology: Developmental perspective on trauma: Theory, research, and intervention* (Vol. 8, pp. 1-32). Rochester, NY: University of Rochester Press.

Finkelhor, D., Ormrod, R., Turner, H., & Hamby, S. L. (2005). The victimization of children and youth: A comprehensive, national survey. *Child Maltreatment, 10*(1), 5-25.

Flanagan, C. (1999). *Early socialization: Sociability and attachment.* New York: Routledge.

Fraley, R. C., Brumbaugh, C. C., & Marks, M. J. (2005). The evolution and function of adult attachment: A comparative and phylogenetic analysis. *Journal of Personal and Social Psychology, 89*(5), 731-746.

Freeman, J. B., & Beck, J. G. (2000). Cognitive interference for trauma cues in sexually abused adolescent girls with posttraumatic stress disorder. *Journal of Clinical Child Psychology, 29*(2), 245-256.

Gemelli, R. (1996). *Normal child and adolescent development.* Washington, DC: American Psychiatric Press.

Goldman, J. D. G., & Padayachi, U. K. (2000). Some methodological problems in estimating incidence and prevalence in child sexual abuse research. *The Journal of Sex Research, 37*(4), 305-314.

Haj-Yahi, M. M., & Tamish, S. (2001). The rates of child sexual abuse and its psychological consequences as revealed by a study among Palestinian university students. *Child Abuse & Neglect, 25*(10), 1303-1327.

Haugaard, J. J. (2000). The challenge of defining child sexual abuse. *American Psychologist, 55*(9), 1036-1039.

Johnson, C. F. (2004). Child sexual abuse. *Lancet, 364*(9432), 462-470.

Jones, L. M., Finkelhor, D., & Kopiec, K. (2001). Why is sexual abuse declining? A survey of state child protection administrators. *Child Abuse & Neglect, 25*(9), 1139-1158.

Jones, L. M., Finkelhor, D., & Halter, S. (2006). Child maltreatment trends in the 1990s: Why does neglect differ from sexual and physical abuse? *Child Maltreatment, 11*(2), 107-120.

Jurkovic, G. H. (1997). *Lost childhoods: The plight of the parentified child.* New York: Brunner & Mazel.

Kandel, E. R. (1983). From metapsychology to molecular biology. *American Journal of Psychiatry, 140,* 1277-1293.

Kandel, E. R. (1998). A new intellectual framework for psychiatry. *American Journal of Psychiatry, 155,* 457-469.

Katsikas, S., Petretic-Jackson, P., & Knowles, E. (1996). *Long-term sequelae of childhood maltreatment: An attachment theory perspective.* Paper presented at the Annual Meeting of the Association for the Advancement of Behavior Therapy, New York.

Kelly, R. J., Wood, J. J., Gonzalez, L. S., MacDonald, V., & Waterman, J. (2002). Effects of mother-son incest and positive perceptions of sexual abuse experiences on the psychosocial adjustment of clinic-referred men. *Child Abuse & Neglect, 26*(4), 425-441.

Kilpatrick, D. G. (2004). What is violence against women: Defining and measuring the problem. *Journal of Interpersonal Violence, 19*(11), 1209-1234.

Kinsey, A. C., Pomeroy, W. B., Martin, C. E., & Gebhard, P. (1953). *Sexual behavior in the human female.* Philadelphia: W.B. Saunders.

Kirby, J. S., Chu, J. A., & Dill, D. L. (1993). Severity, frequency, and age of onset of physical and sexual abuse as factors in the development of dissociative symptoms. *Comprehensive Psychiatry, 34,* 258-263.

Koss, M. P. (1998). *Hidden rape: Sexual aggression and victimization in a national sample of students in higher education.* Wilmington, DE: SR Books/Scholarly Resources, Inc.

Lascaratos, J., & Poulakou-Rebelakou, E. (2000). Child sexual abuse: Historical cases in the Byzantine empire (324-1453 A.D.). *Child Abuse & Neglect, 24*(8), 1085-1090.

Legrand, M., & Reldman, S. (1999). *The Michel Legrand Songbook: Martina* (p. 74, original work 1966). Van Nuys, CA: Alfred Publishing.

Lesniak, L. P. (1993). Penetrating the conspiracy of silence: Identifying the family at risk for incest. *Family and Community Health, 16,* 66-76.

Leventhal, J. M. (2000). Sexual abuse of children: Continuing challenges for the new millennium. *Acta Paediatrica, 89*(3), 268-271.

Luthar, S. S. (1991). Vulnerability and resilience: A study of high-risk adolescents. *Child Development, 62*(3), 600-616.

Luthar, S. S., & Blatt, S. J. (1993). Dependent and self-critical depressive experiences among inner-city adolescents. *Journal of Personality, 61* (3), 365-386.

Lynskey, M. T., & Fergusson, D. M. (1997). Factors protecting against the development of adjustment difficulties in young adults exposed to childhood sexual abuse. *Child Abuse & Neglect, 21*(12), 1177-1190.

MacDonald, K. (1987). Early experience, relative plasticity, and social development. In S. Chess & A. Thomas (Eds.), *Annual progress in child psychiatry and child development 1986* (pp. 86-110). New York: Brunner/Mazel.

Massat, C. R., & Lundy, M. (1998). "Reporting costs" to nonoffending parents in cases of intrafamilial child sexual abuse. *Child Welfare, 77*(4), 371-388.

McCubbin, M. A., & McCubbin, H. I. (1993). Family coping with health crisis: The resiliency model of family stress, adjustment and adaptation. In C. Danielson, B. Hamel-Bissell, & P. Winstead-Fry (Eds.), *Families, health and illness* (pp. 21-64). St. Louis, MO: C. V. Mosby.

McLeer, S. V., Deblinger, E., Atkins, M. S., Foa, E. B., & Ralphe, D. L. (1988). Post-traumatic stress disorder in sexually abused children. *Journal of the American Academy of Child & Adolescent Psychiatry, 27*(5), 650-654.

Melton, G. B., Petrila, J., Poythress, N. G., & Slobogin, C. (1997). *Psychological evaluations for the courts: A handbook for mental health professionals and lawyers* (2nd ed.). New York: Guilford Press.

Miller-Perrin, C. L., & Perrin, R. D. (1999). *Child maltreatment: An introduction.* Thousand Oaks, CA: Sage.

Mitchell, C. W., & Rogers, R. E. (2003). Rape, statutory rape, and child abuse: Legal distinctions and counselor duties [Electronic version]. *Professional School Counseling, 6*(5), 332-338.

Morison, S., & Greene, E. (1992). Juror and expert knowledge of child sexual abuse. *Child Abuse & Neglect, 16*(4), 595-613.

Morrison, J., Frank, S., Holland, C., & Kates, W. (1999). *Emotional development and disorders in young children in the child welfare system*. Baltimore: Paul H. Brookes.

Mosher, C. J., Miethe, T. D., & Phillips, D. M. (2002). *The mismeasure of crime*. Thousand Oaks, CA: Sage.

NCPCA. (2004). *Investigation and prosecution of child abuse* (3rd ed.). Thousand Oaks, CA: Sage.

NIBRS (n.d). *National incidence-based reporting system (NIBRS)*. Retrieved June 23, 2006, from http://www.fbi.gov/ucr/faqs.htm

NIS-4 (n.d). *NIS-4 description*. Retrieved June 23, 2006, from https://www.nis4.org/nis4.asp.

Norman, E. (2000). Introduction: The strengths perspective and resiliency enhancement: A natural partnership. In E. Norman (Ed.), *Resiliency enhancement: Putting the strengths perspective into social work practice* (pp. 1-16). New York: Columbia University Press.

Paolucci, E. O., Genuis, M. L., & Violato, C. (2001). A meta-analysis of the published research on the effects of child sexual abuse. *Journal of Psychology, 135*, 17-36.

Pearce, J. W., & Pezzot-Pearce, T. D. (1997). *Psychotherapy of abused and neglected children*. New York: Guilford Press.

Peddle, N., & Wang, C. (2001). *Current trends in child abuse prevention, reporting, and fatalities: The 1999 fifty-state survey*. Working Paper Number 808. Chicago: Prevent Child Abuse America.

Perkins, D. F., & Jones, K. R. (2004). Risk behaviors and resiliency within physically abused adolescents. *Child Abuse & Neglect, 28*(5), 547-563.

Pillai, M. (2005). Forensic examination of suspected child victims of sexual abuse in the UK: A personal view. *Journal of Clinical and Forensic Medicine, 12*(2), 57-63.

Plummer, C. A. (2001). Prevention of child sexual abuse: A survey of 87 programs. *Violence and Victims, 16*(5), 575-588.

Prentky, R. A., & Burgess, A. W. (2000). *Forensic management of sexual offenders*. New York: Kluwer.

Putnam, F. W. (2003). Ten-year research update review: Child sexual abuse. *Journal of the American Academy of Child and Adolescent Psychiatry, 42*(3), 269-278.

Putnam, F. W., & Trickett, P. K. (1993). Child sexual abuse: A model of chronic trauma. *Psychiatry, 56*(1), 82-95.

Resnick, H. S., Kilpatrick, D. G., Dansky, B. S., Saunders, B. E., & Best, C. L. (1993). Prevalence of civilian trauma and posttraumatic stress disorder in a representative national sample of women. *Journal of Consulting & Clinical Psychology, 61*(6), 984-991.

Rotter, J. B. (1966). Generalized expectancies for internal versus external control of reinforcement. *Psychological Monograph, 80*(1), 1-28.

Ruggiero, K. J., Del Ben, K., Scotti, J. R., & Rabalais, A. E. (2003). Psychometric properties of the PTSD Checklist-Civilian version. *Journal of Traumatic Stress, 16*(5), 495-502.

Russell, D. E. H. (1984). *Sexual exploitation: Rape, child sexual abuse, and workplace harassment.* Beverly Hills, CA: Sage.

Rutter, M. (1990). Psychosocial resilience and protective mechanisms. In J. E. Rolf & A. S. Masten (Eds.), *Risk and protective factors in the development of psychopathology* (pp. 181-214). New York: Cambridge University Press.

Salter, D., McMillan, D., Richards, M., Talbot, T., Hodges, J., Bentovim, A., et al. (2003). Development of sexually abusive behaviour in sexually victimised males: A longitudinal study. *Lancet, 361*(9356), 471-476.

Sawyer, G. K., Tsao, E. H., Hansen, D. J., & Flood, M. F. (2006). Weekly problems scales: Instruments for sexually abused youth and their nonoffending parents in treatment. *Child Maltreatment, 11*(1), 34-48.

Sealander, J. (2003). *The failed century of the child: Governing America's young in the twentieth century.* New York: Cambridge University Press.

Sedlak, A. J., & Broadhurst, D. D. (1996). *Executive summary of the third national incidence study of child abuse and neglect.* Retrieved June 13, 2006, from http://nccanch.acf.hhs.gov/pubs/statsinfo/nis3.cfm.

Sedney, M. A., & Brooks, B. (1984). Factors associated with a history of childhood sexual experience in a nonclinical female population. *Journal of the American Academy of Child Psychiatry, 23*(2), 215-218.

Seidner, A., & Calhoun, K. S. (1984). *Childhood sexual abuse factors related to differential adult adjustment.* Paper presented at the second National Conference for Family Violence Researchers, Durham, NH.

Seligman, M. E., & Maier, S. F. (1967). Failure to escape traumatic shock. *Journal of Experimental Psychology, 74*(1), 1-9.

Seligman, M. E., Maier, S. F., & Geer, J. H. (1968). Alleviation of learned helplessness in the dog. *Journal of Abnormal Psychology, 73*(3), 256-262.

Shapiro, D. L., & Levendosky, A. A. (1999). Adolescent survivors of childhood sexual abuse: The mediating role of attachment style and coping in psychological and interpersonal functioning. *Child Abuse and Neglect, 23*(11), 1175-1191.

Siegel, D. J. (2003). An interpersonal neurobiology of psychotherapy: The developing mind and the resolution of trauma. In M. F. Solomon & D. J. Siegel (Eds.), *Healing trauma: Attachment, mind, body, and brain* (pp. 1-56). New York: W.W. Norton & Co.

Sroufe, L. A. (2005). Attachment and development: A prospective, longitudinal study from birth to adulthood. *Attachment and Human Development, 7*(4), 349-367.

Sroufe, L. A., Carlson, E. A., Levy, A. K., & Egeland, B. (1999). Implications of attachment theory for developmental psychopathology. *Developmental Psychopathology, 11*(1), 1-13.

Stanley, J., & Kovacs, K. (2004). Letter to the editor re: Is child sexual abuse declining? Evidence from a population based survey of men and women in Australia (Dunne, Purdie, Cook, Boyle, & Najman, 2003). *Child Abuse & Neglect, 28*(4), 369-372.

Star, L. D., & Lani, F. M. (2002). Current issues in conducting child sex abuse evaluations. *American Journal of Forensic Psychology, 20*(4), 53-77.

Stein, H., Fonagy, P., Ferguson, K. S., & Wisman, M. (2000). Lives through time: An ideographic approach to the study of resilience. *Bulletin of the Menninger Clinic, 64*(2), 281-305.

Svedin, C. G., Back, C., & Soderback, S. B. (2002). Family relations, family climate and sexual abuse. *Nordic Journal of Psychiatry, 56*(5), 355-362.

Teicher, M. H. (2002). Scars that won't heal: The neurobiology of child abuse. *Scientific American, 286*(3), 68-75.

Van Haeringen, A. R., Dadds, M., & Armstrong, K. L. (1998). The child abuse lottery—Will the doctor suspect and report? Physician attitudes towards and reporting of suspected child abuse and neglect. *Child Abuse and Neglect, 22*(3), 159-169.

Wang, C. T., & Daro, D. (1998). *Current trends in child abuse reporting and fatalities: The results of the 1997 annual fifty-state survey.* Chicago: National Committee to Prevent Child Abuse.

Widom, C. S., & Morris, S. (1997). Accuracy of adult recollections of childhood victimization, Part 2: Childhood sexual abuse. *Psychological Assessment, 9*(1), 34-46.

Wilcox, D. T., Richards, F., & O'Keeffe, Z. C. (2004). Resilience and risk factors associated with experiencing childhood sexual abuse. *Child Abuse Review, 13*(5), 338-352.

Wilsnack, S. C., Wonderlich, S. A., Kristjanson, A. F., Vogeltanz-Holm, N. D., & Wilsnack, R. W. (2002). Self-reports of forgetting and remembering childhood sexual abuse in a nationally representative sample of US women. *Child Abuse & Neglect, 26*(2), 139-147.

Wolin, S., & Wolin, S. (1995). Resilience among youth growing up in substance-abusing families. *Pediatric Clinics of North America, 42*(2), 415-429.

Wurtele, S. K., & Miller-Perrin, C. L. (1992). *Preventing child sexual abuse: Sharing the responsibility.* Lincoln, NE: University of Nebraska Press.

Wyatt, G. E. (1985). The sexual abuse of African American and European American women in childhood. *Child Abuse & Neglect, 9,* 507-519.

Wyatt, G. E., Carmona, J. V., Loeb, T. B., Ayala, A., & Chin, D. (2002). Sexual abuse. In G. M. Wingwood & R. J. DiClemente (Eds.), *Handbook of women's sexual and reproductive health* (pp. 195-216). New York: Kluwer Academic/Plenum Publishers.

Wyatt, G. E., Loeb, T. B., Solis, B., Carmona, J. V., & Romero, G. (1999). The prevalence and circumstances of child sexual abuse: Changes across a decade. *Child Abuse & Neglect, 23*(1), 45-60.

Zellman, G. L. (1990). Child abuse reporting and failure to report among mandated reporters: Prevalence, incidence, and reasons. *Journal of Interpersonal Violence, 5,* 3-22.

Zellman, G. L. (1992). The impact of case characteristics on child abuse reporting decisions. *Child Abuse & Neglect, 16*(1), 57-74.

Chapter 3

Family Dysfunction:
Theoretical Explanations
and Ethnic Considerations

Donna Harrington
Elizabeth Hisle-Gorman
David Dia

INTRODUCTION

The purpose of this chapter is to examine theoretical perspectives of child sexual abuse (CSA) and family dysfunction. Although an exhaustive review of the many theories and models in this area is beyond the scope of this chapter, we review several theories that may be useful for practitioners, policymakers, educators, and others interested in CSA and also explore how CSA is related to family dysfunction. Theories of CSA often emphasize either risk factors or sequelae (Higgins & McCabe, 1994); we focus on risk factors and practice models because of their relevance for developing prevention and treatment efforts. We begin by discussing the importance of theory in research, practice, policy, and education, followed by a brief discussion of different levels of theories, and a review of several theories. We end with an overview of how the theories address ethnic considerations and a section on conclusions and implications.

BACKGROUND

Families in which child sexual abuse occurs are often described as dysfunctional (Kellogg, Burge, & Taylor, 2000), and a number of

Handbook of Social Work in Child and Adolescent Sexual Abuse
© 2008 by The Haworth Press, Taylor & Francis Group. All rights reserved.
doi:10.1300/5804_03

family characteristics have been identified as risk factors for CSA, including poor family functioning and witnessing family or intimate partner violence (Higgins & McCabe, 1994, 2003; Svedin, Back, & Söderback, 2002). Although family dysfunction appears to be common in families that have experienced either intra- or extrafamilial sexual abuse, intrafamilial CSA appears to be associated with more severe family dysfunction (Svedin et al., 2002). Svedin and colleagues (2002) noted that dysfunction in families that have experienced CSA may be a result of, as well as a cause of, the sexual abuse; longitudinal research is needed to determine the direction and patterns of causal relations between CSA and family dysfunction.

CSA often co-occurs with other forms of child abuse, including neglect, physical abuse, and psychological or emotional abuse, making it difficult to disentangle unique causes of and outcomes for CSA or any one type of child maltreatment (Bevan & Higgins, 2002). Some research suggests that family factors, such as other forms of family violence or divorce, may be more predictive of trauma symptomatology than may be the experience of CSA (Higgins & McCabe, 1994). Families experiencing child maltreatment have been described as complex, unstable, and constantly changing; it may be difficult to identify who is part of the family (Paavilainen & Åstedt-Kurki, 2003).

IMPORTANCE OF THEORY

It has been recommended that the treatment of and research in CSA should be theory driven (Hulme, 2004; Trepper & Barrett, 1989). Theory is useful for identifying potential causal mechanisms and treatment modalities. Without theory, research and practice can be haphazard, unorganized, and ultimately ineffective (Ward & Siegert, 2002). With theory, research can proceed in an orderly manner, making investigations more effective and efficient and providing a systematic way of organizing vast amounts of information, especially in areas of practice such as CSA, where there are a large number of potential contributing factors and outcomes. Theory can also guide policy development.

Although all theories are open to criticism and are frequently incomplete, they provide a starting point from which to proceed. Theory development is an iterative process, typically beginning with a theorist identifying or recognizing a problem, describing the problem and then making etiological assumptions about the problem on the basis of theoretical orientation. The next step occurs when theorists from other orientations use different theoretical perspectives to provide input about the same problem, in the form of case studies and clinical examples. Next, treatment programs evolve on the basis of the aforementioned process and descriptive and basic effectiveness data are developed. The final step involves clinical trials that refine and test the theory under controlled situations (Trepper & Barrett, 1989).

The use of theory in organizing and understanding a phenomenon such as CSA has much to offer, but it is also important to recognize potential limitations. Theory offers a systematic approach, which is one of its strengths, but it can also create a systematic bias in how the clinician or policymaker defines the problem and what variables are considered important. Some researchers are concerned that an overreliance on theory can make one mechanistic and create a self-fulfilling prophecy (Turner, 1996). Therefore, when adopting any theoretical orientation, it is important to recognize its strengths and its limitations. Parton (2000) suggests that theory should be considered generative, in that it can help practitioners to think differently by providing new perspectives or insights. One way to overcome the weakness of any one theory is to examine the same problem through the lens of another theory that considers other casual variables. This is why we review several theories in this chapter.

LEVELS OF THEORY

There are many ways to organize or categorize theories; Hulme (2004) uses the classification of macro or grand[1] (often psychosocial or biopsychosocial theories that explain many phenomena), middle range (more limited in focus, such as victimization, but not specific to CSA), and micro (specific to CSA) theories. Using Hulme's classification, ecological, attachment, and resiliency are examples of grand level theories—all can be used to explain not only CSA and family dysfunction, but also many other human behaviors; we briefly review each of these because of their broad relevance for social work. Ward and Siegert's (2002) work provides an example of a micro level theory specific to CSA. We review this model in some detail because

Hanson and Morton-Bourgon (2005) and Whitaker, Lutzker, and Shelley (2005) have cited it as a good example, and it presents a complex and multifactored model, which builds upon the work of other CSA theorists. Some micro theories may also be considered practice theories, and may be very highly operationalized (e.g., Hund and Espelage's [2005] mediation model for CSA, disordered eating, and general distress), but sometimes this specificity limits their applicability to CSA in general. Because of the length of the considerations, we have not reviewed middle range or overly specific micro theories in this chapter.

GRAND THEORIES

As Finkelhor (1998) states, "Sexual abuse does not occur in a vacuum; it occurs in a childhood context that more often than not includes other forms of maltreatment, other traumas, and various degrees of family dysfunction, disruption, and deprivation" (p. 1864). Grand theories can be particularly helpful in identifying this broader context and guiding the examination of the multiple factors that may co-occur with CSA. Although there are many grand theories that can be applied to understanding CSA, we have focused on three—ecological, attachment, and risk and resilience—that can be broadly applied and that place some emphasis on the family. In addition, these three grand theories provide some of the foundation for other middle or micro level theories of CSA. Other grand theories, such as feminist theory (e.g., Lancaster & Lumb, 1999), are beyond the scope of this chapter.

Ecological Perspective

The ecological perspective provides a basic framework for understanding individual change and the connections between individuals and their environment. With roots in biology, ecological theory posits that individuals and their environment interact in a process of adaptation that changes both the person and the environment through a process of mutual accommodation (Bronfenbrenner, 1977; Germain & Gitterman, 1996). As a grand theory, the ecological perspective does not identify a specific explanatory process for CSA. However, it provides a framework for understanding child sexual abuse by examining the etiology of sexual abuse at several levels: the individual and what he or she brings to the situation (ontogenic development), the family (the microsystem), the community (the exosystem), and the society (the macrosystem).

At the ontogenic level, the ecological perspective suggests that the victim child should be included in the equation of understanding (Belsky, 1980). It goes on to say that some preexisting vulnerability may make sexually abused children more likely to be targeted. The theory does not suggest that abuse is the victim's fault, but instead acknowledges that some children with certain characteristics may be more likely to be victimized than others. At the family level, ecological theory suggests that certain characteristics of the family unit would predispose some families to abuse, for example research has found large families and those with closely spaced children may be more likely to be abusive and neglectful in general (Belsky, 1980). At the neighborhood and community level, researchers have found maltreated children and maltreating families more likely to be socially isolated (Garbarino, 1977). Finally, the larger societal system's effect on CSA may be seen in the sexualization of children and teens in the media, and a general belief that parents have ultimate authority over children. As these systems interact, forces can converge to position a child at risk of being sexually victimized. Understanding that multiple levels are involved in causing sexual abuse helps to guide researchers and clinicians beyond the perpetrator and victim dyad to focus on prevention and promote healing at family, community, and societal levels (Belsky, 1980).

Ecological theory also provides some explanation of how being abused can affect an individual, and how this can vary between individuals. Clearly, issues such as the length and severity of the abuse as well as the relationship between the victim and the perpetrator are important. However ecological theory would suggest that these as well as other factors specific to the individual would influence the effect of the abuse. As with biological ecology, the ecological perspective suggests that a stressor may cause difficulty for an individual; however, if sufficient support systems or protective factors are in place, the individual may overcome the negative experience. The stressor, such as CSA, may be too great to overcome, leading to disease and dysfunction. Yet, if individuals appraise their resources as sufficient to overcome the negative experience, they may be able to adapt and achieve positive change in response; this transformation may ultimately provide them with a level of protection or resilience. For example, a child who is abused and immediately tells a protective adult resulting in the removal and arrest of the perpetrator may feel strengthened and feel a renewed sense of his or her own ability to control the environment. An ecological understanding of CSA reminds researchers and clinicians of the role of larger systems and provides a framework for understanding how sexual abuse can have different effects on different individuals. Perhaps the most important contribution of the ecological perspective in understanding CSA and family dysfunction is that it forces researchers, practitioners, and policymakers to examine CSA in the broader context of the community and society, rather than just focusing on individual children and their families.

Risk and Resilience Theory

Risk and resilience theory grew from observation of the real-life phenomena of resilient young people who were doing well despite adversity (Richardson, 2002). General resilience studies find between one-half and two-thirds of children growing up in adverse situations are resilient (Fraser, 1997; Greene, 2002); however studies focused specifically on maltreatment consistently find much lower resilience levels of approximately 5 percent (Bolger & Patterson, 2003). Although research has long focused on risk factors, only recently have researchers also looked at resilience or protective factors and their acquisition in a theoretic way. Though some resilience theorists focus on an individual's internal "motivational force" (Richardson, 2002), much of their work incorporates systems ideas in the understanding that hardiness factors can occur at multiple levels, including individual, familial, and environmental levels (Liem, James, O'Toole, & Boudewyn, 1997). Risk and resilience theory also incorporates ideas consistent with Lazarus's (1990) work on stress and coping and ecological theory's ideas of appraisal (Germain & Gitterman, 1996). Richardson (2002) describes the resiliency model as one in which people have the opportunity to choose the outcome of stressors or life events using protective factors or resources.

Applying these ideas to child sexual abuse, risk and resilience theory informs us that multiple factors affect a child's longer-term response to abuse, and that risk and protective factors occur at multiple levels (as discussed earlier in the chapter), both at the time of abuse and as the child grows to adulthood. Factors such as seeking and finding support outside of the family (Valentine & Feinauer, 1993), a strong relationship with a nonabusing parent (Spaccarelli & Kim, 1995), or environmental factors such as a positive school experience or playing a sport (Romans, Martin, Anderson, O'Shea, & Mullen, 1995) may be important to resilience in victims of sexual abuse.

Cognitive appraisals are also extremely important in risk and resilience theory. Again moving from research to theory, CSA investigations suggest that positive illusions or optimistic distortions of reality (Himelein & McElrath, 1996) and attributing blame externally to the perpetrator (Feinauer & Stuart, 1996) may be important to resilience in survivors of sexual abuse. Internal appraisal of both the world around them (despite the reality of the situation) and internal ascription of blame to the perpetrator are important components of their understanding of the situation and are involved in their "choice" of the outcome. The empirical foundation of risk and resilience theory makes it applicable to the understanding of coping with child sexual abuse, but it may be less useful in guiding clinical interventions because some important factors are vague or not fully operationalized, such as internal working models (derived from attachment theory) or preexisting resources.

Attachment Theory

Attachment theory maintains that an infant's innate attachment behaviors (e.g., calling, crying, clinging, and following) evoke attachment behaviors from the mother or caregiver, forming the foundation of the lasting relationship dynamic between the two. Through interaction with the parent, children build "internal working models" of their self-worth on the basis of the perceptions of caregiver's availability and protection (Bowlby, 1973). Initially theorized by Bowlby (1969), who based his observations on war orphans, empirically examined with Ainsworth, Blehar, Walther, and Wall's (1978) strange situation, and later elaborated by Simpson and Rholes (1998), four attachment styles have been described:

Secure. Children are confident their parents will be available, responsive, and helpful, and as a result feel bold and capable in their exploration of the world.

Anxious Resistant. Uncertain of parents' availability or responsiveness, children exhibit extreme dependence in an attempt to gain attention, are prone to separation anxiety, and are hesitant about exploring the world.

Anxious Avoidant. Children expect to be rebuffed when seeking care, and thus avoid the attachment figures to avoid rejection; children tend to become emotionally self-sufficient and live without the love and support of others (Bowlby, 1988).

Disorganized. Resulting from unpredictability of parents, children are unsure of what to make of the world (Simpson & Rholes, 1998).

Research suggests that these attachment styles are stable over time, and that parents often pass their own attachment styles to their children, so that securely attached parents have securely attached children, and insecurely attached parents have insecurely attached children (Alexander, 1992; Bacon & Richardson, 2001).

Child abuse and neglect often occur within a context of insecure attachment (see Morton & Brown, 1998 for review), and child physical abuse may produce anxious attachments (Bacon & Richardson, 2001). Because child sexual abuse often co-occurs with other types of maltreatment, it is difficult to separate the specific relationship between attachment and child sexual abuse. Furthermore, in the application of attachment theory, the victim-abuser dyad cannot be singled out and all familial connectedness must be examined. Looking at the family unit, Alexander (1992) suggests the following hypotheses for the connection between child sexual abuse and attachment:

Avoidant. In this attachment style, it is hypothesized that a rejecting mother is unavailable, and that an authoritarian father, who views his wife and children as property and subject to fulfilling his needs, perpetrates child sexual abuse.

Resistant. Within this attachment style, Alexander postulates that the victim child is parentified, the nonabusing parent then feels that this parentified child should nurture them as opposed to caring for and nurturing the child, and the abusive parent may feel as though the child should meet their sexual needs as well.

Disorganized. This type of attachment usually occurs in chaotic families in which there is fear and unresolved trauma, and there would likely be substance abuse, physical abuse, and indiscriminate sexual behavior; the nonabusing parent may be so disorganized that he or she does not see the evidence of abuse, or ignores the evidence out of fear of the family breaking up.

This system of understanding sexual abuse within an attachment framework theorized by Alexander (1992) is empirically untested. However, it can serve a clinical function in reminding the professionals who help that even when an immediate threat of abuse is eliminated, the underlying family structure that allowed the abuse may exist, necessitating treatment focused on family structure to ensure ongoing safety of the child.

Liem and Boudewyn (1999) provide an example of how attachment theory may explain individual coping strategies in reaction to CSA. Children who have internal working models of others as caring and supportive may seek social support to help them cope with CSA. However, those who expect others to be unresponsive, hostile, or betraying may experience self-blame or anxious dependence on attachment figures, resulting in ineffective use of social support. Children experiencing multiple forms of child maltreatment may be at risk for insecure attachments, consequently resulting in less successful coping when CSA occurs. Using theory in this way can lead to specific hypotheses about adult outcomes of CSA, which may ultimately provide guidance for treatment. Bolen (2000) cautions that though many of the hypotheses derived from attachment theory have been supported by research, support "remains equivocal, and the limits of the theory are not clearly defined" (p. 128).

Although none of the grand theories reviewed here was developed specifically as explanations for the phenomenon of CSA, all of them can provide some guidance for understanding CSA. In brief, the ecological perspective identifies the importance of examining CSA in the broader community and societal context; risk and resilience reminds us to look for factors related to resilient outcomes; and attachment theory guides examination of the important relationship between children and caregivers, and how it is related to the occurrence and outcomes of CSA.

MICRO LEVEL THEORIES

Micro level theories can build on grand level theories, by providing operationalization of some of the abstract constructs used, or by integrating aspects of several grand theories. We briefly review one such micro level theory: Ward and Siegert's (2002) comprehensive theory of CSA, which includes some aspects of each of the grand theories discussed earlier in the chapter.

Ward and Siegert's Comprehensive Theory of Child Sexual Abuse

Ward and Siegert (2002) used a theory knitting approach to integrate three influential theories of CSA: Finkelhor's precondition model of CSA (Finkelhor & Araji, 1986; Ward & Hudson, 2001), Hall and Hirschman's quadripartite model (Ward, 2001), and Marshall and Barbaree's integrated theory (Ward, 2002). According to Ward and Siegert (2002), all three theories have strengths and weaknesses; they attempted to create a "comprehensive etiological theory" by integrating the best components of the three. As Ward (2002) states:

> Finkelhor's theory nicely links offenders' psychological vulnerabilities with the offence process, Hall and Hirschman comprehensively address the issue of typology, while Marshall and Barbaree lucidly describe the way developmental adversity can result in the abuse of a child. (p. 226)

Ward and Siegert (2002) identify multiple causal mechanisms, including "developmental adversity, cultural values and belief systems, family context, biological variables, psychological deficits, and situational variables" (p. 331). Specifically, they identify four distinct, interacting mechanisms of child molesters: (1) intimacy and social skills deficits, resulting from insecure attachment related to abusive or neglectful early environments; (2) distorted sexual scripts due to early abuse; (3) emotional disregulation, which might be a function of "dysfunctional goals (e.g., to avoid feelings), inadequate coping strategies (e.g., use of alcohol), inability or disinclination to utilise coping skills, or poorly modulated affective states" (p. 333); and (4) cognitive distortions. Each of these four mechanisms represents potentially separate causal pathways, and each may result in unique symptoms and patterns. According to Ward and Siegert (2002), all instances of CSA involve all four mechanisms, resulting in five pathways through which CSA may occur.

Pathway one: Intimacy deficits. The onset of sexual offending occurs in adulthood, often triggered by rejection or sustained loneliness. Though offenders may have normal sexual scripts, they may offend at specific times, such as when a preferred partner is not available, because of intimacy deficits caused by insecure attachment styles "and subsequent problems establishing satisfactory relationships with adults" (Ward & Siegert, 2002, p. 336).

Pathway two: Deviant sexual scripts. Like pathway one, onset of sexual offending in pathway two also begins in adulthood, and tends to be episodic in nature. However, pathway two differs from pathway one in that it involves distortions in sexual scripts interacting with dysfunctional relationship schemas or attachment styles. Offenders in pathway two may have been sexually abused as children, may confuse sex with intimacy, may abuse after rejection by adults, and may choose children as sexual partners because of opportunity and sexual or emotional need (Ward & Siegert, 2002).

Pathway three: Emotional disregulation. Within pathway three, onset of sexual offending may occur during adolescence or adulthood, especially during stressful periods because sex may be used to ameliorate mood. This pathway is marked by problems in the emotional regulation system, such as "problems identifying emotions, a lack of capacity to modulate negative emotions, or an inability to utilise social supports in times of emotional distress" (Ward & Siegert, 2002, p. 337). Sex and emotional well-being become linked as sex is used as a means of increasing self-esteem or mood.

Pathway four: Antisocial cognitions. Within pathway four, sexual offending may begin during childhood or adolescence and may be diagnosed as conduct disorder. CSA may reflect the offenders' general antisocial tendencies, pro-criminal attitudes and beliefs, patriarchal attitudes toward children, and feelings of their own superiority (Ward & Siegert, 2002).

Pathway five: Multiple dysfunctional mechanisms. The fifth pathway includes "individuals who have developed distorted sexual scripts, usually reflecting a history of sexual abuse or exposure to sexual material or activity at a young age. . . . [They are] likely to exhibit a multitude of offence related deficits and constitute 'pure' pedophiles" (Ward & Siegert, 2002, p. 339).

Ward and Siegert (2002) identify the five pathways as explanations for why someone may begin sexually abusing children, but not why they may continue; while the vulnerability factors identified for each pathway may be linked to continued sexual abuse, it is not necessary and it is expected that positive and negative reinforcement will maintain the sexually abusive behavior. Sexual abuse occurs in the context of situational triggers interacting with the predispositions outlined in the pathways.

The findings from a recent meta-analysis of sexual offender recidivism studies are consistent with the model in terms of different factors being associated with initial as compared with continued abuse and that situational triggers may be important in recidivism (Hanson & Morton-Bourgon, 2005). It is important to note that CSA experienced as a child is an important vulnerability factor for pathways two and five, but not all who have been sexually abused will become perpetrators of CSA, and whether they will become sexual offenders is moderated by how others respond to the abuse, duration and severity of abuse, and other factors. These factors increase or decrease the chances of becoming an abuser, which is "mediated by the degree of distortion of the sexual script, and/or, the absence of marked disruptions to other socioemotional mechanisms (e.g., emotional regulation)" (Ward & Siegert, 2002, p. 341).

Ward and Siegert (2002) present the pathways model as a provisional framework in need of refining. As they note, the theory is lacking a substantive evidential base. The data that support its major ideas tend to come from other areas in psychology, and there is little direct support from the sexual offending domain. However, there is preliminary evidence to support the existence of multiple offense pathways, intimacy deficits, self-regulation deficits, and deviant sexual scripts and preferences (Ward & Siegert, 2002).

The pathways model is important for examining child sexual abuse because it identifies multiple causal mechanisms and acknowledges the importance of cultural factors. It also suggests that different vulnerability factors interacting with environmental factors will increase or decrease the likelihood that child sexual abuse will occur. Finally, though the pathways model does not identify particular treatment interventions for each pathway, it does suggest that different treatment options may be necessary for each pathway.

Practice Theory and the Multiple Systems Model

While Ward and Siegert's (2002) theory does not provide specific treatment guidelines, other micro level practice theories specifically address treatment options for CSA. A practice theory affords clinicians working within the same or similar practice model ease of communication, provides a systematic way of conducting the assessment and planning treatment, and, finally, helps clinicians clarify their own assumptions and values surrounding how a problem is defined and treatment is conducted (Trepper & Barrett, 1989). Practice theory also helps with recognizing relationships and interactions, predicting future outcomes, and offering assurance to the clinician (Turner, 1996).

Social work practitioners and clinicians engage in practice theory building or theory testing (Turner, 1996). Typically, clinicians conduct an assessment and then generate a treatment plan to achieve some desirable goal. There is an assumption inherent in this process that the situation can be understood and that by modifying the situation the desired outcome can be achieved. Turner (1996) suggests that in essence, this becomes a theory building or theory testing exercise; gaps in the knowledge base are identified when the situation cannot be understood or clearly explained or the clinician obtains an outcome that was not predicted.

One practice theory of CSA, more specifically incest, is a multiple systems model (MSM), which is an integration of three different theoretical models (the perpetrator-victim, family systems, and the ecosystemic models) and provides a comprehensive explanation of the potential causal pathways for CSA. The MSM approach incorporates the perpetrator-victim model in which abuse is viewed as an aggressive act of a pathological nature with the adult being the perpetrator against an innocent victim (Trepper & Barrett, 1989). The strength of the perpetrator-victim model is that it places responsibility on the offending person and identifies children as needing protection; however, the model misses larger familial and societal influences. The MSM draws from the family system model to emphasize that abuse is viewed as a product of a problematic family in which all family members share in the responsibility for the cause and the maintenance of the abuse. Families in which sexual abuse occurs have dysfunctional family boundaries and are typically defined as enmeshed (Minuchin, Rosman, & Baker, 1978). The advantage of the family systems model is that it considers the family influence, but may unduly put the child at risk or place blame on the victim. The final model incorporated into the MSM is the ecosystemic model, which looks at the larger social and environmental factors that influence CSA and how the family interacts with the environment. The MSM incorporates all of the most salient features of each of these models.

Central to the MSM is the acknowledgment of vulnerability factors. These vulnerability factors include factors that occur within the socioenvironmental system, family of origin system, current family system, and individual system. Clinicians need to assess each of these system levels. The theory suggests that the collection of vulnerability factors occurs in the presence of some precipitating event (e.g., father going on an alcohol binge), which is then mediated by the person's coping mechanism. If the person's coping mechanisms are weak, this leads to abuse. If abuse occurs, it then contributes to an exacerbation of the vulnerability factors. An advantage of this model is that it incorporates multiple theoretical perspectives in a manageable format for the practicing clinician (see Trepper & Barrett, 1989, for more detail on this model).

ETHNIC AND CULTURAL CONSIDERATIONS

Though most theories of CSA and family dysfunction acknowledge possible cultural effects, none of the theories reviewed does an adequate job of examining or explaining ethnic and cultural issues. In her cross-cultural research, Patterson (2005) concludes "that incest, like its avoidance, remains a largely 'cultural' phenomenon" (p. 111); in her research, the definition of relatedness (i.e., of family or father-daughter relationships) varied by culture, and, as such, the definitions of sexual abuse or unacceptable sexual behavior between family members varied. Patterson's (2005) work suggests that future research needs to consider how the family is defined for those involved in CSA and broader cultural factors. Theories should not be assumed to be universally applicable across or within cultures until research provides proof that this is the case (Fontes, 1998).

There is still a lack of consensus about definitions for most forms of child maltreatment, including CSA, and it is possible that differences across states and localities may reflect regional differences in acceptable parenting norms (Whitaker, Lutzker, & Shelley, 2005). It is also important to consider the ethnic and cultural issues related to CSA for the practitioners who will provide services to children, adolescents, and adults who may have experienced CSA. Research suggests that nurses and other practitioners usually do not ask about sexual issues, including CSA. Warne and McAndrew (2005) suggest that not being prepared to work with these issues "results from the mental health nurses' own internal psyche, which has been influenced by their own social, cultural and political identity" (p. 681). The association between CSA and mental health problems means that mental health nurses, social workers, and other professionals are likely to work with clients who have experienced CSA, and mental health practitioners need to be able to discuss these issues with their clients.

"There is also a need to tailor programs to various cultural and racial and ethnic groups, ensuring the materials, format delivery, and language of certain intervention components are appropriate" (Whitaker, Lutzker, & Shelley, 2005, p. 252). Culturally sensitive intervention models have been described recently. For example, Lawrence-Webb (2003) provides a culturally sensitive model on the basis of feminist theory, cognitive-behavioral techniques, and an Afrocentric perspective of group work for African-American children who have experienced sexual abuse. Baker and Dwairy (2003) describe "a culturally sensitive model of intervention" (p. 109) for Arab families that build on the strengths of Palestinian families living in Israel. However, though this model potentially advances culturally competent interventions, it may leave victims at risk and more work is needed (Fontes, 2003).

Finally, within efforts to create culturally sensitive theories and interventions, it may be important to examine subgroups within cultures. For example, Fontes (2002) points out that there is not a unitary Latino culture because this group is very heterogeneous. Such heterogeneity is likely within other cultural groups as well, and much work is needed to understand how current practices influence subgroup treatment and outcomes within larger cultures. The theories presented here are based primarily on quantitative research. Qualitative examination of family functioning and child maltreatment is emerging (e.g., Paavilainen & Åstedt-Kurki, 2003) and may be particularly useful in understanding the cultural and ethnic aspects and relevance of the theories presented.

CONCLUSION

According to Whitaker and colleagues (2005), "The process by which maltreatment leads to negative outcomes . . . is not fully understood. This is primarily because of the lack of well-developed theory and methodologically rigorous studies examining factors related to child maltreatment. . . . Theoretical work is needed to identify how different types of maltreatment lead to specific negative outcomes" (p. 251). The Centers for Disease Control listed the following as one of its top priorities: "Develop conceptual models that address mechanisms and processes of the origin and perpetuation of child maltreatment for all four types of child maltreatment," including CSA (Whitaker, Lutzker, & Shelley, 2005, p. 257).

It is important to note that although this chapter has focused on theories of CSA and family dysfunction, CSA often co-occurs with other types of child maltreatment; Higgins and McCabe (2003) found that sexual abuse was significantly related to physical abuse, psychological maltreatment, neglect, and witnessing family violence. Because children and adolescents who experience one form of maltreatment are likely to experience other forms of victimization (e.g., other types of maltreatment, witnessing family violence, etc.) (Finkelhor, Ormrod, Turner, & Hamby, 2005), it may ultimately be important to develop theories that examine how CSA and other forms of victimization are related with each other and with family dysfunction. Clearly, additional theory development is needed. "Theory generation is not a luxury" (Ward & Hudson, 2001, p. 291), it is a necessary component of developing effective prevention and intervention programs.

NOTE

1. Hulme (2004) uses the term "macro"; however, because this term may be used to describe community or organizational social work theories, we will use the more general term "grand" in this chapter.

REFERENCES

Ainsworth, M. D. S., Blehar, M. C., Waters, E., & Wall, S. (1978). *Patterns of attachment: A psychological study of the strange situation.* Hillsdale, NJ: Erlbaum.

Alexander, P. (1992). Application of attachment theory to the study of sexual abuse. *Journal of Consulting and Clinical Psychology, 60,* 185-195.

Bacon, H., & Richardson, S. (2001). Attachment theory and child abuse: An overview of the literature for practitioners. *Child Abuse Review, 10,* 377-397.

Baker, K. A., & Dwairy, M. (2003). Cultural norms versus state law in treating incest: A suggested model for Arab families. *Child Abuse & Neglect, 27,* 109-123.

Belsky, J. (1980). Child maltreatment: An ecological integration. *American Psychologist, 35,* 320-335.

Bevan, E., & Higgins, D. J. (2002). Is domestic violence learned? The contribution of five forms of child maltreatment to men's violence and adjustment. *Journal of Family Violence, 17,* 223-245.

Bolen, R. M. (2000). Validity of attachment theory. *Trauma, Violence & Abuse, 1,* 128-153.

Bolger, K., & Patterson, C. (2003). Sequelae of child maltreatment. In S. Luthar (Ed.), *Resilience and vulnerability: Adaptation in the context of childhood adversity* (pp. 156-181). New York: Cambridge University Press.

Bowlby, J. (1969). *Attachment and loss: Volume 1. Attachment.* New York: Basic Books Inc.

Bowlby, J. (1973). *Attachment and loss: Volume 2. Separation.* New York: Basic Books Inc.

Bowlby, J. (1988). *A secure base: Clinical applications of attachment theory.* London: Routledge.

Bronfenbrenner, U. (1977). Toward an experimental ecology of human development. *American Psychologist, 32,* 513-531.

Feinauer, L., & Stuart, D. (1996). Blame and resilience in women sexually abused as children. *The American Journal of Family Therapy, 24*(1), 31-40.

Finkelhor, D. (1998). Improving research, policy, and practice to understand child sexual abuse [Editorials]. *Journal of the American Medical Association, 280,* 1864-1865.

Finkelhor, D., & Araji, S. (1986). Explanations of pedophilia: A four factor model. *The Journal of Sex Research, 22,* 145-161.

Finkelhor, D., Ormrod, R., Turner, H., & Hamby, S. L. (2005). The victimization of children and youth: A comprehensive, national survey. *Child Maltreatment, 10,* 5-25.

Fontes, L. A. (1998). Ethics in family violence research: Cross-cultural issues. *Family Relations, 47,* 53-61.

Fontes, L. A. (2002). Child discipline and physical abuse in immigrant Latino families: Reducing violence and misunderstandings. *Journal of Counseling & Development, 80,* 31-40.

Fontes, L. A. (2003). Re: Cultural norms versus state law in treating incest: A suggested model for Arab families, by K. Abu Baker and M. Dwairy [Letter to the Editor]. *Child Abuse & Neglect, 27,* 1335-1336.

Fraser, M. (1997). The ecology of childhood: A multisystems perspective. In M. Fraser (Ed.), *Risk and resilience in childhood: An ecological perspective* (pp. 1-9). Washington, DC: NASW Press.

Garbarino, J. (1977). The human ecology for child maltreatment: A conceptual model for research. *Journal of Marriage and the Family, 39,* 721-736.

Germain, C., & Gitterman, A. (1996). *The life model of social work practice.* New York: Columbia University Press.

Greene, R. (2002). Human behavior theory: A resilience orientation. In R. Green (Ed.), *Resiliency: An integrated approach to practice, policy and research* (pp. 1-28). Washington, DC: NASW Press.

Hanson, R. K., & Morton-Bourgon, K. E. (2005). The characteristics of persistent sexual offenders: A meta-analysis of recidivism studies. *Journal of Consulting and Clinical Psychology, 73,* 1154-1163.

Higgins, D. J., & McCabe, M. P. (1994). The relationship of child sexual abuse and family violence to adult adjustment: Toward an integrated risk-sequelae model. *The Journal of Sex Research, 31,* 255-266.

Higgins, D. J., & McCabe, M. P. (2003). Maltreatment and family dysfunction in childhood and the subsequent adjustment of children and adults. *Journal of Family Violence, 18,* 107-120.

Himelein, M., & McElrath, J. (1996). Resilient child sexual abuse survivors: Cognitive coping and illusion. *Child Abuse & Neglect, 20,* 747-758.

Hulme, P. A. (2004). Theoretical perspectives on the health problems of adults who experienced childhood sexual abuse. *Issues in Mental Health Nursing, 25,* 339-361.

Hund, A. R., & Espelage, D. L. (2005). Childhood sexual abuse, disordered eating, alexithymia, and general distress: A mediation model. *Journal of Counseling Psychology, 52,* 559-573.

Kellogg, N. D., Burge, S., & Taylor, E. R. (2000). Wanted and unwanted sexual experiences and family dysfunction during adolescence. *Journal of Family Violence, 15,* 55-68.

Lancaster, L., & Lumb, J. (1999). Bridging the gap: Feminist theory and practice reality in work with the perpetrators of child sexual abuse. *Child and Family Social Work, 4,* 119-129.

Lawrence-Webb, C. (2003). New perspectives in group work for working with sexually abused African-American children. In N. E. Sullivan, E. S. Mesbur, N. C. Lang, D. Goodman, & L. Mitchell (Eds.), *Social work with groups: Social justice through personal, community and societal change* (pp. 135-146). Binghamton, NY: The Haworth Press.

Lazarus, R. (1990). Theory-based stress measurement. *Psychological Inquiry, 1,* 3-13.

Liem, J. H., & Boudewyn, A. C. (1999). Contextualizing the effects of childhood sexual abuse on adult self- and social functioning: An attachment theory perspective. *Child Abuse & Neglect, 23,* 1141-1157.

Liem, J., James, J., O'Toole, J., & Boudewyn, A. (1997). Assessing resilience in adults with histories of childhood sexual abuse. *American Journal of Orthopsychiatry, 67,* 594-606.

Minuchin, S., Rosman, B. L., & Baker, L. (1978). *Psychosomatic families: Anorexia nervosa in context.* Cambridge: Harvard University Press.

Morton, N., & Brown, K. D. (1998). Theory and observation of attachment and its relationship to child maltreatment: A review. *Child Abuse and Neglect, 22*(11), 1093-1105.

Paavilainen, E., & Åstedt-Kurki, P. (2003). Functioning of child maltreating families: Lack of resources for caring within the family. *Scandinavian Journal of Caring Sciences, 17*(2), 139-147.

Parton, N. (2000). Some thoughts on the relationship between theory and practice in and for social work. *British Journal of Social Work, 30,* 449-463.

Patterson, M. (2005). Coming too close, going too far: Theoretical and cross-cultural approaches to incest and its prohibitions. *The Australian Journal of Anthropology, 16*(1), 95-115.

Richardson, G. (2002). The metatheory of resilience and resiliency. *Journal of Clinical Psychology, 58,* 307-321.

Romans, S., Martin, J., Anderson, J., O'Shea, M., & Mullen, P. (1995). Factors that mediate between child sexual abuse and adult psychological outcome. *Psychological Medicine, 25*(1), 127-142.

Simpson, J., & Rholes, W. S. (Eds.) (1988). *Attachment theory and close relationships.* New York: The Guilford Press.

Spaccarelli, S., & Kim, S. (1995). Resilience criteria and factors associated with resilience in sexually abused girls. *Child Abuse and Neglect, 19,* 1171-1182.

Svedin, C. G., Back, C., & Söderback, S.-B. (2002). Family relations, family climate and sexual abuse. *Nordic Journal of Psychiatry, 56,* 355-362.

Trepper, T. S., & Barrett, M. J. (1989). *Systemic treatment of incest: A therapeutic handbook.* New York: Brunner/Mazel.

Turner, F. J. (1996). *Social work treatment* (4th ed.). New York: The Free Press.

Valentine, L., & Feinauer, L. (1993). Resilience factors associated with female survivors of childhood sexual abuse. *The American Journal of Family Therapy, 21,* 216-224.

Ward, T. (2001). A critique of Hall and Hirshman's quadripartite model of child sexual abuse. *Psychology, Crime & Law, 7,* 333-350.

Ward, T. (2002). Marshall and Barbaree's integrated theory of child sexual abuse: A critique. *Psychology, Crime & Law, 8,* 209-228.

Ward, T., & Hudson, S. M. (2001). Finkelhor's precondition model of child sexual abuse: A critique. *Psychology, Crime & Law, 7,* 291-307.

Ward, T., & Siegert, R. J. (2002). Toward a comprehensive theory of child sexual abuse: A theory knitting perspective. *Psychology, Crime & Law, 8,* 319-351.

Warne, T., & McAndrew, S. (2005). The shackles of abuse: Unprepared to work at the edges of reason. *Journal of Psychiatric and Mental Health Nursing, 12,* 679-686.

Whitaker, D. J., Lutzker, J. R., & Shelley, G. A. (2005). Child maltreatment prevention priorities at the Centers for Disease Control and Prevention. *Child Maltreatment, 10,* 245-259.

Chapter 4

Intrafamilial Child and Adolescent Sexual Abuse

Theresa A. Gannon
Elizabeth Gilchrist
Kimberly A. Wade

INTRODUCTION

Seeking to understand why some men choose to sexually offend against their immature family members is always a work in progress, as is work examining treatment efforts with these men. What we do know about these issues stems from a wide variety of theoretical perspectives. However, these perspectives have not always communicated effectively with one another, resulting in a somewhat fragmented knowledge base. We do, however, hold a more sophisticated understanding of intrafamilial offenders and their abuse than we did two decades ago, which is testament to the many research studies undertaken to understand intrafamilial abuse more fully.

A number of questions seem pertinent to understanding intrafamilial abuse. For example, what differing forms does intrafamilial abuse take? How different are intrafamilial abusers from the average man on the street? How do intrafamilial abusers begin to engage in sexually abusive acts with their immature dependents? What effects does intrafamilial abuse have on its victims and other family members? What types of psychological characteristics typify intrafamilial abusers? And, how do professionals use current understanding of intrafamilial abuser characteristics in rehabilitative programs for offenders? These are all questions that have become increasingly re-

Handbook of Social Work in Child and Adolescent Sexual Abuse
© 2008 by The Haworth Press, Taylor & Francis Group. All rights reserved.
doi:10.1300/5804_04

searched over the past two decades, and so we aim to structure this chapter along these main subheadings. Throughout this chapter, when we use the term *intrafamilial offender* or *intrafamilial abuse* we are referring to the abuse of children or adolescents under the age of sixteen. Children and adolescents are not systematically differentiated as the literature rarely distinguishes between the two.

INTRAFAMILIAL OFFENDERS: A DEFINITION

The term *intrafamilial offender* is used inconsistently in the child sexual abuse literature. For example, some professionals use the term to describe a subset of child sexual abusers whose behavior is *incestuous* in nature (i.e., offenders who sexually abuse a child who is a *blood* relative). Thus, professionals using the term in this sense are referring to *involuntary incest* as opposed to *voluntary* incest, which may exist between consenting adults. Other professionals, however, use the term intrafamilial offender to describe offenders who are related to their victim through adoption, or marriage (i.e., stepfather), who hold a temporary familial relationship with their victim (i.e., a foster parent), or represent leading father-type figures in the community (e.g., clergy members). Thus, the term intrafamilial offender is used to refer to any one abuser type, or combination of abuser types outlined earlier in the chapter (see Rice & Harris, 2002, for an example). Furthermore, to add confusion, the term *intrafamilial offender* is often substituted by the term incest for any one or more of the aforementioned abuser relationships (see Ballard et al., 1990; Hanson, Gizzarelli, & Scott, 1994; Hartley, 2001). Clearly, this lack of definitional clarity creates confusion in the literature and greatly impedes our ability to make meaningful comparisons across differing research studies.

In this chapter, we would like to focus our attention on biological fathers or stepfathers who abuse their daughters because this is a common form of intrafamilial abuse (Bolen, 2001; Gibbens, Soothill, & Way, 1978; Rice & Harris, 2002). We do this for two main reasons. First, men whose offense characteristics fall out of this remit may hold differing offense dynamics (Studer, Clelland, Aylwin, Reddon, & Monro, 2000; Williams & Finkelhor, 1990). Second, this focus allows us to draw upon a more mature evidence base since molesters of daughters or stepdaughters are those most commonly researched in the extant sexual abuse literature. Other forms of intrafamilial abuse (i.e., female-perpetrated, sibling-perpetrated) we believe require separate focused attention.

The basic presumption that child sexual abuse perpetrated within the family should be conceptualized as fundamentally different from other forms of child sexual abuse appears to have stemmed from a variety of sources (e.g., family dysfunction theory; Hoorwitz, 1983, evolutionary theory; Westermarck, 1891, psychodynamic typological distinction; Groth, Hobson, & Gary, 1982, and early recidivism studies; McGrath, 1991). For example, Groth et al.'s (1982) fixated-regressed typology[1] conceptualized very clear demarcations between familial and nonfamilial abuse. Within Groth et al.'s typology, familial offenders were primarily associated with the *regressed* offender, who was hypothesized to primarily prefer age-mates for sexual relationships, yet regressed toward children for sexual comfort in the face of adverse life events (e.g., marital or work pressures). In contrast, nonfamilial offenders were primarily associated with the *fixated* offender, who was hypothesized to hold a primary sexual fixation on children. This preference was hypothesized to drive strong emotional congruence with children, as well as persistent and premeditated sexual offending.

Such clear-cut distinctions appear to have driven the widespread and somewhat misguided consensus that (1) intrafamilial offenders pose no risk to children outside of the family, and (2) intrafamilial offenders require little, if any, treatment compared with nonfamilial offenders (Rice & Harris, 2002; Studer et al., 2000). Current wisdom, however, suggests that intrafamilial offenders do not represent a distinct group, who pose no risk to children and require little treatment. For example, although intrafamilial offenders generally have less pervasive sexual and nonsexual conviction histories, this does not necessarily indicate that offending has been or will be limited to the family (Becker, 1994; Beech, 1998; Rice & Harris, 2002). Further, research shows that, like all child sexual abusers, intrafamilial offenders are driven by multifactorial issues, and show considerable diversity in their psychological characteristics (Rice & Harris, 2002; Ward & Siegert, 2002). To illustrate, Beech (1998) has argued that *psychological deviance* is important for understanding intrafamilial offenders' treatment needs rather than offense characteristics per se. Using a battery of psychometric tests that tapped deviant sexual interests, socioaffective functioning, and offense-supportive attitudes (and relevant nonoffender norms), Beech was able to classify a diverse group of molesters as either high or low deviancy. In short, Beech found that a good deal of situational or intrafamilial offenders (just under one-third) tended to hold pervasive deficits indicating high deviancy; in other words they were high risk, with pervasive treatment needs (see also Beech, Fisher, & Beckett, 1999). In summary, sexual abuse identified within the family is a poor predictor of offenders' true sexual misdemeanors, risk levels, and treatment needs (see Abel, Becker, Cunningham-Rathner, Mittelman, & Rouleau, 1988; Heil, Ahlmeyer, & Simons, 2003; Studer et al., 2000).

WHO IS THE INTRAFAMILIAL ABUSER?

As we have already noted, intrafamilial offenders have classically been viewed as a distinct group. Not surprisingly then, professionals have been keen to establish whether intrafamilial offenders are characterized by specific personality traits or sociodemographic features. In accordance with the intrafamilial offender diversity already highlighted, results have been disappointing. Apart from commonly documented passivity and dependency (see Cole, 1992 or Williams & Finkelhor, 1990), research has been unable to pinpoint any defining typological personality profiles for intrafamilial men (Conte, 1985; Firestone, Dixon, Nunes, & Bradford, 2005). Researchers have also been unable to pinpoint any core demographical features distinguishing intrafamilial offenders from other men (Ballard et al., 1990; Herman & Hirschman, 1981). Thus, intrafamilial offenders are not obviously distinct as a group of sexual offenders, and may be described as "everyman" since they are indistinguishable from the average man on the street (Marshall, 1996).

WHAT DOES THE INTRAFAMILIAL OFFENDER DO?

In this section, we will explore how intrafamilial offenders gain the child's trust, the sexually abusive behaviors typically perpetrated by intrafamilial men, and the postoffense strategies used by intrafamilial offenders to minimize the child's disclosure of the abuse. Both intrafamilial sexual offenders and victims have provided accounts of the rituals and behaviors associated with intrafamilial abuse (see Berliner & Conte, 1990; Craven, Brown, Gilchrist, & Cushway, 2005; Lang & Frenzel, 1988; Phelan, 1995; Smallbone & Wortley, 2000, 2001). Both accounts are critical for gaining a true understanding of offenders' behaviors, and so we refer to both resources in our descriptions in the sections that follow.

Gaining the Child's Trust

When people think about the sexual abuse of children, they generally focus on the sexual behavior itself. The sexual abuse of children, however, is not typically reported by offenders or victims as being a random event of thoughtless sexual action[2] (see Christiansen & Blake, 1990; Elliott, Browne, & Kilcoyne, 1995). Instead, both extrafamilial and intrafamilial offenders prepare the child for the intended forthcoming sexual interaction (a process commonly termed "grooming") through employing a series of strategies aimed at securing the child's trust and compliance (Christiansen & Blake, 1990; Craven et al., 2005; Elliott et al., 1995; Smallbone & Wortley, 2001; van Dam, 2001).

Christiansen and Blake (1990) reviewed the intrafamilial abuser and victim literature and concluded that intrafamilial grooming includes the establishment of trust, alienation of the child from significant others, demands of secrecy from the child, and violation of the child's boundaries through, for example, watching or helping them bathe.

Smallbone and Wortley (2000, 2001) asked seventy-nine intrafamilial sexual offenders to anonymously complete a self-report modus operandi questionnaire and compared their answers to extrafamilial offenders. The results showed that intrafamilial offenders gained their victim's trust before the abuse through spending time with the victim (70.9 percent), by engaging in lots of nonsexual physical closeness with the victim (67.1 percent), and by being extra attentive to the child (64.6 percent). These strategies did not dramatically differ from those used by extrafamilial offenders. However, compared with extrafamilial molesters, intrafamilial offenders did not need to develop elaborate strategies to gain access to the child finding it relatively easy to spend time alone with the child at home (57.7 percent).

Having developed a special and close relationship with the child, intrafamilial offenders—like their extrafamilial counterparts—report strategies aimed at *desensitizing* the child to sexual stimuli. Typically this involves lots of nonsexual touching, attention, compliments, and violation of boundaries (Christiansen & Blake, 1990; Smallbone & Wortley, 2000, 2001). For example, Lang and Frenzel (1988) found intrafamilial offenders reported using multiple strategies to desensitize the child to sexual touching. A large number reported "accidentally" touching their victim before the abuse (75 percent), cuddling the child (55 percent), or using accidental sexual touching during games to stimulate the child's natural curiosity (59 percent). Craven et al.'s (2005) study with intrafamilial abuse victims appears to support these general findings.

The Sexually Abusive Behavior

Having set up a situation for the sexual abuse, intrafamilial men often make sexual advances within the home environment (Lang & Frenzel, 1988; Smallbone & Wortley, 2001). The offenders interviewed in Lang and Frenzel's study admitted using a whole range of methods that helped them trick or force the child into having sexual contact with them. A large number of fathers (78 percent) misinformed their daughters or used their superior intellect to talk their daughters into having sexual contact with them (80 percent). More aggressive strategies were also reported and included aggressive intimidation (63 percent), physical assault (35 percent), bribes (37 percent), and withholding privileges (25 percent). The extrafamilial men's tactics did not appear dramatically different. However, it could be argued that intrafamilial fathers' tactics are more influential as they hold significantly more power over their child's life and daily living.

Smallbone and Wortley (2001) specifically focused on capturing the actual *types* of sexual behaviors exhibited by intrafamilial men. In their study, they found many similarities between intrafamilial and extrafamilial men in terms of their sexual behaviors with children. Unsurprisingly, both intrafamilial and extrafamilial abusers were prone to sexually touch the child (i.e., on the child's bottom, breasts, or genitals), or get the child to touch their own (i.e., the abuser's) penis. However, intrafamilial men reported perpetrating somewhat less oral sex on their victims than did extrafamilial offenders. Further, intrafamilial offenders appear more likely to engage in, or attempt to engage in, sexual intercourse with their victims compared with extrafamilial offenders (see Smallbone & Wortley, 2001), and this is a finding supported by victim data also (see Kercher & McShane, 1984).

Postoffense Behaviors

Like all child molesters, intrafamilial men typically attempt to minimize the child's disclosure of the abuse through a variety of means (Phelan, 1995; Smallbone & Wortley, 2000, 2001). Offenders in Smallbone and Wortley's study used their special relationship with the child. For example, many men told the child that they would get put in jail if anyone found out (41.8 percent) and hoped that the child would worry about losing the special attention lavished on them (35.4 percent); a finding not too dissimilar for extrafamilial offenders. Phelan (1995) reports an example of the type of threat made by intrafamilial abusers in her interview study:

> I told her not to tell anybody. I told her I'd go to jail, and your mother and I will get a divorce. (Phelan, 1995, p. 12)

This father was clearly able to use the wider family context as a tool for inducing fear in his daughter, so that she would not disclose the abusive relationship. Similarly, fathers may threaten to hurt or sexually abuse other family members to ensure the abused child remains silent (NCH Action for Children, 1997). This may, in part, explain why some intrafamilial abuse continues—undisclosed—for months or sometimes years (see Smallbone & Wortley, 2000; Wilson, 2004a).

In summary, like all child sexual abusers, intrafamilial abusers use a range of strategies to groom the child and persuade them not to tell anyone about the secret sexual activity. As we have already noted, intrafamilial men are similar to their extrafamilial counterparts in many ways. However, we believe that intrafamilial men's grooming may be somewhat harder to detect as many of their behaviors may be misperceived as functional and supportive relationships between family members. In addition, the powerful position of the father role within the family not only allays suspicions concerning close adult child contact but also provides more opportunities for creating the abusive relationship (e.g., through being home alone with the child), and maintaining it (e.g., through using the family structure to stop the child from disclosing). Finally, it should be noted that offenders regarded as "intrafamilial" may simply represent highly successful extrafamilial groomers who have targeted a vulnerable family to gain access to child victims.

WHAT IS THE DAMAGE DONE?

As we have already noted, intrafamilial victims are typically forced to endure lengthy periods of sexual abuse, which is perpetrated by an emotionally significant figure in their home. Little wonder then that intrafamilial victims have been found to experience a number of adverse physical and psychological effects, which are believed to be more pervasive and long lasting than those experienced by victims of extrafamilial abuse (Browne & Finkelhor, 1986; Goodwin, McCarthy, & DiVasto, 1981). In this section, we describe both the short- and long-term effects of intrafamilial abuse on victims. We will also consider the effects of intrafamilial abuse on other family members though the literature is less plentiful on this issue.

Since there appears to be no longitudinal research tracking survivors from childhood to adulthood, we have split the victim effects literature into two parts. We use the descriptor *short-term* to describe studies documenting the effects of abuse during childhood or adolescence and *long-term* to describe studies documenting effects during adulthood.

Short-Term Damage to the Primary Victim

The general consensus regarding the short-term psychological symptoms of intrafamilial abuse is that child or adolescent victims suffer significant problems in their psychological health and behavioral functioning. For example, in a comprehensive review of the research literature, Cole and Putnam (1992) concluded that children experienced significant difficulties in functioning of the *self* (i.e., depression, low self-esteem, substance abuse, attempted suicide and self-harm, somatic issues, body image distortions, and post-traumatic stress disorder; PTSD). Cole and Putnam (1992) also report significant issues in children's social functioning (i.e., aggression, conduct problems, and sexual behavior problems). Levitt, Owen, and Truchsess (1991) reported similar short-term effects after interviewing the primary caregivers of children abused within the family.

Long-Term Damage to the Primary Victim

A good number of studies exist that focus on problems experienced by intrafamilial sexual abuse victims during adulthood (see Cole & Putnam, 1992 or Stevenson, 1990). Here, a range of effects appears to exist at worrying levels, mirroring many of the problems noted in short-term studies (Cole & Putnam, 1992). For example, personality disorders in the form of borderline personality disorder and multiple personality disorder are commonly noted, as are eating, somatization, and substance abuse disorders (Cole & Putnam, 1992). Like the short-term studies outlined earlier, intrafamilial abuse survivors commonly report self-esteem issues, depression, anxiety, self-harming and suicidal behaviors, and PTSD (see Cole & Putnam, 1992, for a review).

Researchers have also found that intrafamilial abuse victims—like other child abuse victims—very often report a whole host of other interpersonal functional difficulties. These include poor relationships with partners (DiLillo & Long, 1999; Meiselman, 1978), problems with sexual functioning (Meiselman, 1978; Steele & Alexander, 1981), and poor child-rearing activities and relationships with their offspring (Burkett, 1991; Cole & Woolger, 1989; Lubell & Peterson, 1998). For example, using videotapes of mother and child interactions, Burkett (1991) found that women incest survivors tended to be more self-focused than child-focused compared with a comparison group of mothers. The sexually abused mothers also appeared to role reverse the mother-child relationship, using their children for significant emotional support and comfort. Finally, research has identified a "grooming shadow" that affects survivors long after the abusive experience (see Craven et al., 2005). Here, the actual process of *grooming* seems to leave its mark over and above the abuse itself. For example, individuals feel worthless and blameworthy as they hold dissonant feelings of both loving and hating their perpetrator (Craven et al., 2005).

The basic message about the effects of sexual abuse appears clear from the aforementioned studies. However, it would be misleading to conclude that all intrafamilial abuse victims experience each of these short- and long-term symptoms in much the same way. Instead, research suggests great diversity in the adjustment of abuse survivors, with suggestions that victim age, victim coping styles, degree of violence, length of victimization, familial support, family dysfunction, and court involvement may all play a role (see Bennett, Hughes, & Luke, 2000; Kendall-Tackett, Williams, & Finkelhor, 1993; or Ray, 1993). For example, victims whose sexual abuse began during adolescence (as opposed to childhood) are more robust to the negative psychological effects of child sexual abuse (see Schultz, Braun, & Kluft, 1989).

Damage to Other Family Members

The disclosure of sexual abuse within the family represents a short-term "crisis" for other family members (Bagley & King, 1990; Levenson & Morin, 2001). For example, from the day of initial disclosure, the nonoffending mother is likely to have taken on many urgent and stressful responsibilities such as finding money to pay legal fees, attending court, dealing with questioning social workers and police officers, and coping with the anticipated or actual loss of the offending parent and the child or children (Levenson & Morin, 2001). Not surprising then, researchers have found that the majority of families rocked by the disturbance of sexual abuse report this as being the most stressful life event experienced over the past three years (Levitt et al., 1991). From clinical experience of working with nonoffending parents, Levenson and Morin (2001) argue that denial is common in nonoffending mothers, since to face up to the truth unleashes an impossible conflict in loyalty between child and partner. In short, the nonoffending mother is likely to feel anger and bitterness toward the offender (and perhaps even the child) and may feel ashamed, guilty, or inadequate over a whole host of issues. For example, she may experience shame surrounding adequacy as a partner (e.g., *Why did he turn to our children for sex?*) or as a mother (e.g., *Why didn't I see that this was happening?*) (Levenson & Morin, 2001). In support of this, Reis and Heppner (1993) found that the mothers of intrafamilial victims had low confidence and perception of personal control. Similarly, Wagner (1991) found that 50 percent ($n = 16$) of intrafamilial mothers felt moderately depressed following abuse disclosure.

The siblings of the victim may have been only too aware of the abuse (e.g., they may have been made to watch it or were in the same room) or, they may have had no idea of its occurrence. Either event has the potential to create problems. For example, a sibling may feel guilty about having escaped the abusive actions, or hostile and bitter toward the victim for "special treatment," "making too much out of nothing," or "making Dad move out" (Bagley & King, 1990; de Young, 1982; DiGiorgio-Miller, 2002). Wilson (2004b), citing a study by Kroth (1979), has argued that nonabused siblings do not tend to show extreme emotional disturbances on the whole. In Kroth's study, for example, only 18 percent of nonabuse siblings displayed signs of nervous tendencies upon intake to a treatment center. A definition of such nervous tendencies is not given.

It may not necessarily be the abuse per se that kick starts damage to the siblings of the victim, but associated occurrences or events. For instance, intrafamilial abuse—as we shall see later—is commonly associated with some family dysfunction, which may make its own independent and negative impact on the nonabused sibling. In addition, being placed in foster care is a particularly likely occurrence for the nonabused sibling and is associated with various psychological disturbances (Wilson, 2004a). In summary, it seems that intrafamilial abuse has an effect not only on the immediate victim, but also on other family members. This highlights the need for service providers to be sensitive and responsive to such issues when handling intrafamilial child sexual abuse cases. Intrafamilial abuse is a disturbing event for nonabused family members as well as the primary victim and should not be ignored or downplayed.

WHY DO MEN SEXUALLY ABUSE THEIR OWN CHILDREN?

Given the obvious damage caused by intrafamilial abuse, it is of paramount importance that we try to explain why some fathers sexually abuse their own children. Historically, a host of theoretical perspectives have attempted to explain why men would offend within their own family unit. Each of these emphasize a single main process, namely evolution, society, or family dysfunction.[3]

Evolutionary Theory

Evolutionary approaches to incest use the principles of evolutionary biology to explain the development of *incest avoidance* (see Wolfe & Durham, 2004). That is, why do humans generally show distaste toward incest? Understanding why humans generally avoid incest is hypothesized to provide valuable clues concerning the *failure* of incest avoidance mechanisms. An example is that of Westermarck's hypothesis (1891). In brief, Westermarck was interested in trying to explain why children who were raised together appeared to develop such a deeply ingrained incest avoidance mechanism. He believed humans had evolved an innate biological aversion to inbreeding with individuals from the same familial pool and that the cue driving this aversion was childhood association. Research has indeed shown that unrelated individuals raised in the same family household display a distinct distaste concerning sexual relations with one another (Shepher, 1983; Wolfe, 1970). Adults, too, who have played a part in raising a child should, by Westermarck's account, show considerable aversion to sexual relations with that child (Seto, Lalumière, & Kuban, 1999). Using this hypothesis, intrafamilial abuse may occur as a result of poor paternal association. There has been some support for this hypothesis. For example, Parker and Parker (1986) observed that a large number of intrafamilial abusers were absent, or partially absent from the family household during the initial three years of their daughters' lives compared with a comparison group (i.e., 59 percent versus 14 percent). Intrafamilial fathers were also less likely to be involved with the day-to-day caring of the child when they were at home suggesting that bonding might have been compromised.

Feminist Approaches

Feminists provide a sociocultural explanation of intrafamilial abuse (see Bell, 1993; Ward, Polaschek, & Beech, 2005). In their view, intrafamilial abuse is a patriarchal cultural problem played out within the family context (although it is of note that there is considerable variation in feminist explanations of child sexual abuse). Generally, however, all child sexual abuse (including intrafamilial abuse) is believed to stem from some form of power imbalance between men and women in society explaining why sexual abuse is mainly male-perpetrated. Feminism has contributed greatly to the acknowledgment of cultural factors associated with sexual offenders (Ward et al., 2005) and has advocated recognition of incest as a significant social problem (Barrett, Trepper, & Stone-Fish, 1990). There is also support for the proposal that intrafamilial men are characterized by attitudes of sexual entitlement (see Hanson et al., 1994), a point that we return to later in the chapter.

Family Psychiatry Approaches

The family dysfunction approach—first advocated as an explanatory framework for a number of disorders during the 1940s—maintains that incest is the result of overall family dysfunction (Maisch, 1973). Thus, all members of the family are believed to play some part in facilitating the abuse, although they may not consciously be aware of this fact (e.g., a mother who fails to provide sex for her husband and nurturance for her child provides the breeding ground for incest; see Salter, 1988). Generally, research and clinical intuition suggests that incestuous abuse occurs in the midst of a large amount of general family disorganization (Saunders, Lipovsky, & Hanson, 1995; Williams & Finkelhor, 1990). Research shows that incestuous families are characterized by family conflict (Dadds, Smith, & Webber, 1991), marital issues (Gruber & Jones, 1983; Swanson & Biaggio, 1985), poor family cohesion and lack of boundaries (Dadds et al., 1991), isolation (Dadds et al., 1991), and rigid organization (Dadds et al., 1991; Madonna, Van Scoyk, & Jones, 1991). For example, Dadds et al. (1991) gave families in which incest had occurred and matched control group families a battery of psychometric tests designed to examine quality of family environment. The results showed that the incestuous families were characterized by significantly more family pathology compared with controls; they were in conflict, isolated, lacked cohesiveness and intimacy, and were bound by strict rules and family positions. It is unclear, however, the degree to which this familial dysfunction is present *prior* to abuse disclosure (Cole, 1992).

The mothers within incestuous families have also been studied to investigate whether their characteristics may play a facilitatory or protective role in their child's abuse. Traditionally, researchers have proposed that mothers—aware of the abusive relationship—do little or nothing to intervene (Forward & Buck, 1978), or play a more central role through, for example, encouraging the abuse (see Kaufman, Peck, & Tagiuri, 1954). Other researchers have suggested that poor mother-child relationships or role reversal may provide optimal opportunities for father-child incest (Herman & Hirschman, 1981; Lipovsky, Saunders, & Hanson, 1992). Generally, however, researchers believe that the lack of strictly controlled empirical evidence in this area makes it nearly impossible to draw solid conclusions about the mother's role (e.g., Faust, Runyon, & Kenny, 1995). Recent research suggests there is significant heterogeneity in the family organization characteristics of families affected by intrafamilial abuse (see Alexander & Schaeffer, 1994). In other words, although family context is an important factor to be considered in clinical formulation, considerable diversity is likely to exist, calling for skillful clinical interpretation and management.

The diversity between each of the previous theoretical perspectives serves as a timely reminder of the multifaceted issues likely to facilitate intrafamilial abuse. However, the majority of these perspectives treat intrafamilial abuse as a *special* problem in need of explanation and downplay the contribution of the offender's own psychological characteristics to the abusive relationship. Thus, in the section that follows, we focus on four main psychological problems typically associated with intrafamilial offenders (and child molesters generally) that are targeted in offender treatment to promote offense abstinence. It should be noted that although we aim to discuss intrafamilial men in particular there is likely to be considerable diversity on the characteristics we describe and so these psychological characteristics are best described as vulnerability factors. Nevertheless, each of these factors has become an important building block for principal models of child molestation etiology and effective treatment in the Western world.

PSYCHOLOGICAL FACTORS RELATED TO INTERFAMILIAL OFFENDING

There are four main factors believed to be relatively common in child molesters, which should be examined in any comprehensive assessment of intrafamilial offenders: deviant sexual interests, intimacy deficits, offense-supportive beliefs and attitudes, and emotional regulation (Beech & Ward, 2004; Hanson, 2006; Hanson & Morton-Bourgon, 2004). It should be noted that such characteristics are believed to have developed from and exist within a complex interplay of factors (i.e., ecology, biology, and culture; see Marshall & Barbaree, 1990; Ward & Beech, 2006).

Deviant Sexual Interest

While extrafamilial child molesters appear to hold distinct sexual preferences for children (Hanson & Bussière, 1998), the picture is decidedly less clear for intrafamilial child molesters (see Marshall, Anderson, & Fernandez, 1999; Rice & Harris, 2002; Seto et al., 1999; Williams & Finkelhor, 1990). For example, some research has shown that intrafamilial child molesters exhibit less deviant sexual interest in children compared with men who molest outside of the family (Frenzel & Lang, 1989; Freund, Watson, & Dickey, 1991; Marshall, Barbaree, & Christophe, 1986; Seto et al., 1999), while other research has been unable to differentiate intrafamilial offenders from extrafamilial offenders on the basis of deviant sexual interests (Abel, Becker, Murphy, & Flanagan, 1981; Langevin & Watson, 1991; Murphy, Haynes, Stalgaitis, & Flanagan, 1986). The method often used to measure deviant sexual arousal is the penile plethysmograph (PPG), which is an instrument that measures erection size change while the individual watches or listens to sexual material (Gannon, Ward, & Polaschek, 2004).

Interestingly, Firestone et al. (2005) attempted to compare intrafamilial men who had offended against young victims (i.e., youngest child victim younger than six years) with intrafamilial men who had offended against adolescents (i.e., youngest victim = twelve to sixteen years) on deviant sexual interest. Both groups showed problematic profiles (i.e., the results were *clinically* significant). Thus, on the basis of the pattern of results described earlier, it is fair to conclude that some intrafamilial men appear to show distinct sexual preferences for children, although their profiles do not appear comparable with extra-familial offenders (Rice & Harris, 2002).

Intimacy and Social Skills Deficit

A common observation made about child molesters in general is that they lack the skills necessary to relate well with others and, as a consequence of this, they experience high levels of loneliness (Araji & Finkelhor, 1986; Garlick, Marshall, & Thornton, 1996; Hudson & Ward, 1997; Marshall, 1989; Segal & Marshall, 1985). Marshall (1989), for example, has hypothesized that child molesters generally experience negative early attachments to their caregivers leaving them fearful and unable to deal with intimate adult relationships (i.e., intimacy and social skills deficits; see also Ward, Hudson, Marshall, & Siegert, 1995). This hypothesis has been supported in the child molester literature generally, and more specifically with intrafamilial offender subgroups (Bogaerts, Vervaeke, & Goethals, 2004; Parker, 1984; Quinn, 1984; Seidman, Marshall, Hudson, & Robertson, 1994; Smallbone & Dadds, 1998; Strand, 1986). For example, Smallbone and Dadds (1998) found that intrafamilial child molesters were partic-ularly likely to report experiencing adverse early relationships with their mothers (i.e., inconsistent and unresponsive, or rejecting and abu-sive mothering) compared with other sexual offenders and nonsexual offending comparison groups. In fact, general parental instability and rejection are commonly noted in intrafamilial molesters' childhood histories (see Ballard et al., 1990; Hartley, 1998). During adulthood, Bumby and Hansen (1997) found that intrafamilial molesters were more likely to be characterized by intimacy deficits and emotional loneliness compared with offender and community control groups (see also Seidman et al., 1994). Other studies have reported varying degrees of apparent ineptness among intrafamilial offenders (see Wil-liams & Finkelhor, 1990, for a review). For example, research shows that intrafamilial men are characterized by few close friendships (Ballard et al., 1990; Parker, 1984), social introversion (Kirkland & Bauer, 1982; Scott & Stone, 1986), and low self-esteem (Ballard et al., 1990). There is also some evidence to suggest that intrafamilial fathers shy away from group activities (see Williams & Finkelhor's

[1990] description of two doctoral theses by Quinn, 1984, and Strand, 1986).

Offense-Supportive Cognition

Both intrafamilial and extrafamilial offenders say things such as "she wanted it to happen," "she started it," or "she will get over it" when talking about their own victims (see Gannon & Polaschek, in press; Neidigh & Krop, 1992; Phelan, 1995; Pollock & Hashmall, 1991; Veach, 1997). Over the past two decades, researchers and clinicians have argued that offense supportive statements such as these are key indicators of *offense-supportive beliefs* (sometimes referred to as *cognitive distortions;* see Ward, Hudson, Johnston, & Marshall, 1997). Ward and his colleagues (Drake, Ward, Nathan, & Lee, 2001; Ward, 2000; Ward & Keenan, 1999) have recently argued that child molesters' offense-supportive beliefs are likely to be the product of ingrained offense-supportive schemas (or as he calls them *implicit theories*). In brief, Ward argues that child molesters use these schemas to interpret, predict, and understand their complex surrounding world. For example, a molester could interpret the innocent cuddle received from a young child as being some type of flirtatious provocation (a belief most likely to be accompanied by deviant sexual arousal; Ward & Beech, 2006). Ward hypothesizes that intrafamilial molesters are likely to be characterized by such offense-supportive schemas, although the strength and content of these schemas will vary across individuals. Specifically, more pervasive schemas are thought to be characteristic of men with more pervasive sexual offending histories.

On questionnaires, intrafamilial men have been found to respond favorably to items depicting children as sexually motivated and unharmed by abuse in relation to comparison groups (Bumby, 1996; Hanson et al., 1994). Intrafamilial men also appear more likely to respond favorably to items supporting the sexual entitlement of males (Hanson et al., 1994). Wilson (1999) reports that intrafamilial abusers are more likely to see their victim as adultlike unlike nonfamilial homosexual abusers who show a strong emotional identification with children.

It should be noted, however, that there is no *experimental* evidence illustrating that intrafamilial molesters misinterpret social information using offense-supportive beliefs to date (see Gannon, Wright, Beech, & Williams, 2006). In addition, nothing is currently known about when offense-supportive beliefs and attitudes may develop, or whereabouts in the offense process these structures exert an etiological influence (Beech & Mann, 2002).

Emotional Self-Management

A number of researchers have argued that emotional self-management plays an important role in sexual offense abstinence generally (Ward, Hudson, & Keenan, 1998). A close examination of intrafamilial offenders' offense descriptions shows that, like extrafamilial men, they often report having felt significantly emotionally disturbed around the time of their offending (i.e., feeling angry, anxious, sad, or depressed; Ballard et al., 1990; Cole, 1992; Hartley, 1998). But how do these emotional disturbances translate into sexually offensive behavior toward a child or adolescent family member? It may be that offenders' adverse early experiences diminish molesters' abilities to develop adequate coping mechanisms. This would explain why, when faced with life stressors, intrafamilial men appear to choose clearly inadequate coping mechanisms. For example, some interfamilial child sexual abuse cases appear to be associated with excessive drug or alcohol use (see Williams & Finkelhor, 1990).

Until relatively recently, researchers largely presumed that molestation both in and outside of the family was associated with *negative affect* such as those outlined earlier (Pithers, 1990; Pithers, Kashima, Cumming, Beal, & Buell, 1988). Recent research, however, has suggested that molestation may also be accompanied by positive affect (e.g., excitement), which is highly problematic as it facilitates appetitive sexual offending (Ward, Louden, Hudson, & Marshall, 1995). Both negative and positive affective states (or pathways to offending) are hypothesized to be goal related, where negative affect is associated with a strong desire to avoid offending and positive affect is associated with a desire to seek out sexual offending (see the pathways model; Ward & Hudson, 1998). Interestingly, recent research has shown that intrafamilial abusers are not always characterized by avoidant goals, as the classical literature would have us believe (see Groth et al., 1982), but a good portion of these men (50 percent; $n = 24$) appear to follow an *approach* goal pathway (Yates, Kingston, & Hall, 2003). Clearly, this illustrates the heterogeneity of intrafamilial offenders, and raises important considerations for their risk assessment and treatment.

In addition to these four main factors, some researchers have argued that men offend sexually against their immature family members because they lack *empathy,* perhaps due to a lack of bonding during the early childhood years (see Marshall et al., 1999; Parker & Parker, 1986; Williams & Finkelhor, 1990). To recall what Parker and Parker found: Intrafamilial offenders had very often been absent during their daughter's formative years and therefore did not take part in important child rearing activities. In brief, it appears that these findings would explain why intrafamilial men have problems empathizing with their own children but not with others (Hayashino, Wurtele, & Klebe, 1995; Marshall et al., 1999). In other words, intrafamilial abusers appear to have *specific* but not globalized empathy deficiencies. Williams and Finkelhor (1990) have quite rightly pointed out that there is a general tendency, in the literature, to characterize incest victims as having been *exceptionally special* to their offender (i.e., Daddy's favorite girl). This lack of fit with the empathy and bonding hypothesis may well be the product of some of the grooming features that we outlined earlier in this chapter (i.e., making the potential victim feel special and wanted), and may not be indicative of genuine strong father-daughter bonds (Williams & Finkelhor, 1990).

TREATMENT FOR INTRAFAMILIAL OFFENDERS

A variety of treatment options have been proposed for intrafamilial offenders that generally fall under the rubric of being either offender- or family-focused. Offender-focused treatment is typically implemented using cognitive-behavioral treatment (CBT) methods. Other methods are documented (e.g., psychodynamic therapy) but we shall refrain from describing them here since they are not as widely used or empirically supported.

Cognitive-Behavioral Treatment

The most widely implemented and successful treatment method used in the Western world is cognitive-behavioral in orientation (see

Marshall et al., 1999, for a review). Within this type of therapy, mixed groups of sexual offenders (i.e., intrafamilial and extrafamilial child molesters, and sometimes offenders against adults) are taught how to modify their cognition and the behavioral mechanisms driving their offending behavior. In brief, the behavioral part of the program teaches men procedures aimed at changing deviant sexual behavior using behavior therapy principles. For example, for men who hold deviant sexual interests in child, *masturbatory reconditioning* may be used. Here, men are required to sexually arouse themselves however they wish and then engage in more prosocial fantasies (i.e., consenting adult intercourse) up until ejaculation thus strengthening sexual arousal to prosocial stimuli. To weaken inappropriate arousal, men are asked to engage in deviant sexual fantasies *following* ejaculation (Ward, 2003). Other behavioral components of therapy may include covert sensitization (learning to associate deviant sexual arousal with negative consequences), modeling (in which the therapist models a prosocial behavior), and behavioral rehearsal of desirable skills (see Fisher, Ward, & Beech, in press).

The cognitive part of treatment tackles any maladaptive thinking that appears to contribute to sexual offending, encouraging new alternative ways of thinking and feeling where possible. For example, tackling offense-supportive beliefs (more recently in the form of schemas or implicit theories) is a vital component of most major treatment programs. Here, offenders are educated about how such beliefs may facilitate and maintain sexually offensive behaviors (see Mann & Shingler, 2006), and alternative ways of seeing the world are encouraged and developed. As we have seen, for intrafamilial offenders, themes of entitlement appear to be important, and so these offenders should be encouraged to recognize the existence of such a schema, and to look for alternative ways of viewing the world when challenged with a particularly difficult situation. Other cognitive components of therapy may include victim empathy training (recognizing the impact of one's offending the victim), cognitive problem solving (i.e., anticipating, identifying, and responding to problems), and mood management training (in which offenders are taught how to identify and deal with affective states associated with their offending).

The general rehabilitative philosophy guiding CBT is risk management (or the risk-needs model; Andrews & Bonta, 2003),which has received impressive empirical support (see Hollin, 2004). Within this model, the psychological deficits we described earlier, such as deviant sexual interests, intimacy deficits, offense-supportive beliefs, and emotion regulation are conceptualized as *stable-dynamic risk* factors that require reduction so as to prevent future offending. More recently, some treatment providers have begun to adopt a "good lives" rehabilitative approach alongside the standard risk-needs-model approach (Ward, 2002; Ward & Stewart, 2003). Within the good lives approach, each offender's previous offending life is analyzed to give the therapist an idea of what types of activities or *primary human goods* the offender strives for. For example, is the offender interested primarily in gaining mastery at work, or maintaining an intimate relationship? If so, it is important to ensure that his future treatment plan takes this into account, otherwise, he is likely to lack the internal motivation necessary to desist from offending long term. As yet, however, no follow-up programs that investigate the effectiveness of a combined risk-needs and good lives approach have been completed.

Family Therapy

Despite the limitations of intrafamilial abuse being viewed as a family-only problem, family systems therapy is still recognized as a fundamental treatment method. Typically, such therapy involves a multifaceted approach in which each individual, the parents, and the family receive therapy (DiGiorgio-Miller, 2002). Giarretto (1989) is often cited as the leader of this therapeutic approach. In brief, Giarretto developed the Child Sexual Abuse Treatment Program in the 1970s to target the familial dysfunction hypothesized to be associated with intrafamilial abuse. Since its establishment, it has been deemed a success for intrafamilial families wishing to reunite (Giarretto, 1982), although Becker (1994) believes that more information regarding recidivism rates is needed for an adequate assessment.

IS IT POSSIBLE TO REUNIFY THE FAMILY?

Whether or not a child should live within the family home with an identified sexual offender is an extremely difficult question to answer, and the subject of much debate (Becker, 1994; Levenson &

Morin, 2001; Wilson, 2004a,b). Yet often therapists are asked to establish a family's suitability for reunification (Levenson & Morin, 2001). Levenson and Morin (2001) warn therapists to ensure that three main conditions are met before contemplating a decision recommending reunification. First, they argue that the intrafamilial offender should have *successfully finished* an Association for the Treatment of Sexual Abusers endorsed treatment program (i.e., offender treatment that is cognitive-behavioral in nature and evidence based). Second, the intrafamilial offender should receive a polygraph examination to ensure that the father is adhering appropriately to his treatment plan and is not engaging in any high-risk behaviors (e.g., deviant sexual fantasies). A suitably qualified polygraph examiner should conduct all examinations. Finally, if the family is keen for the father and victim to be reunited, the victim's therapist should be contacted as the very first step in the process. Only if the therapist feels reunification will be beneficial for the victim should a reunification recommendation be approved.

Levenson and Morin (2001) believe that some features of the nonoffending parent and/or family structure, in their clinical experience, increase the likelihood of family reunification being recommended and successful. In short, if the nonoffending mother is unable to help provide the necessary conditions for the father to carry out his treatment plan, then the father may experience a relapse (see also Powell & Ilett, 1992). For example, a nonoffending mother may be unable (through depression) or reluctant (through financial dependency) to inform therapists of any notable high-risk behaviors (DiGiorgio-Miller, 2002; Levenson & Morin, 2001). Similarly, there may be a noticeable power differentiation between the couple (e.g., domestic violence) impeding the mother's ability to act in a supervisory role (NCH Action for Children, 1997). As a general rule, professionals believe that the family unit should be openly communicative, respectful, and supportive for safe family reunification to be achieved (Levenson & Morin, 2001). It should be noted, however, that these features are not clear empirical predictors, as yet, of family reunification success.

CONCLUSION

In this chapter, we examined how intrafamilial offenders are typically defined, distinguishing characteristics of intrafamilial offenders, their modus operandi, the damage they cause to their primary victim and other nonoffending family members; theories were proposed to explain intrafamilial abuse; and current treatment perspectives aimed at promoting offense abstinence were explored. Overall, we have found that intrafamilial offenders are defined in many ways, creating confusion in the literature and hindering our ability to make meaningful comparisons across differing research programs. Despite these obstacles, however, research has now shown that intrafamilial abuse does not represent the discrete offense category that researchers once believed to be true. Instead, intrafamilial offenders appear to be categorized—like all child sexual offenders—by heterogeneity, and do not evidence a unique intrafamilial profile. However, they are likely to hold a number of core psychological deficits that should be targeted in CBT for successful offense desistence. Overall, we have argued that the focus should shift from family dynamic detection, which treats incest as a unique family problem, since this minimizes the role of the offender's own psychological characteristics in sexual offending. In short, though we believe that family context may be an important consideration for assessing the offender's own issues and future treatment considerations, it may not be helpful to view incest as a problem generated solely from within the family structure. To do so minimizes important psychological features of the offender that require treatment for future offense abstinence.

NOTES

1. See also Howells's (1981) preference-situational typology.

2. Although it should be noted that some offenders do report seemingly unplanned, impulsive sexual behaviors with children (see Gannon, Keown, & Polaschek, in preparation).

3. We do not examine psychodynamic theory here due to space limitations but refer the interested reader to Theunissen (2005).

REFERENCES

Abel, G. G., Becker, J. V., Cunningham-Rathner, J., Mittelman, M. S., & Rouleau, J. L. (1988). Multiple paraphilic diagnoses among sex offenders. *Bulletin of the American Academy of Psychiatry and the Law, 16,* 153-168.

Abel, G. G., Becker, J. V., Murphy, W. D., & Flanagan, B. (1981). Identifying dangerous child molesters. In R. Stuart (Ed.), *Violent behavior: Social learning approaches to prediction, management and treatment* (pp. 116-137). New York: Brunner/Mazel.

Alexander, P. C., & Schaeffer, C. M. (1994). A typology of incestuous family is based on cluster analysis. *Journal of Family Psychology, 8,* 458-470.

Andrews, D. A., & Bonta, J. (2003). The psychology of criminal conduct (3rd ed.). Cincinnati, OH: Anderson Publishing Co.

Araji, S., & Finkelhor, D. (1986). Abusers: A review of the research. In D. Finkelhor (Ed.), *A sourcebook on child sexual abuse* (pp. 89-118). Beverly Hills: Sage.

Bagley, C., & King, K. (1990). *Child sexual abuse: The search for healing.* London: Routledge.

Ballard, D. T., Blair, G. D., Devereaux, S., Valentine, L. K., Horton, A. L., & Johnson, B. L. (1990). A comparative profile of the incest perpetrator: Background characteristics, abuse history, and use of social skills. In A. L. Horton, B. L. Johnson, L. M. Roundy, & D. Williams (Eds.), *The incest perpetrator: A family member no one wants to treat* (pp. 43-64). London: Sage.

Barrett, M. J., Trepper, T. S., & Stone-Fish, L. (1990). Feminist-informed family therapy for the treatment of intra-family child sexual abuse. *Journal of Family Psychology, 4,* 151-166.

Becker, J. V. (1994). Offenders: Characteristics and treatment. *The Future of Children, 4,* 176-197.

Beech, A. R. (1998). A psychometric typology of child abusers. *International Journal of Offender Therapy and Comparative Criminology, 42,* 319-339.

Beech, A. R., Fisher, D., & Beckett, R. C. (1999). *An evaluation of the prison sex offender treatment programme.* U.K. Home Office occasional report (available from Home Office Information Publications Group, Research, Development and Statistics Directorate, Room 201, 50 St Anne's Gate, London SW1 9AT). Available electronically from: www.homeoffice.gov.uk/rds/pdfs/occ-step3.pdf.

Beech, A. R., & Mann, R. (2002). Recent developments in the assessment and treatment of sexual offenders. In J. McGuire (Ed.), *Offender rehabilitation and treatment: Effective programmes and policies to reduce re-offending* (pp. 259-288). Chichester, UK: Wiley.

Beech, A. R., & Ward, T. (2004). The integration of etiology and risk in sex offenders: A theoretical model. *Aggression and Violent Behavior, 10,* 31-63.

Bell, V. (1993). *Interrogating incest: Feminism, foucault, and the law.* London: Routledge.

Bennett, S. E., Hughes, H. M., & Luke, D. A. (2000). Heterogeneity in patterns of child sexual abuse, family functioning, and long-term adjustment. *Journal of Interpersonal Violence, 15,* 134-157.

Berliner, L., & Conte, J. R. (1990). The process of victimization: The victim's perspective. *Child Abuse and Neglect, 14,* 29-40.

Bogaerts, S., Vervaeke, G., & Goethals, J. (2004). A comparison of relational attitude and personality disorders in the explanation of child molestation. *Sexual Abuse: A Journal of Research and Treatment, 16,* 37-47.

Bolen, R. M. (2001). *Child sexual abuse: Its scope and our failure*. New York: Kluwer Academic.

Browne, A., & Finkelhor, D. (1986). Impact of child sexual abuse: A review of the research. *Psychological Bulletin, 99,* 66-77.

Bumby, K. M. (1996). Assessing the cognitive distortions of child molesters and rapists: Developments and validation of the MOLEST and RAPE scales. *Sexual Abuse: A Journal of Research and Treatment, 8,* 37-54.

Bumby, K. M., & Hansen, D. J. (1997). Intimacy deficits, fear of intimacy, and loneliness among sexual offenders. *Criminal Justice and Behavior, 24,* 315-331.

Burkett, L. P. (1991). Parenting behaviors of women who were sexually abused as children in their families of origin. *Family Process, 30,* 421-434.

Christiansen, J. R., & Blake, R. H. (1990). The grooming process in father-daughter incest. In A. L. Horton, B. L. Johnson, L. M. Roundy & D. Williams (Eds.), *The incest perpetrator: A family member no one wants to treat* (pp. 88-98). London: Sage.

Cole, W. (1992). Incest perpetrators: Their assessment and treatment. *Clinical Forensic Psychiatry, 15,* 689-701.

Cole, P. M., & Putnam, F. W. (1992). Effect of incest on self and social functioning: A developmental psychopathology perspective. *Journal of Consulting and Clinical Psychology, 60,* 174-184.

Cole, P. M., & Woolger, C. (1989). Incest survivors: The relation of their perception perceptions of their parents and their own parenting attitudes. *Child Abuse and Neglect, 13,* 409-416.

Conte, J. R. (1985). Clinical dimensions of adult sexual abuse of children. *Behavioral Sciences and the Law, 3,* 341-354.

Craven, S., Brown, S., & Gilchrist, E., (2006). Sexual grooming: Review of literature and theoretical considerations. *Journal of Sexual Aggression, 12*(3), 287-299.

Craven, S., Brown, S., Gilchrist, E., & Cushway, D. (2005). *What is sexual grooming?* Paper presented at the National Organisation for the Treatment of Sexual Abusers, Dublin.

Dadds, M., Smith, M., & Webber, Y. (1991). An exploration of family and individual profiles following father-daughter incest. *Child Abuse and Neglect, 15,* 575-586.

de Young, M. (1982). *The sexual victimisation of children*. Jefferson, NC: McFarland.

DiGiorgio-Miller, J. (2002). A comprehensive approach to family reunification following incest in an era of legislatively mandated community notification. *Journal of Offender Rehabilitation, 35,* 83-91.

DiLillo, D., & Long, P. J. (1999). Perceptions of couple functioning among female survivors of child sexual abuse. *Journal of Child Sexual Abuse, 7,* 59-76.

Drake, C., Ward, T., Nathan, P., & Lee, J. (2001). Challenging the cognitive distortions of child molesters: An implicit theory approach. *Journal of Sexual Aggression, 7,* 25-40.

Elliott, M., Browne, K., D., & Kilcoyne, J. (1995). Child sexual abuse: What offenders tell us. *Child Abuse and Neglect, 19,* 579-594.

Firestone, P., Dixon, K. L., Nunes, K. L., & Bradford, J. M. (2005). A comparison of incest offenders based on victim age. *The Journal of the American Academy of Psychiatry and the Law, 33,* 223-232.

Faust, J., Runyon, M. K., & Kenny, M. C. (1995). Family variables associated with the onset and impact of intrafamilial childhood sexual abuse. *Clinical Psychology Review, 15,* 443-456.

Fisher, D., Ward, T., & Beech, A. R. (2006). Pedophilia. In J. E. Fisher & W. T. O'Donohue (Eds.), *Practitioner's guide to evidence-based psychotherapy.* New York: Springer.

Forward, S., & Buck, C. (1978). *Betrayal of innocence: Incest and its devastation.* New York: Penguin Books.

Frenzel, R. R., & Lang, R. A. (1989). Identifying sexual preferences in intrafamilial and extrafamilial child sexual abusers. *Annals of Sex Research, 2,* 255-275.

Freund, K., Watson, R., & Dickey, R. (1991). Sex offenders against female children perpetrated by men who are not paedophiles. *Journal of Sex Research, 28,* 409-423.

Gannon, T. A., Keown, K., & Polaschek, D. L. L. (in preparation). Comparing child molesters' cognitive distortions across interviews and questionnaires.

Gannon, T. A., & Polaschek, D. L. L. (2006). Cognitive distortions in child molesters: A re-examination of key theories and research. *Clinical Psychology Review. 26*(8), 1000-1019.

Gannon, T. A., Ward, T., & Polaschek, D. L. L. (2004). Child sexual offenders. In M. Connolly (Ed.), *Violence in society: New Zealand perspectives* (pp. 31-47). Christchurch: Te Awatea Press.

Gannon, T. A., Wright, D. B., Beech, A. R., & Williams, S. A. (2006). Do child molesters have cognitive distortions? What does their memory recall tell us? *Journal of Sexual Aggression, 12,* 5-18.

Garlick, Y., Marshall, W. L., & Thornton, D. (1996). Intimacy deficits and attribution of blame among sexual offenders. *Legal and Criminological Psychology, 1,* 251-258.

Giarretto, H. (1982). A comprehensive child sexual abuse treatment programme. *Child Abuse and Neglect, 6,* 263-278.

Giarretto, H. (1989). Community-based treatment of the incest family. *Psychiatric Clinics of North America, 12,* 351-361.

Gibbens, T. C. N., Soothill, K. L., & Way, C. K. (1978). Sibling and parent-child incest offenders. *British Journal of Criminology, 18,* 40-52.

Goodwin, J., McCarthy, T., & DiVasto, P. (1981). Prior incest in mothers of abused children. *Child Abuse and Neglect, 5,* 87-96.

Groth, A. N., Hobson, W. F., & Gary, T. S. (1982). The child molester: Clinical observations. In J. Conte & D. A. Shore (Eds.), *Social work and child sexual abuse* (pp. 129-144). Binghamton, NY: The Haworth Press.

Gruber, K., & Jones, R. (1983). Identifying determinants of risk and sexual victimisation of youth. *Child Abuse and Neglect, 7,* 17-24.

Hanson, R. K. (2006). Stability and change: Dynamic risk factors for sexual offenders. In W. L. Marshall, Y. M. Fernandez, L. E. Marshall & G. A. Serran (Eds.), *Sexual offender treatment: Controversial issues* (pp. 17-33). Chichester, UK: Wiley.

Hanson, R. K., & Bussière, M. T. (1998). Predicting relapse: A meta-analysis of sexual offender recidivism studies. *Journal of Consulting and Clinical Psychology, 66,* 348-362.

Hanson, R. K., Gizzarelli, R., & Scott, H. (1994). The attitudes of incest offenders: Sexual entitlement and acceptance of sex with children. *Criminal Justice and Behavior, 21,* 187-202.

Hanson, R. K., & Morton-Bourgon, K. (2004). *Predictors of sexual recidivism: An updated meta-analysis.* (User Report 2004-02). Ottawa, Canada: Public Safety and Emergency Preparedness.

Hartley, C. (1998). How incest offenders overcome internal inhibitions through the use of cognitions and cognitive distortions. *Journal of Interpersonal Violence, 13,* 25-39.

Hartley, C. (2001). Incest offenders' perceptions of their motives to sexually offend within their past and current life context. *Journal of Interpersonal Violence, 16,* 459-475.

Hayashino, D. S., Wurtele, S. K., & Klebe, K. J. (1995). Child molesters: An examination of cognitive factors. *Journal of Interpersonal Violence, 10,* 106-116.

Heil, P., Ahlmeyer, S., & Simons, D. (2003). Crossover sexual offences. *Sexual Abuse: A Journal of Research and Treatment, 15,* 221-236.

Herman, J. C., & Hirschman, L. (1981). *Father-daughter incest.* Cambridge, MA: Harvard University Press.

Hollin, C. R. (2004). To treat or not to treat? An historical perspective. In C. R. Hollin (Ed.), *The essential handbook of offender assessment and treatment* (pp. 1-13). London: John Wiley.

Hoorwitz, A. N. (1983). Guidelines for treating father-daughter incest. *Social Casework: Journal of Contemporary Social Work, 64,* 515-524.

Howells, K. (1981). Adult sexual interest in children: Considerations relevant to theories of aetiology. In M. Cook & K. Howells (Eds.), *Adult sexual interest in children* (pp. 55-94). London: Academic Press.

Hudson, S., & Ward, T. (1997). Intimacy, loneliness, and attachment style in sex offenders. *Journal of Interpersonal Violence, 12,* 323-339.

Kaufman, I., Peck, A. L., & Tagiuri, C. K. (1954). The family constellation and overt incestuous relations between father and daughter. *American Journal of Orthopsychiatry, 24,* 266-277.

Kendall-Tackett, K. A., Williams, L. M., & Finkelhor, D. (1993). Impact of sexual abuse on children: A review and synthesis of recent empirical studies. *Psychological Bulletin, 113,* 164-180.

Kercher, G., & McShane, M. (1984). The prevalence of child sexual abuse victimization in an adult sample of Texas residents. *Child Abuse and Neglect, 8,* 495-501.

Kirkland, K., & Bauer, C. (1982). MMPI traits of incestuous fathers. *Journal of Criminal Psychology, 38,* 645-649.

Kroth, J. A. (1979). *Child sexual abuse: Analysis of a family therapy approach.* Springfield, IL: Charles C. Thomas Pub Ltd.

Lang, R. A., & Frenzel, R. R. (1988). How sex offenders lure children. *Annals of Sex Research, 1,* 303-317.

Langevin, R., & Watson, R. (1991). A comparison of incestuous biological and stepfathers. *Sexual Abuse: A Journal of Research and Treatment, 4*(2), 141-150.

Levenson, J. S., & Morin, J. W. (2001). *Treating nonoffending parents in child sexual abuse cases: Connections for family safety.* London: Sage.

Levitt, C., Owen, G., & Truchsess, J. (1991). Families after sexual abuse: What helps? What is needed? In M. Patton (Ed.), *Frontline research and evaluation* (pp. 39-56). Newbury Park, CA: Sage.

Lipovsky, J. A., Saunders, B. E., & Hanson, R. F. (1992). Parent-child relationships of victims and siblings in incest families. *Journal of Child Sexual Abuse, 1,* 35-49.

Lubell, A. K. N., & Peterson, C. (1998). Female incest survivors: Relationships with mothers and female friends. *Journal of Interpersonal Violence, 13*(2), 193-205.

Madonna, P. G., Van Scoyk, S., & Jones, D. (1991). Family interactions within incest and non-incest families. *American Journal of Psychiatry, 148,* 46-49.

Maisch, H. (1973). *Incest* (translated by Colin Bearne). London: Andre Deutsch.

Mann, R. E., & Shingler, J. (2006). Schema-driven cognition in sexual offenders: Theory, assessment and treatment. In W. L. Marshall, Y. M. Fernandez, L. E. Marshall, & G. A. Serran (Eds.), *Sexual offender treatment: Controversial issues* (pp. 173-185). Chichester, UK: Wiley.

Marshall, W. L. (1989). Intimacy, loneliness, and sexual offenders. *Behaviour Research and Therapy, 27*(5), 491-503.

Marshall, W. L. (1996). The sexual offender: Monster, victim, or everyman. *Sexual Abuse: A Journal of Research and Treatment, 8,* 317-335.

Marshall, W. L., Anderson, D., & Fernandez, Y. M. (1999). *Cognitive behavioral treatment of sexual offenders.* Chichester, UK: Wiley.

Marshall, W. L., & Barbaree, H. E. (1990). An integrated theory of sexual offending. In W. L. Marshall, D. R. Laws, & H. E. Barbaree (Eds.), *Handbook of sexual assault: Issues, theories and treatment of the offender* (pp. 363-385). New York: Plenum.

Marshall, W. L., Barbaree, H. E., & Christophe, D. (1986). Sexual offenders against female children: Sexual preferences for age of victims and type of behaviour. *Canadian Journal of Behavioural Science, 18,* 424-439.

McGrath, R. J. (1991). Sex offender risk assessment and disposition planning: A review of empirical and clinical findings. *International Journal of Offender Therapy and Comparative Criminology, 35,* 328-350.

Meiselman, K. C. (1978). *Incest: A psychological study of causes and effects with treatment recommendations.* San Francisco, CA: Jossey-Bass.

Murphy, W. D., Haynes, M. R., Stalgaitis, S. J., & Flanagan, B. (1986). Differential sexual responding among four groups of sexual offenders against children. *Journal of Psychopathology and Behavioural Assessment, 8,* 339-353.

NCH Action for Children (1997). *Making a difference: Working with women and children experiencing domestic violence.* Rochester, UK: Chapel Press.

Neidigh, L., & Krop, H. (1992). Cognitive distortions among child sexual offenders. *Journal of Sex Education and Therapy, 18,* 208-215.

Parker, H. (1984). Intrafamilial sexual child abuse: A study of the abusive father. *Dissertation Abstracts International, 45,* 3757A.

Parker, H., & Parker, S. (1986). Father-daughter sexual abuse: An emerging perspective. *American Journal of Orthopsychiatry, 56,* 531-549.

Phelan, P. (1995). Incest and its meaning: The perspectives of fathers and daughters. *Child Abuse and Neglect, 19,* 7-24.

Pithers, W. D. (1990). Relapse prevention with sexual aggressors: A method for maintaining therapeutic gain and enhancing external supervision. In W. L. Marshall, D. R. Laws, & H. E. Barbaree (Eds.), *Handbook of sexual assault: Issues, theories and treatment of the offender* (pp. 346-361). New York: Plenum.

Pithers, W. D., Kashima, K. M., Cumming, G. F., Beal, L. S., & Buell, M. M. (1988). Relapse prevention in sexual aggression. In R. A. Prentky & V. L. Quinsey (Eds.), *Human sexual aggression: Current perspectives* (pp. 244-260). New York: New York Academy of Science.

Pollock, N. L., & Hashmall, J. M. (1991). The excuses of child molesters. *Behavioral Sciences and the Law, 9,* 53-59.

Powell, M. B., & Ilett, M. J. (1992). Assessing the incestuous family's readiness for reconstitution. *Families in Society: The Journal of Contemporary Human Services, 73,* 417-423.

Quinn, T.M. (1984). Father-daughter incest: An ecological model. *Dissertation Abstracts International, 45*(12), 3957B.

Ray, S. L. (1993). *Incest survivors: Selected review of the literature.* Retrieved May 5, 2006 from http://www.mirror.org/wayne.ray/review.html.

Reis, S. D., & Heppner, P. P. (1993). Examination of coping resources and family adaptation in mothers and daughters of incestuous versus non-clinical families. *Journal of Counseling Psychology, 40,* 100-108.

Rice, M. E., & Harris, G. T. (2002). Men who molest their sexually immature daughters: Is a special explanation required? *Journal of Abnormal Psychology, 111,* 329-339.

Saunders, B. E., Lipovsky, J. A., & Hanson, R. F. (1995). Couple and familial characteristics of father-child incest families. *Journal of Family Social Work, 1,* 5-25.

Salter, A. (1988). *Treating child sex offenders and victims.* Newbury Park, CA: Sage.

Schultz, R., Braun, B. G., & Kluft, R. P. (1989). Multiple personality disorder: Phenomenology of selected variables in comparison to major depression. *Dissociation, 2,* 45-51.

Scott, R. L., & Stone, D. (1986). MMPI profile consolation in incest families. *Journal of Consulting and Clinical Psychology, 54,* 364-368.

Segal, Z. L., & Marshall, W. L. (1985). Heterosexual social skills in a population of rapists and child molesters. *Journal of Consulting and Clinical Psychology, 53,* 55-63.

Seidman, B. T., Marshall, W. L., Hudson, S. M., & Robertson, P. J. (1994). An examination of intimacy and loneliness in sex offenders. *Journal of Interpersonal Violence, 9,* 518-534.

Seto, M. C., Lalumière, M. L., & Kuban M. (1999). The sexual preferences of incest offenders. *Journal of Abnormal Psychology, 108,* 267-272.

Shepher, J. (1983) *Incest: A biosocial view.* New York: Academic Press.

Smallbone, S. W., & Dadds, M. R. (1998). Childhood attachment and adult attachment in incarcerated adult male sex offenders. *Journal of Interpersonal Violence, 13,* 555-573.

Smallbone, S., & Wortley, R. (2000). *Child sexual abuse in Queensland: Offender characteristics and modus operandi.* Brisbane: Queensland Crime Commission.

Smallbone, S., & Wortley, R. (2001). Child sexual abuse: Offender characteristics and modus operandi. *Trends and issues in crime and criminal justice. No. 193.* Canberra: Australian Institute of Criminology.

Steele, B., & Alexander, H. (1981). Long-term effects of sexual abuse in childhood. In P. Mrazek & C. Kempe (Eds.), *Sexually abused children and their families* (pp. 223-234). Oxford: Pergamon.

Stevenson, J. (1990). The treatment of the long-term sequelae of child abuse. *Journal of Child Psychology and Psychiatry, 40,* 89-111.

Strand, V. (1986). Parents in incest families: A study in differences. *Dissertation Abstracts International, 47*(8), 3191a.

Studer, L. H., Clelland, S. R., Aylwin, A. S., Reddon, J. R., & Monro, A. (2000). Rehinking risk assessment for incest offenders. *International Journal of Law and Psychiatry, 23,* 15-22.

Swanson, L., & Biaggio, M. K. (1985). Therapeutic perspectives on father-daughter incest. *American Journal of Psychiatry, 142,* 667-674.

Theunissen, C. (2005). Sexual attachments: A theoretical psychoanalytical perspective on incest. *Psychoanalytic Psychotherapy, 19,* 259-278.

van Dam, C. (2001). *Identifying child molesters: Preventing child sexual abuse by recognizing the patterns of the offenders.* Binghamton, NY: The Haworth Press.

Veach, T. A. (1997). Cognitive therapy techniques in treating incestuous fathers: Examining cognitive distortions and levels of denial. *Journal of Family Psychotherapy, 8,* 1-20.

Wagner, W. G. (1991). Depression in mothers of sexually abused vs. mothers of nonabused children. *Child Abuse and Neglect, 15,* 99-104.

Ward, T. (2000). Sexual offenders' cognitive distortions as implicit theories. *Aggression and Violent Behavior, 5,* 491-507.

Ward, T. (2002). Good lives and the rehabilitation of offenders: Promises and problems. *Aggression and Violent Behavior, 7,* 513-528.

Ward, T. (2003). The explanation, assessment and treatment of child sexual abuse. *International Journal of Forensic Psychology, 1,* 10-25.

Ward, T., & Beech, T. (2006). An integrated theory of sexual offending. *Aggression and Violent Behavior, 11,* 44-63.

Ward, T., & Hudson, S. M. (1998). A model of the relapse process in sexual offenders. *Journal of Interpersonal Violence, 13,* 700-725.

Ward, T., Hudson, S. M., Johnston, L., & Marshall, W. L. (1997). Cognitive distortions in sex offenders: An integrative review. *Clinical Psychology Review, 17,* 479-507.

Ward, T., Hudson, S. M., & Keenan, T. (1998). A self-regulation model of the sexual offense process. *Sexual Abuse: A Journal of Research and Treatment, 10,* 141-157.

Ward, T., Hudson, S., Marshall, W., & Siegert, R. (1995). Attachment style and intimacy deficits in sex offenders: A theoretical framework. *Sexual Abuse: A Journal of Research and Treatment, 7,* 317-335.

Ward, T., & Keenan, T. (1999). Child molesters' implicit theories. *Journal of Interpersonal Violence, 14,* 821-838.

Ward, T., Louden, K., Hudson, S. M., & Marshall, W. L. (1995). A descriptive model of the offense chain for child molesters. *Journal of Interpersonal Violence, 10,* 452-472.

Ward, T., Polaschek, D. L. L., & Beech, A. R. (2005). *Theories of sexual offending.* Chichester, UK: Wiley.

Ward, T., & Siegert, R. (2002). Toward a comprehensive theory of child sexual abuse: A theory knitting perspective. *Psychology, Crime, and Law, 8,* 319-351.

Ward, T., & Stewart, C. A. (2003). Criminogenic needs or human needs: A theoretical critique. *Psychological, Crime, & Law, 9,* 125-143.

Westermarck, E. (1891). *The history of the human marriage.* London: McMillan and Co.

Williams, L. M., & Finkelhor, D. (1990). The characteristics of incestuous fathers: A review of recent studies. In W. L. Marshall, D. R. Laws, & H. E. Barbaree (Eds.), *Handbook of sexual assault: Issues theories and treatment of the offender* (pp. 231-255). New York: Plenum.

Wilson, R. F. (2004a). Recognizing the threat posed by an incestuous parent to the victim's siblings: Part I: Appraising the risk. *Journal of Child and Family Studies, 13,* 143-162.

Wilson, R. F. (2004b). Recognizing the threat posed by an incestuous parent to the victim's siblings: Part II: Improving legal responses. *Journal of Child and Family Studies, 13,* 263-276.

Wilson, R. J. (1999). Emotional congruence in sexual offenders against children. *Sexual Abuse: A Journal of Research and Treatment, 11,* 33-47.

Wolfe, A. P. (1970). Childhood association and sexual attraction: A further test of the Westermarck hypothesis. *American Anthropologist, 72,* 503-515.

Wolfe, A. P., & Durham W. H. (2004). *Inbreeding, incest, and the incest taboo: The state of knowledge at the turn of the century.* Palo Alto, CA: Stanford University Press.

Yates, P. M., Kingston, D., & Hall, K. (2003). *Pathways to sexual offending: Validity of Hudson and Ward's (1998) self-regulation model and relationship to static and dynamic risk among treated high risk sexual offenders.* Presented at the 22nd annual research and treatment conference of the Association for the Treatment of Sexual Abusers (ATSA). St. Louis, MO.

Chapter 5

The Nonfamily Sex Offender

Carolyn Hilarski

INTRODUCTION

Thousands of American children are substantiated as sexual abuse victims each year (DHHS, 2006a) with many more unreported or unconfirmed cases left in the hands of sexual perpetrators (Webster, O'Toole, O'Toole, & Lucal, 2005). It is estimated that nonfamily members sexually harm more than 11 percent of the annual established child abuse cases, either alone or with one or more of the victim's caregivers (DHHS, 2006b). The rate of discontinuance and the risk and protective factors relating to the extrafamilial[1] sex offender is currently only suggestive (Saleh & Guidry, 2003). A dominating issue around the paucity of child sexual abuse research is the public's willingness to deny or minimize its existence. To illustrate, Hanson, Scott, and Steffy (1995) suggest that it is difficult for individuals to imagine their family's friends or neighbors as sexual perpetrators. Rush (1996) proposed that sexual abuse accusations were thought to be oedipal acting out by female children. These and other examples are supported by estimates that 90 percent or more of sexual victimization goes unreported (Cheit & Freyd, 2005; Russell, 1983). Public policy relating to sex offenders and offending is often based on myths and misperceptions[2] that can seriously undermine appropriate assessment and treatment[3] (Sample & Bray, 2003).

This chapter's intent is to inform professionals and policy makers working with child sex offenders of the current understanding

Handbook of Social Work in Child and Adolescent Sexual Abuse
© 2008 by The Haworth Press, Taylor & Francis Group. All rights reserved.
doi:10.1300/5804_05

regarding the personal characteristics and the likelihood of the extra-familial type perpetrator discontinuing harm to children. Although, this category of offender is common, related literature is uncommonly wanting (Bolen, 2000). It is imperative that professionals and policy makers working with child sex offenders be informed to increase the likelihood of effective assessment and treatment and reduce child victimization.

WHAT IS SEX OFFENDING?

The definition of sex offending is not standardized among states or legal authorities. However, those who have attempted to characterize the term tend to describe it as a sexual act committed by one or more persons against a less powerful other (Wells & Sirotnak, 2004).

The clinical definition describes sexual offending as deviant sexual interests and behaviors that continue for six months or longer and cause impairment in an individual's social and occupational functioning. The diagnosis is understood as *paraphilias* and is found under the heading of sexual and gender identity disorder in the *Diagnostic and Statistical Manual of Mental Disorders,* Fourth Edition, Text Revision (APA, 2000). The person who engages in paraphilia may exhibit sexual behaviors that include (but are not limited to) exhibitionism (sexual exhibition), fetishism (sexual pleasure from inanimate objects), transvestic fetishism (dressing is clothing of the opposite sex), frotteurism (sexual touching), necrophilia (sexual arousal from a corpse), pedophilia (sexual assaults on children by adults), sexual sadism or masochism (sexual pleasure through pain either to the self or others), telephone scatologia (obscene telephone calls), and voyeurism (watching others' sexual activity or undressing). The disorder is most often observed around puberty and is frequently found comorbid with other disorders.[4] However, many, if not most, paraphiliac go undiagnosed; moreover some paraphiliac disorders are not considered criminal (Saleh & Guidry, 2003). Sex offenders, generally, engage in more than one type of paraphiliac behavior, judged legal and illegal (Abel, Becker, Cunningham-Rathner, Mittelman, & Rouleau, 1988), although arrest data show that of all sex offender types child molesters present the greatest tendency to specialize.[5]

CHARACTERISTICS OF THE CHILD
SEX OFFENDER

Sexual perpetrators are not generally distinguishable by race, religion, income, employment, gender, or age, although nonfamily predators of children are most often male (Bolen, 2000). They do, however, share one essential element: they break the law, though few are apprehended after the first offense, and many are never detected, especially those who harm children. With only 5 percent of sexual offenders having a criminal record, profiling them is almost impossible (Beyko & Wong, 2005).

Offense predilections range from the kind of victim chosen[6] to the type of behavior.[7] Nonfamily sexual predators often select victims who are limited in their ability or circumstances to report victimizing behavior. Emotionally vulnerable children, very young females, members of troubled families, or children with developmental disabilities are all vulnerable targets (Bolen, 2000). Moreover, children with insecure attachments often possess belief systems that love must be earned through "pleasing." These youth appear more vulnerable to grooming techniques (Marshall & Marshall, 2000) and experience greater consequences from perceived trauma (Smallbone & McCabe, 2003).

Nonfamily sex offenders victimize children and youth most often in perceived "safe" locations, for example, while children are walking in their own or another "good" neighborhood, or, are in their own home or a friend's home. The perpetrator's methods of contact are varied and resourceful (Bolen, 2000) and may include pleasant and nonviolent interaction, sadism, or masochism (Goldstein, 1999).

Commonly, sexual perpetrators are distinguished as preferential or situational (Dietz, 1983). The *preferential* offender prefers children[8] and the *situational* perpetrator is an equal opportunity offender. In other words, whoever is available (Bolen, 2000), although vulnerable victims such as young children or the mentally or physically challenged are most often targeted (Davis & Mcshane, 1995). Nevertheless, the *situational* offender usually has an ongoing sexual relationship with an adult. His sexual interactions with children are episodic, whereas the *preferential* offender is compelled to engage sexually with children in consistently decided ways (Goldstein, 1999; Lanning, 2001).

Preferential sex offenders display several distinguishing patterns of behavior (see Goldstein, 1999). For example, the *seducer,* often an extrovert and a respected person in the community, will initially captivate his victims with friendship, kindness, gifts, and loyalty. Then, he will use threats of violence to silence them. This type of offender is predisposed to "child sex rings" and is most often apprehended after he has rejected one or more of his victims[9] (Goldstein, 1999; Lanning, 1992).

The *introverted preferential* offender does not have the necessary skills to attract or interact with child prey. Consequently, this type of offender might employ a child prostitute or engage in obscene conversation or exposure with unknown victims. Some will enter into a relationship in which there are children in their target group, or they may have biological children to abuse them beginning in infancy (Goldstein, 1999).

Sadists must hurt their victims, either physically and/or emotionally, to satisfy their sexual urges. This type of criminal will most often abduct or murder children (Goldstein, 1999).

Overall, *preferential* sex offenders are predictable in that they have a difficult time relating to peers. When apprehended, they are often in their late twenties or older, not married (although they may have been), living alone or with a family member, markedly focused on children from early adolescence, with no long-term employment history. They engage in hobbies that attract children, especially in their age preference, and have varied collections of pornography depending on their socioeconomic level (Davis & Mcshane, 1995; Goldstein, 1999; Lanning, 2001).

Emotions

Rage, poor self-esteem, depression, or feeling inadequate are associated with sexual aggression (Scheff & Retzinger, 2003). Violence is used as a defensive technique meant to manage irresistible thoughts and feelings (Hall & Barongan, 1997). The suggestion is that this type of behavior is a coping style learned from childhood sexual abuse experiences (Lee, Jackson, Pattison, & Ward, 2002) that include rape and physical abuse (Simons, Wurtele, & Heil, 2002). The outcome of their acting out behavior is impaired relationships with others

(Knight & Prentky, 1990b). Sexual perpetrators frequently express self-depreciating thoughts resulting from feelings of loneliness and isolation (Hudson & Ward, 2000). Disorganized and/or anxious attachment with the primary caregiver is related to the negative self-talk and social interaction difficulty (Marshall & Marshall, 2000). Inconsistent or avoiding caregiver response can create long-lasting insecurity (Marshall, Serran, & Cortoni, 2000). The individual feels unlovable and vulnerable to rejection. Choosing intimate and social interactions that can be controlled enhances the perpetrator's sense of safety (Smallbone & Dadds, 2000).

In sum, it seems that no single model is sufficient for explaining sexual offending. Instead, it appears that a combination of factors influence sexual victimizing behavior (Dube et al., 2001; Rind, Tromovitch, & Bauserman, 1998), although it is important to remember that any discussion of sexual perpetrator characteristics is suspect, since most offenders go unnoticed (Miethe, Olson, & Mitchell, 2006).

CAN CHILD SEX OFFENDERS STOP VICTIMIZING?

Understanding the reasons that offenders choose not to offend is less complex and more transferable to treatment than attempting to find the causal variables for criminal offending or reoffending according to Uggen and Piliavin (1998). However, there is limited research on desistance across criminal behavior and almost none relating to sexual offending. Most of the literature relates to treatment outcome with recidivism, reoffending, or criminal career criteria as derived measures. The section that follows discusses these separate but overlapping concepts.

CRIMINAL CAREERS AND SPECIALIZATION

Important information relating to the sex offender's history is the onset, frequency, seriousness, and duration of the offending behavior. Public policy and treatment modalities are based on these parameters. The current assumption is that sexual perpetrators are lifelong "career specialists" and laws meant to hinder these behaviors are seen in chemical castration, extended sentencing, offender registration, and community notification (Winick & LaFond, 2003). Interestingly, the literature does not fully support the common perception that all perpetrators will chronically offend in the same manner (Sample & Bray, 2003; Zimring, 2004). With few exceptions, most criminals engage in varying types of crime (Miethe et al., 2006). Moreover, when compared with other types of criminals, certain categories of sexual perpetrators are significantly less likely to reoffend (Langan, Schmitt, & Durose, 2003) and if they do reoffend it is unusual for them to commit a similar sexual crime (see Sample & Bray, 2003).

RECIDIVISM

Recidivism is sometimes termed a "relapse" (Pithers, 1990), or being arrested for a new crime when there has been a previous detainment and incarceration (Zgoba & Simon, 2005). The crime could be any type, as certain sex offenders are known to engage in sexual and nonsexual offending (Olver & Wong, 2006).

The current suggestion is that sexual deviancy, chaotic lifestyle, and hostile attributions are risk factors for recidivism (Gacono, Meloy, & Bridges, 2000; Hildebrand, de Ruiter, & de Vogel, 2004; Prentky, Knight, & Lee, 1997).

Two types of factors delineate sex offending and recidivism: static and dynamic characteristics. The static risk factors are not subject to change and include the age (often young) or race of the offender (currently understood as disproportionately a minority), in addition to the number of prior offenses (Hanson & Bussiere, 1998b).

The dynamic risk factors are changeable elements, such as, deviant sexual interest and fantasies, identifying as a victim, denial, and negative beliefs about women (Hanson et al., 2001). Skill deficits relating to anger, problem solving, and social issues are also included (Craig, Browne, & Stringer, 2003).

Other risk factors include an extensive history of sexual offenses and victimization, in addition to nonsexual criminal behavior,[10] substance abuse, noncompliance with treatment, cultural socialization, and the presence of a personality disorder or other comorbid mental health issue[11] (Carich & Mussack, 2001).

Offenders obtaining treatment in the community are likely to have different criminal histories than incarcerated offenders (Firestone et al., 2000; Hanson, Steffy, & Gauthier, 1993). For example, Zgoba and Simon (2005) found that incarcerated sex offenders were more likely than sex offenders involved in a community-based treatment (CBT) to commit a violent rape against a female (27.8 percent versus 8.1 percent), while those in CBT preferred to violate children under the age of ten (44.4 percent versus 34.5 percent).

Recent literature suggests that sexual reoffending may not be as prevalent as previously or universally assumed, although, recidivism rates should be viewed with caution and considered to be underestimates. Greenberg (1998) conservatively estimated that nonfamily sex offenders of children reoffend at a rate of 10 to 20 percent. A later study that was in agreement, however, added that sex offenders with a varied criminal background who target unknown children are particularly susceptible to recidivism (37-42 percent) (Greenberg, Bradford, Firestone, & Curry, 2000).

DESISTANCE

What is "desistance?" It refers to the *termination* of offending behavior (Laub & Sampson, 2001). However, there are those who might suggest that "termination" is too polarized a concept (Maruna, 2001). Bottoms, Shapland, Costello, Holmes, and Muir (2004), for example, suggest that desistance be defined as "crime free gaps" or an abstinence period from offending (p. 370). In contrast to reoffending or recidivism, desistance is the cumulative time during which no criminal behavior is presented (Maruna, 2001).

The literature on sexual victimization and desistance suggests that suspension of offending is associated with previous sexual offending or "other" convictions, age, and a willingness to take responsibility for behaviors. To illustrate, Escarela, Francis, and Soothill (2000) found that 88 percent of their first time sexual offenders under the age of sixteen and 60 percent of those offenders of age thirty with no convictions for ten years were likely to maintain desistance from offending.

Sex offenders derive pleasure from their victimizing behavior. Moreover, they appear to be limited in their skills to acquire this pleasure by any other means. They verbalize a lack of awareness regarding the consequences of their actions and show insufficient impulse control (Farrington, 1995). It is suggested that for desistance to take place, the perpetrator must first desire a behavior modification; then he must come to believe that he or she has the ability to self-soothe[12] and problem solve perceived stressful circumstances (Walters, 2002). The catalyst for this willingness to change may be a valued job (Kruttschnitt, Uggen, & Shelton, 2000), a relationship (Laub, Nagin, & Sampson, 1998), or a culminating distaste for legal sanctions (Laub & Sampson, 2001) that arise at a certain developmental age.[13] Indeed, employed offenders over the age of twenty-six are more likely to maintain desistance over unemployed offenders (Uggen, 2000).

Theoretical explanations for desisting behavior have included *rational choice* (Piliavin, Gartner, & Thornton, 1986) and *opportunity theory* (Uggen & Shelton, 1996). However, it is of note that Uggen and Piliavin (1998) did not find that *rational choice* theory explained their findings adequately. Kruttschnitt et al.'s (2000) study of 422 sex offenders (predominantly child molesters) on probation supported the *age graded theory of informal social control.*[14] In general, they found as their participant's age increased desistance time increased. However, age became less significant when employment and marriage was controlled. Their conclusion was that sexual offenders with stable employment, in a meaningful partner relationship, and/or who are involved in treatment appear more likely to maintain desistance. They added that instead of long-term incarceration for this level of offender they should be given probation that includes treatment and employment opportunities (Kruttschnitt et al., 2000; Meloy, 2005).

CONCLUSION

There is no single distinct profile of sex offender (Saleh & Guidry, 2003). Previous attempts to categorize sexual perpetrators have resulted in confusing and overlapping categories (Knight & Prentky, 1990a). It does appear that extrafamilial sex offenders commit the preponderance of sexual victimization against children (Bolen, 2000; Danni & Hampe, 2000). The rate at which they reoffend is relatively unknown due mostly to victim underreporting followed by mortality and longer incarcerations. However, there are inferences that recidivism is low among certain types of sexual offenders (Hall, DeGarmo, Eap, Teten, & Sue, 2006). Moreover, recent literature proposes that sexually victimizing behavior will naturally desist, influenced by external events, at some point along the life-course continuum.[15] Thus, individuals are not trapped in "life-course trajectories." Rather, they have choices within the context of their environments[16] (Sampson & Laub, 2003, 2005), where desistance may be an integral part of the "change" process (Bushway, Thornberry, & Krohn, 2003) and must be respected and valued as an essential component of sexual offender treatment (McNeil, 2003).

NOTES

1. "Extrafamilial sexual abuse is sexual abuse by anyone other than a relative" (Bolen, 2000, p. 1137). *Nonfamily* and *extrafamilial* will be used interchangeably in this book.

2. For example, the myth that all sex offenders are very dangerous and never stop offending (Sample & Bray, 2003), or that sex offenders are all mentally ill "dirty old men" who hang around schools (Rudin, Zalewski, & Bodman-Turner, 1995).

3. To illustrate, DNA studies have shown that sex offenders have nonsexual criminal histories (Stevens, 2001). Consequently, several U.S. states are now demanding DNA collection from burglars to hamper potential sexual victimization (Sample & Bray, 2003). However, such reoffending is not substantiated in literature reviews (see Hanson & Bussiere, 1998a), and in a sample of Illinois inmates where 93 percent of sex offenders desisted over a five-year period, only 2 percent of convicted burglars went on to commit a sexual crime (Sample & Bray, 2003).

4. ADHD, conduct disorder, and substance abuse (see Kafka & Hennen, 2002).

5. "Specialization implies some degree of repetition of the same offense behavior over time" (Miethe et al., 2006, p. 208).

6. For example, rapists tend to choose victims close to their own age (Freeman-Longo, 2000). Preferential offenders often have age and gender inclinations (Goldstein, 1999).

7. There are "hands off" offenses (e.g., exhibitionism), hands on (e.g., fondling), and, at the complete end of the spectrum, mortal wounding (Freeman-Longo, 2000).

8. Preferential offenders are sophisticated and diligent in their quest and often use the child's family or their profession to gain access to their victim (Shoop, 2004). In addition, they are less likely to be apprehended because of the age and powerlessness of their victim. They tend to abuse large numbers of children especially offenders who choose extrafamilial victims (Davis & Mcshane, 1995). Moreover, they prefer varied sexual experiences and, if they have an age preference, they require another child once their victim "ages out" (Lanning, 1992).

9. These children become dependent on their abusers for everything including their emotional needs. When abandoned, they retaliate (Goldstein, 1999).

10. To illustrate, Zgoba and Simon (2005) found that offenders with two or more mixed offenses (sexual and nonsexual) were five times more likely to commit a new sexual offense and offenders with three or more prior convictions were nine times more likely than those with no prior criminal history to sexually reoffend.

11. Diverse sexual offending behaviors with unknown child male victims and the diagnosis of antisocial personality disorder appear to predict reoffending (Hanson & Bussiere, 1998a), especially nonfamily offenders (Kruttschnitt et al., 2000).

12. Related to attachment with primary caregiver.

13. For example, getting married at a very young age may initiate or exacerbate criminal behavior (Kolvin, Miller, Fleeting, & Kolvin, 1988). Involvement in a relationship at the appropriate developmental stage for that individual can be beneficial in relation to problem behavior (Born, Chevalier, & Humblet, 1997). The proposal is thus: "Work and marriage have age-specific effects rather than uniform effects on crime" (Uggen, 2000, p. 1).

14. See Sampson and Laub (1993).

15. Indeed, offender characteristics or type of offense is not related to the process or predictors for desistance (Laub & Sampson, 2001).

16. For example, Warr (1998) suggests that a positive marriage helps the individual to reidentify and divorce deviant peer groups.

REFERENCES

Abel, G. G., Becker, J. V., Cunningham-Rathner, J., Mittelman, M., & Rouleau, J. L. (1988). Multiple paraphilic diagnoses among sex offenders. *Bulletin of American Academy of Psychiatry in Law, 16*(2), 153-168.

American Psychiatric Association (APA). (2000). *Diagnostic and statistical manual of mental disorders: DSM-IV-TR* (4th ed., text revision). Washington, DC: American Psychiatric Association.

Beyko, M. J., & Wong, S. C. (2005). Predictors of treatment attrition as indicators for program improvement not offender shortcomings: A study of sex offender treatment attrition. *Sex Abuse, 17*(4), 375-389.

Bolen, R. M. (2000). Extrafamilial child sexual abuse: A study of perpetrator characteristics and implications for prevention. *Violence Against Women, 6,* 1137-1169.

Born, M., Chevalier, V., & Humblet, I. (1997). Resilience, desistance and delinquent career of adolescent offenders. *Journal of Adolescence, 20*(6), 679-694.

Bottoms, A., Shapland, J., Costello, A., Holmes, D., & Muir, G. (2004). Towards desistance: Theoretical underpinnings for an empirical study. *The Howard Journal, 43*(4), 368-389.

Bushway, S. D., Thornberry, T. P., & Krohn, M. D. (2003). Desistance as a developmental process: A comparison of static and dynamic approaches. *Journal of Quantitative Criminology, 19,* 129-153.

Carich, M. S., & Mussack, S. E. (2001). *Handbook for sexual abuser assessment and treatment.* Brandon, VT: The Safer Society Press.

Cheit, R. E., & Freyd, J. (2005). Let's have an honest fight against child sex abuse. *Brown University Child & Adolescent Behavior Letter, 21*(6), 8.

Craig, L. A., Browne, K. D., & Stringer, I. (2003). Risk scales and factors predictive of sexual offence recidivism. *Trauma, Violence, & Abuse, 4*(1), 45-69.

Danni, K. A., & Hampe, G. D. (2000). An analysis of predictors of child sex offender types using pre-sentence investigation reports. *International Journal of Offender Therapy and Comparative Criminology, 44,* 490-504.

Davis, L., & Mcshane, M. D. (1995). Controlling computer access to pornography: Special conditions for sex offenders. *Federal Probation, 59*(2), 43-49.

DHHS. (2006a). *Chapter 3, victims; child maltreatment 2004.* Retrieved September 11, 2006, from http://www.acf.hhs.gov/programs/cb/pubs/cm04/chapterthree.htm#types.

DHHS. (2006b). *Child maltreatment 2004: Figure 3-6 victims by perpetrator relationship.* Retrieved September 11, 2006, from http://www.acf.hhs.gov/programs/cb/pubs/cm04/figure3_6.htm.

Dietz, P. E. (1983). Sex offenses: Behavioral aspects. In S. Kadish (Ed.), *Encyclopedia of crime and justice* (Vol. 4, pp. 1485-1493). New York: Free Press.

Dube, S. R., Anda, R. F., Felitti, V. J., Chapman, D. P., Williamson, D. F., & Giles, W. H. (2001). Childhood abuse, household dysfunction, and the risk of attempted suicide throughout the life span: Findings from the Adverse Childhood Experiences Study. *Journal of the American Medical Association, 286*(24), 3089-3096.

Escarela, G., Francis, B., & Soothill, K. (2000). Competing risks, persistence, and desistance in analyzing recidivism. *Journal of Quantitative Criminology, 16*(4), 385-414.

Farrington, D. P. (1995). The twelfth Jack Tizard memorial lecture. The development of offending and antisocial behaviour from childhood: Key findings from the Cambridge study in delinquent development. *Journal of Child Psychology and Psychiatry, 36*(6), 929-964.

Firestone, P., Bradford, J. M., McCoy, M., Greenberg, D. M., Curry, S., & Larose, M. R. (2000). Prediction of recidivism in extrafamilial child molesters based on court-related assessments. *Sex Abuse, 12*(3), 203-221.

Freeman-Longo, R. E. (2000). Children, teens, and sex on the Internet. *Sexual Addiction & Compulsivity, 7,* 75-90.

Gacono, C. B., Meloy, J. R., & Bridges, M. R. (2000). A Rorschach comparison of psychopaths, sexual homicide perpetrators, and nonviolent pedophiles: Where angels fear to tread. *Journal of Clinical Psychology, 56*(6), 757-777.

Goldstein, S. L. (1999). *The sexual exploitation of children: A practical guide to assessment, investigation, and intervention* (2nd ed.). New York: CRC Press.

Greenberg, D. M. (1998). Sexual recidivism in sex offenders. *Canadian Journal of Psychiatry, 43*(5), 459-465.

Greenberg, D. M., Bradford, J. M., Firestone, P., & Curry, S. (2000). Recidivism of child molesters: A study of victim relationship with the perpetrator. *Child Abuse & Neglect, 24*(11), 1485-1494.

Hall, G. C., DeGarmo, D. S., Eap, S., Teten, A. L., & Sue, S. (2006). Initiation, desistance, and persistence of men's sexual coercion. *Journal of Consulting and Clinical Psychology, 74*(4), 732-742.

Hall, G. C. N., & Barongan, C. (1997). Prevention of sexual aggression: Socio-cultural risk and protective factors. *American Psychologist, 52*(1), 5-14.

Hanson, R. F., Saunders, B., Kilpatrick, D., Resnick, H., Crouch, J. A., & Duncan, R. (2001). Impact of childhood rape and aggravated assault on adult mental health. *American Journal of Orthopsychiatry, 71*(1), 108-119.

Hanson, R. K., & Bussiere, M. T. (1998a). Predicting relapse: A meta-analysis of sexual offender recidivism studies. *Journal of Consulting and Clinical Psychology, 66*(2), 348-362.

Hanson, R. K., & Bussiere, M. T. (1998b). Predicting relapse: A meta analysis of sexual offender recidivism studies. *Journal of Consulting and Clinical Psychology, 66,* 348-362.

Hanson, R. K., Scott, H., & Steffy, R. (1995). A comparison of child molesters and nonsexual criminals: Risk predictors and long-term recidivism. *Journal of Research in Crime and Delinquency, 32,* 325-337.

Hanson, R. K., Steffy, R. A., & Gauthier, R. (1993). Long-term recidivism of child molesters. *Journal of Consulting and Clinical Psychology, 61*(4), 646-652.

Hildebrand, M., de Ruiter, C., & de Vogel, V. (2004). Psychopathy and sexual deviance in treated rapists: Association with sexual and nonsexual recidivism. *Sex Abuse, 16*(1), 1-24.

Hudson, S. M., & Ward, T. (2000). Relapse prevention: Assessment and treatment implications. In D. R. Laws, S. M. Hudson, & T. Ward (Eds.), *Remaking relapse prevention with sex offenders: A sourcebook* (pp. 102-122). Newbury Park, CA: Sage.

Kafka, M. P., & Hennen, J. (2002). A DSM-IV Axis I comorbidity study of males (n = 120) with paraphilias and paraphilia-related disorders. *Sex Abuse, 14*(4), 349-366.

Knight, R. A., & Prentky, R. A. (1990a). Classifying sex offenders: The development and corroboration of taxonomic models. In W. L. Marshall, D. R. Laws, & H. E. Barbaree (Eds.), *Handbook of sexual assault* (pp. 23-52). New York: Plenum Press.

Knight, R. A., & Prentky, R. A. (1990b). Classifying sexual offenders: The development and corroboration of taxonomic models. In W. L. Marshall, D. R. Laws, & H. E. Barbaree (Eds.), *Handbook of sexual assault: Issues, theories, and treatment of the offender* (pp. 23-52). New York: Plenum Press.

Kolvin, I., Miller, F. J., Fleeting, M., & Kolvin, P. A. (1988). Social and parenting factors affecting criminal-offence rates. Findings from the Newcastle Thousand Family Study (1947-1980). *British Journal of Psychiatry, 152,* 80-90.

Kruttschnitt, C., Uggen, C., & Shelton, K. (2000). Predictors of desistance among sex offenders: The interaction of formal and informal social controls. *Justice Quarterly, 17*(1), 61-87.

Langan, P., Schmitt, E. L., & Durose, M. R. (2003). *Recidivism of sex offenders released from prison in 1994* (Bureau of Justice Statistics Special Report, November 2003). Washington, DC: U.S. Department of Justice.

Lanning, K. V. (1992). *Child molesters: A behavioral analysis* (3rd ed.). Quantico, VA: Federal Bureau of Investigation.

Lanning, K. V. (2001). Child molesters and cyber pedophiles: A behavioral perspective. In R. R. Hazelwood & A. W. Burgess (Eds.), *Practical aspects of rape investigations: A multidisciplinary approach* (3rd ed.). Boca Raton, FL: CRC Press.

Laub, J. H., Nagin, D. S., & Sampson, R. J. (1998). Good marriages and trajectories of change in criminal offending. *American Sociological Review, 63,* 225-238.

Laub, J. H., & Sampson, R. J. (2001). Understanding desistance from crime. *Crime and Justice, 28,* 1-70.

Lee, J. K., Jackson, H. J., Pattison, P., & Ward, T. (2002). Developmental risk factors for sexual offending. *Child Abuse & Neglect, 26*(1), 73-92.

Marshall, W. L., & Marshall, L. E. (2000). The origins of sexual offending. *Trauma, Violence, & Abuse, 1,* 250-263.

Marshall, W. L., Serran, G. A., & Cortoni, F. A. (2000). Childhood attachments, sexual abuse, and their relationship to adult coping in child molesters. *Sexual Abuse: A Journal of Research and Treatment, 12*(1), 17-26.

Maruna, S. (2001). *Making good: How ex-convicts reform and rebuild their lives.* Washington, DC: American Psychological Association.

McNeil, F. (2003). Desistance focused probation practice. In W. H. Chui & M. Nellis (Eds.), *Moving probation forward: Evidence, arguments, and practice* (pp. 146-162). Harlow: Pearson Longman.

Meloy, M. L. (2005). The sex offender next door: An analysis of recidivism, risk factors, and deterrence of sex offenders on probation. *Criminal Justice Policy Review, 16*(2), 211-236.

Miethe, T. D., Olson, J., & Mitchell, O. (2006). Specialization and persistence in the arrest histories of sex offenders: A comparative analysis of alternative measures and offense types. *Journal of Research in Crime and Delinquency, 43*(3), 204-229.

Olver, M. E., & Wong, S. C. (2006). Psychopathy, sexual deviance, and recidivism among sex offenders. *Sex Abuse, 18*(1), 65-82.

Piliavin, I., Gartner, R., & Thornton, C. (1986). Crime, deterrence, and rational choice. *American Sociological Review, 51,* 101-119.

Pithers, W. (1990). Relapse prevention with sexual aggression: A method for maintaining therapeutic gain and enhancing external supervision. In W. Marshall, D. R. Laws, & H. E. Barbaree (Eds.), *Handbook of sexual assault: Issues, theories, and treatment of the offender* (pp. 343-361). New York: Plenum Press.

Prentky, R. A., Knight, R. A., & Lee, A. F. (1997). Risk factors associated with recidivism among extrafamilial child molesters. *Journal of Consulting and Clinical Psychology, 65*(1), 141-149.

Rind, B., Tromovitch, P., & Bauserman, R. (1998). A meta-analytic examination of assumed properties of child sexual abuse using college samples. *Psychological Bulletin, 124,* 22-53.

Rudin, M., Zalewski, C., & Bodman-Turner, J. (1995). Characteristics of child sexual abuse victims according to perpetrator gender. *Child Abuse & Neglect, 19,* 963-973.

Rush, F. (1996). The Freudian coverup. *Feminism & Psychology, 6,* 261-276.

Russell, D. E. (1983). The incidence and prevalence of intrafamilial and extra-familial sexual abuse of female children. *Child Abuse & Neglect, 7,* 133-146.

Saleh, F. M., & Guidry, L. L. (2003). Psychosocial and biological treatment consider-ations for the paraphilic and nonparaphilic sex offender. *Journal of the American Academy of Psychiatry and the Law, 31*(4), 486-493.

Sample, L. L., & Bray, T. M. (2003). Are sex offenders dangerous? *Criminology and Public Policy, 3*(1), 59-82.

Sampson, R. J., & Laub, J. H. (1993). *Crime in the making: Pathways and turning points through life*. Cambridge: Harvard University Press.

Sampson, R. J., & Laub, J. H. (2003). Life course desisters? Trajectories of crime among delinquent boys followed to age 70. *Criminology, 41*(3), 555-592.

Sampson, R. J., & Laub, J. H. (2005). A life-course view of the development of crime. *Annals of the American Academy of Political and Social Science, 602,* 12-45.

Scheff, T. J., & Retzinger, S. M. (2003). Shame, anger, and the social bond: A theory of sexual offenders and treatment. In M. Silberman (Ed.), *Violence and society: A reader* (pp. 301-311). Upper Saddle River, NJ: Prentice Hall.

Shoop, R. J. (2004). *Sexual exploitation in schools: How to spot it and stop it.* Thousand Oaks, CA: Sage.

Simons, D., Wurtele, S. K., & Heil, P. (2002). Childhood victimization and lack of empathy as predictors of sexual offending against women and children. *Journal of Interpersonal Violence, 17,* 1291-1305.

Smallbone, S. W., & Dadds, M. R. (2000). Attachment and coercive sexual be-havior. *Sexual Abuse: A Journal of Research and Treatment, 12,* 3-15.

Smallbone, S. W., & McCabe, B. A. (2003). Childhood attachment, childhood sex-ual abuse, and onset of masturbation among adult sexual offenders. *Sexual Abuse: A Journal of Research and Treatment, 15*(1), 1-9.

Stevens, A. P. (2001). Arresting crime: Expanding the scope of DNA databases in America. *Texas Law Review, 79,* 921-961.

Uggen, C. (2000). Work as a turning point in the life course of criminals: A duration model of age, employment, and recidivism. *American Sociological Review, 67,* 529-546.

Uggen, C., & Piliavin, I. (1998). Asymmetrical causation and criminal desistance. *The Journal of Criminal Law and Criminology, 88*(4), 1399-1422.

Uggen, C., & Shelton, K. S. (1996). *Work, crime, and drug use: An integrated model of desistance from deviant roles.* Paper presented at the American Society of Criminology, Chicago, IL.

Walters, G. D. (2002). Developmental trajectories, transitions, and nonlinear dy-namical systems: A model of crime deceleration and desistance. *International Journal of Offender Therapy and Comparative Criminology, 46*(1), 30-44.

Warr, M. (1998). Life-course transitions and desistance from crime. *Criminology, 36*(2), 183-216.

Webster, S. W., O'Toole, R., O'Toole, A. W., & Lucal, B. (2005). Overreporting and underreporting of child abuse: Teachers' use of professional discretion. *Child Abuse & Neglect, 29*(11), 1281-1296.

Wells, K. M., & Sirotnak, A. (2004). The medical evaluation of abuse and neglect. In C. Brittain & D. E. Hunt (Eds.), *Helping in child protective services: A competency based casework handbook* (2nd ed.). New York: Oxford University Press.

Winick, B. J., & LaFond, J. Q. (2003). *Protecting society from sexually dangerous offenders: Laws, justice, and therapy.* Washington, DC: American Psychological Association.

Zgoba, K. M., & Simon, L. M. J. (2005). Recidivism rates of sexual offenders up to 7 years later: Does it matter? *Criminal Justice Review, 30*(2), 155-173.

Zimring, F. E. (2004). *An American travesty: Legal responses to adolescent sexual offending.* Chicago, IL: University Chicago Press.

Chapter 6

Current Empirical
Assessment Methods

Grant James Devilly
Tracey Varker
Fallon Cook
Marie Bee Hui Yap

INTRODUCTION

Childhood sexual abuse raises strong emotions not just within the greater community but also within academic and therapeutic circles. With this in mind, there is little doubt that the use of carefully considered, timely, and reliable assessment procedures is of paramount importance in cases of suspected and/or corroborated abuse. The purpose of this chapter is to outline some of the factors to be borne in mind during the assessment process and to outline some of the assessment devices available. This chapter does not aim to provide an exhaustive review of all available devices and to comment on all context specific issues that occur during the assessment stages. Rather, we aim to provide the generic counselor/agency worker with more domain specific knowledge regarding the issues related to evaluation. To achieve this goal we first outline some of the generic factors to be considered when assessing children for abuse. This includes issues of disclosure, comorbidity, ethnicity, gender, family functioning, legal, child protection responsibilities, and the possibility of creating a trauma myth. We then outline common structured and semistructured interviews and self-report instruments used during assessment. Although it is accepted that individualized case formulations require the use of

Handbook of Social Work in Child and Adolescent Sexual Abuse
© 2008 by The Haworth Press, Taylor & Francis Group. All rights reserved.
doi:10.1300/5804_06

psychometric assessments covering many presentations (e.g., depression, anxiety, general internalizing or externalizing behaviors), the current review focuses mainly on the evaluation of trauma symptoms. This is followed by a short introduction into the developing area of psychophysiological assessment.

ASSESSMENT ISSUES

There are a myriad of relevant issues for consideration when assessing suspected child or adolescent victims of child sexual abuse, and only a few can be outlined here. The issues covered include disclosure-related matters, physical and psychiatric comorbidity, gender, ethnicity, family functioning/dysfunction, and legal/child protection matters. However, first, we wish to draw attention to the need to be careful not to create a trauma myth where none had occurred or had not been perceived by the child.

Trauma Myth

Therapeutic process and assessment requires the suspension of disbelief. On the other hand, objective assessment, as in the case of a forensic evaluation, requires the suspension of belief and an impartial approach to the "suspicions" or accusations of the referrer/source of information. This requires a delicate balance between outward disbelief and disenfranchisement of the victim and the need to obtain unprejudiced information. In effect it is necessary to acknowledge that the assessment process can have unintended consequences. For example, it is possible to transmit to the abused child that something exceptionally terrible has happened to them when, in fact, he or she has not perceived this to be the case and are consequentially asymptomatic. At the other end there is the possibility of creating a trauma history in the child's mind when, in fact, one has not occurred. For these reasons, the assessor should at least be aware of growing research related to memory distortion from child assessments.

A large body of research indicates that memory is fallible, that memory can be influenced and distorted, and that confabulation in memory can easily occur. This has been shown to be the case for both traumatic and nontraumatic memories with many types of people studied or treated (e.g., victims of sexual abuse, nonvictims of sexual abuse, eye witnesses to crimes, etc.; Hyman & Loftus, 1998; McNally, Clancy, & Schacter, 2001; Nourkova, Bernstein, & Loftus, 2004; Wells, Wright, & Bradfield, 1999; Zoellner, Foa, & Brigidi, 2000). Distortion of memory can also occur at any of the three stages of memory: at the time of encoding, during the period of storage, and during retrieval. Furthermore, inaccurate memories can be believed by the individual and described convincingly in as much detail as accurate memories (Garven, Wood, & Malpass, 2000; Schooler, Bendiksen, & Ambadar, 1997). For example, Garven, Wood, Malpass, and Shaw (1998) investigated iatrogenesis and suggestion in school-children in relation to the highly publicized "daycare ritual abuse cases." These authors found that the interviewing techniques used during the cases at the McMartin School contained at least six serious leading and reinforcing strategies and that when the investigators used these strategies 58 percent of a classroom made false accusations regarding a classroom visitor compared with only 17 percent of a group who were questioned with simply "suggestive" questions.

In essence, six interviewing techniques that were identified through viewing the tapes of the original McMartin interviews and should be avoided during assessment of child populations, include the following:

1. Providing negative consequences for "denial of problem," such as criticizing an answer
2. Repetitive questioning although a "nonpreferred" answer has already been given
3. Inviting speculation on what "might" have occurred if it happened
4. Suggestive questions introducing new material into the interview, for example, "When your dad put you to bed at night . . ."
5. Conformity pressure by claiming that "others" or cowitnesses have already told you similar stories and hence normalizing an "expected or desired" answer
6. Providing positive consequences such as praising a "preferred answer" or providing "special" treatment for this "special" population

This study was followed by Garven et al. (2000) who found that even when only two elements of the "McMartin" interviewing techniques were used (reinforcement and cowitness information) more children made false allegations about a classroom visitor compared with children who were asked questions that were only "suggestive" in nature. However, the largest difference between the two groups was on highly implausible and fantastic false accusations (such as a visitor taking the child flying in a helicopter—which never happened) where 52 percent of those assessed with the McMartin interview agreed that this had occurred, compared with only 5 percent agreement made by the controls. Of even more importance here, though, is that even after the interviewing techniques of reinforcement and cowitness testimony had been discontinued, the children repeated the allegations and, when challenged, the children insisted that their reports were based on their personal observations. Garven et al. (2000) also found that reinforcement had a greater effect than providing cowitness enticements to agree with accusations. These authors noted that positive reinforcement in eyewitness testimony cases can alter "confidence of adult eyewitnesses in false identifications and change their retrospective reports in forensically important ways" (p. 45).

Indeed, there is evidence that false memories are easily introduced during assessment and therapeutic processes with adults, incorrect recalls are more confidently held (Devilly, Varker, Hansen, & Gist, 2007) and are more stable than true memories (particularly related to child memories; Brainerd, Reyna, & Brandse, 1995). It is hypothesized that this could be due to true memories being based on unstable narratives while false memories are based on relatively stable ideas.

Disclosure

The timing and circumstances surrounding the disclosure of abuse by the child or adolescent victim can have significant implications on child outcomes. It is crucial to keep in mind before assessing the child for abuse and making professional judgments about the child's needs that disclosure of abuse by a child or adolescent victim does not necessarily entail a termination of the abuse or even the child's distress (Palmer, Brown, Rae-Grant, & Loughlin, 1999). The responses received by these children to their disclosure have long-term effects on their self-esteem and later family functioning in adulthood. In fact, a follow-up study of child sexual abuse (CSA) victims revealed that children who voluntarily disclosed their abuse received less support and treatment than children whose abuse was accidentally discovered by an adult. Consequently, it has been argued that the latter group had better outcomes at the one-year follow-up (Nagel, Putnam, Noll, & Trickett, 1997).

Findings from a recent study of eight- to thirteen-year-old sexually abused children highlight the importance of assessing children's reactions as soon as possible after disclosure of abuse. Sexually abused children who exhibit symptoms of avoidance, anxiety/arousal, and dissociation, either during or immediately following disclosure of abuse, were at increased risk of developing post-traumatic stress disorder (PTSD) symptoms at a later date (Kaplow, Dodge, Amaya-Jackson, & Saxe, 2005). In particular, the younger the child, the more likely he or she is to demonstrate anxiety/arousal symptoms, and to use avoidant coping on disclosure of his or her abuse. Kaplow et al. (2005) attributed the latter finding to the limited language capacity and emotion identification abilities of these young children. Furthermore, children who displayed dissociative symptoms immediately after disclosure were at greater risk of later developing PTSD symptoms, purportedly because these dissociative responses prevent the open expression of trauma-related emotions and cognitions. These findings suggest the importance of tailoring assessments more sensitively to these children's needs, in order to address their dissociative, arousal-based, and avoidant responses.

The assessment and treatment planning process needs to allow for asymptomatic presentations, and/or "sleeper effects" in some children who present with few or no symptoms on disclosure, but deteriorate in the medium to long term (Briere, 1992). Some reasons proposed to explain some children's asymptomatic presentation include the possibility that they had relatively minor abuse experiences, they did not experience the events as traumatic and hence forgot the specific events, they are more resilient, or they have adopted an avoidant coping style (Finkelhor & Berliner, 1995; McNally, Clancy, Barrett, & Parker, 2004). However, the limited longitudinal data available suggest that 10 to 20 percent of asymptomatic children deteriorate over the first twelve to eighteen months (Kendall-Tackett, Williams, & Finkelhor, 1993; Mannarino, Cohen, Smith, & Mooremotily, 1991), with some evidence that such deterioration is especially likely in children who present with the least initial symptoms (Gomes-Schwartz, Horowitz, Cardarelli, & Sauzier, 1990). However, as discussed earlier, this may be exacerbated by other factors, such as repeated questioning by well intentioned but misguided assessors. Furthermore, family and abuse-related variables did not emerge as good predictors of five-year-outcome in sexually abused children, although children who were sad or depressed and had low self-esteem at intake were likely to have continuing problems in these areas (Tebbutt, Swanston, Oates, & O'Toole, 1997).

Given the disclosure-related matters discussed earlier in the chapter, some recommendations for assessment are proposed. First, asymptomatic children should not necessarily be "force questioned" under the assumption that something is wrong yet not evident. However, this does not detract from the need to also assess for additional risk factors such as family substance abuse, mental illness, domestic violence, or other family dysfunction (Putnam, 2003). Second, children who present with avoidance symptomatology at initial assessment, or on disclosure, may need extra monitoring over time for deterioration, especially if their avoidance seems to be contributing to their asymptomatic presentation. Third, children who present with depressive, dissociative and anxiety/arousal symptoms, and those with low self-esteem may be at risk for unrelenting and/or increasing depressive and post-traumatic problems. Therefore, assessment should include measures of such symptomatology and functioning and be conducted in a structured and reliable way.

Comorbidity

Given the usual traumatic nature of child sexual abuse, comorbid psychiatric and physical problems may be present, hence presenting a major challenge for assessment and diagnosis. CSA has been associated with a whole range of disorders in children and adolescents, including major depression, PTSD, phobias, obsessive-compulsive disorder, eating disorders, somatization disorder, substance abuse disorders, sexual disturbances and behavior problems (Putnam, 2003;

Wolfe & Kimerling, 1997; Wonderlich, Brewerton, Jocic, Dansky, & Abbott, 1997). Other concerns include adverse health outcomes (Seng, Graham-Bermann, Clark, McCarthy, & Ronis, 2005) and increased suicidality (Brand, King, Olson, Ghaziuddin, & Naylor, 1996; Sansonnet-Hayden, Haley, Marriage, & Fine, 1987), especially in victims of chronic sexual abuse.

Among these potential problems, depression and PTSD comorbidity seem to be most common in both male and female victims of CSA (Wolfe & Kimerling, 1997). Notably, some research evidence suggests that a history of childhood abuse may alter the clinical presentation of major depression, such as the reversal of neurovegetative signs (Levitan et al., 1998). A further challenge to the assessment of child and adolescent victims is the difficulty of determining whether depressive symptoms following trauma constitute an independent disorder or are primarily correlates of PTSD.

A variety of behavior and conduct problems, especially sexualized behaviors, is very closely linked to CSA (Putnam, 2003). Several studies have found that sexually abused children display more sexualized behaviors than various comparison groups, including nonabused psychiatric inpatients, especially if they are younger, were abused at a younger age, and were assessed relatively proximal to the abusive experiences (Cosentino, Meyerbahlburg, Alpert, Weinberg, & Gaines, 1995; Friedrich et al., 2001; McClellan et al., 1996; Paolucci, Genuis, & Violato, 2001). Although these overtly sexualized behaviors may decrease over time, adolescents with a history of CSA have a significantly increased arrest rate for sex crimes and prostitution, and are at heightened risk for early pregnancy, pregnancy-related complications, and human immunodeficiency virus risk-related behaviors (Putnam, 2003). However, it should be kept in mind that such behaviors should not be seen as indicative of a "hidden" abuse history when one has not been reported, but rather the evidence shows that those with diagnosed conditions following corroborated abuse histories are at greater risk for developing these behaviors.

Gender

Certain gender issues should be attended to as part of the assessment process. For example, while maltreated children and adolescents with

PTSD had smaller intracranial and cerebral volumes than matched controls, males with PTSD showed evidence of a greater volume decrease than females with PTSD (De Bellis et al., 1999). This finding is noteworthy given that decreased brain volume is associated with earlier onset of PTSD, longer duration of trauma, and more symptoms of intrusive thoughts, avoidance, hyperarousal, or dissociation. A more recent study also found that boys are more likely to display avoidant behaviors on disclosure of sexual abuse (Kaplow et al., 2005).

A different angle on gender issues is the effect of the perpetrator's gender on child protection professionals' decisions and attitudes concerning CSA, and on child outcomes. Research evidence suggests that although police and social workers considered CSA perpetrated by females to be a serious issue warranting intervention, some decisions made by these professionals suggest a minimization of female-perpetrated, in comparison with male-perpetrated, abuse (Hetherton & Beardsall, 1998). In particular, male social workers considered that social service involvement and investigation were less warranted when the perpetrator was a woman. Both professional groups considered case registration and imprisonment of a male perpetrator more important. Another study found that both psychiatrists and the police viewed sexual abuse by women as less harmful than sexual abuse by men (Denov, 2001). Moreover, it was noted that both professional groups made efforts, either consciously or unconsciously, to transform the female sex offender and her offense, realigning them with more culturally acceptable notions of female behavior. This ultimately led to a denial of the problem. Notably, a recent qualitative study of the long-term effects of CSA found evidence to dispute the perceptions of the general public and child welfare professionals that sexual abuse by women is relatively harmless and inconsequential as compared with sexual abuse by men (Denov, 2004). Specifically, almost all participants (93 percent) reported that the sexual abuse by women was harmful and damaging. In fact, all respondents who were abused by men and women reported that the sexual abuse by women was more harmful and detrimental than the sexual abuse they had experienced by men.

It is, therefore, important for professionals involved in the assessment and treatment of child victims of abuse to be mindful of the gender biases underlying their professional attitudes and decisions.

Ethnicity

To determine whether a presenting behavior signals clinical distress, an important consideration for assessment and diagnosis is how it compares to its normal rate in a specific child within that child's particular sociocultural environment (Ronen, 2002). Importantly, although race and ethnicity do not seem to be risk factors for CSA, preliminary research suggests that they may influence symptom expression (Mennen, 1995; Shaw, Lewis, Loeb, Rosado, & Rodrieguez, 2001) and rates of rape victimization later in life (Urquiza & Goodlin-Jones, 1994). Unfortunately, although children of certain ethnicities may be overrepresented in the child welfare system, they may also be underrepresented in preventive or treatment services (Webb & Harden, 2003). Hence, mental health services need to address ethnic minority groups' unique cultural needs and incorporate culturally sensitive strategies for assessment and intervention. For instance, the language of assessment instruments and scales can often be a challenge to assessing ethnic minorities whose native language is not English, or who have different perceptions of numbers. An example described by Ronen (2002) illustrates this challenge well: when eight- to ten-year-old Israeli children were asked to rate their anxiety on a scale of 0 to 7, they were confused and unable to use the scale because they were accustomed to the school grading scale of 0 to 10 where "10 is always the best." Hence, the maximum rating (10 rather than 7) and the direction of the scale had to be modified to accommodate the children's language and way of thinking. Nonetheless, minor changes in wording of questions can change the meaning of the question in an instrument; hence it is important to use standard, recommended changes as suggested, for example, in manuals provided for the instruments (Nader, 1997). Where necessary and possible, translation of instruments may be conducted, but accurate translations involving at least one back-translation that has been reviewed by the author(s) are essential to maintain the integrity and validity of the assessment (Nader, 1997).

Family Functioning/Dysfunction

Research has clearly demonstrated that the family context has implications for the level of distress and speed of recovery in child trauma victims. Such contextual factors include parental support (Everson, Hunter, Edelsohn, & Coulter, 1989), maternal distress (Newberger, Gremy, Waternaux, & Newberger, 1993), and help seeking (Waterman, 1993) in response to family crisis, as well as general family functioning, including cohesion and healthy conflict management (Conte & Schuerman, 1987). Parental impairments, especially maternal illness, maternal alcoholism, extended maternal absences, serious marital conflicts, parental substance abuse, social isolation, and punitive parenting, are all associated with increased risk for CSA in some studies (e.g., Fergusson, Lynskey, & Horwood, 1996; Nelson et al., 2002). Family (especially parental) functioning has implications for assessment not only because it influences parental report of child functioning, but also because of the potential for the transmission of anxiety symptoms from parent to child, such that child's responses and behaviors become in part a reflection of his or her parents' reactions (Ronen, 2002; Stover & Berkowitz, 2005). This challenge to assessment is especially important if the parent is displaying PTSD symptoms himself or herself, because of the high correlation between parent and child PTSD symptomatology (Laor, Wolmer, & Cohen, 2001; Wolmer, Laor, Gershon, Mayes, & Cohen, 2000). However, caution is required here owing to inconsistent research. For example, in one study, age, gender, injury severity, threat appraisal, and maternal PTSD did not significantly contribute to child trauma symptoms (Landolt, Vollrath, & Timm, 2005).

Specifically related to child PTSD, as opposed to the event of child sexual abuse, it should also be noted that Kilpatrick and Williams (1997) found an increased prevalence of trauma reactions among children who witnessed domestic violence as compared with children who did not witness such violence. Together with Canadian research suggesting that 37 percent of adults who reported they were assaulted by a spouse also reported that their children had heard or seen the violence take place (Dauvergne & Johnson, 2001), this makes for worrying possibilities.

Legal and Child Protection Issues

A whole range of legal, ethical, and child protection issues is involved in the assessment and reporting of sexual abuse in children and adolescents. For example, in most states of America and Australia there is a mandatory reporting requirement for certain groups of professionals (e.g., medical practitioners, police, teachers) to report their belief or suspicion, on reasonable grounds, that a child has suffered or is likely to suffer significant harm. This extends to the child's parents or caregivers who have demonstrably not protected, or are unlikely to protect, the child from harm (Victorian Government Department of Human Services, 1999). In some European countries and in the United Kingdom where there are no mandatory reporting laws, most professionals who work with children and families have internal procedures to follow if they have concerns about the welfare of a child (NSPCC Library and Information Service, 2006). However, researchers in Europe, the United States, Canada, and Australia have revealed that despite mandatory reporting laws, medical practitioners and teachers continue to have low overall reporting rates. Various reasons cited for this include ethical concerns about confidentiality, mistrust of state services, ignorance about reporting laws and procedures, and fear of making an inaccurate report (Scottish Executive, 2002). Moreover, there is some research evidence suggesting that mandatory reporting is inefficient and ineffective because mandatory reporting systems were overburdened with notifications, many of which proved to be unsubstantiated, yet were time-consuming and costly (Ainsworth, 2002). Some ethical dilemmas inherent in mandatory reporting include first, the possibility that even after the report and alerting the alleged offending adult, the child may remain under the custody of this adult and hence be at greater risk for continued and further harm. Second, by reporting abuse when there has in fact been no abuse, one is essentially creating not just one victim, but two or more.

Another noteworthy legal/child protection matter is the potential conflict of priorities between child protection authorities and child and family mental health professionals, especially with regard to the role of the parent in decision making. For example, investigations through Child Protection Services, and decisions about placements that may result in removal from parental custody, or even termination of parental rights, are inherently adversarial (Webb & Harden, 2003), and some procedures may be perceived as inflicting more harm on the child and the family. An additional complication to the matter is where nonoffending parents of CSA victims have substance abuse (U.S.

Department of Health and Human Services, 1999) or mental health problems that impair their ability to exercise judgment about appropriate services for their children (Webb & Harden, 2003). Nonetheless, some recent changes in the U.S. Child Protection Services entailing the offer of assessment and services to families where there is no ongoing threat to the child's safety, who otherwise might have been subjected to investigation (Webb & Harden, 2003), represent a promising step toward improving the overall assessment and intervention services to young CSA victims.

STRUCTURED AND SEMISTRUCTURED INTERVIEWS

General Assessment Issues

Currently, few well-validated, DSM-IV-based standardized interviews exist. Many of the older scales have not been developed explicitly for children, or are based on old definitions of the underlying constructs. Newer scales are often designed to overcome these problems, but have not been used for long enough for definitive conclusions regarding their reliability or validity to be reached (Balaban, 2006). Many interviews lack usable norms, meaning that a clinician is unable to interpret a given score based on its statistical extremity in the general population, making it impossible to determine the extent to which this score represents dysfunction (Brier & Elliot, 1997).

Increasingly clinicians and researchers use a multimodal, multi-informant approach for assessment and diagnosis of psychiatric disorders in children and adolescents (Hawkins & Radcliffe, 2006). Although there is often low agreement between parent and child reports of diagnostic conditions, with children reporting more symptoms than their parents report for them (e.g., Earls, Smith, Reich, & Jung, 1988; Handford et al., 1986; Korol, Green, & Gleser, 1999), both informants provide valuable information. The quality and accuracy of a child's report depends on many factors, including the child's developmental level, questions posed, the manner in which questions are asked, and factors about the event itself (Hawkins & Radcliffe, 2006).

EMPIRICALLY BASED ASSESSMENT INTERVIEWS

In this section a number of the most frequently used and methodologically sound structured (or semistructured) clinical interviews assessing trauma symptomatology in children and adolescents are reviewed. The interviews were divided into three categories based on administration method: child interview with companion parent interview, child/adolescent interview, and parent interview.

Child/Adolescent Interview with Companion Parent Interview

Child and Adolescent Psychiatric Assessment (CAPA; Angold et al., 1995)

A psychiatric interview for children aged nine to seventeen years, the CAPA is an interview designed to be used with parents and children separately, using different interviewers. Diagnosis can be made using the *Diagnostic and Statistical Manual of Mental Disorders,* Fourth Edition (DSM-IV) (American Psychiatric Association, 1994), or the *International Classification of Diseases and Related Health Problems,* Tenth Revision (ICD-10) (World Health Organization, 1992) criteria. Interviewees are asked whether during the past three months a number of symptoms have occurred. Unlike most of the other interviews discussed here, it does not provide a lifetime diagnosis. When a symptom is reported, questions are asked to find out exactly when the symptom occurred. Parents and children are first asked three screening questions to establish whether the core symptoms of PTSD are present in the child. They are first asked whether painful recall or reexperiencing has occurred, then, if the answer is yes, they are asked about hypervigilance and avoidance. For events where severity is of relevance (e.g., physical or sexual abuse), this is also determined. The measure has relatively good reliability and discriminant validity for both the child version and the adult version (Costello, Angold, March, & Fairbank, 1998), although this assessment was based on a relatively small sample (nine youths with PTSD).

The Childhood PTSD Interview Child Form (CPTSDI-C)/
Childhood PTSD Interview–Parent (CPTSDI-P; Fletcher, 1996)

Both this clinician-administered child interview and the companion parent interview are designed to assess PTSD symptomatology in children and adolescents who have been exposed to traumatic events. Both the child and parent are asked questions assessing PTSD symptoms. Additional questions are included to capture associated features of PTSD such as depression, denial, dissociation, self-destructive behavior and survivor guilt. Each interview takes approximately forty minutes to administer and the measure was developed with the incorporation of DSM-IV criteria. Good internal consistencies have been reported although these are based on a sample of ten children with a history of significant trauma exposure, and twenty children without (Fletcher, 1996).

Diagnostic Interview for Children and Adolescents–Revised
(DICA-R; Welner & Reich, 1997)

The DICA-R is a semistructured interview designed to assess present and lifetime common psychiatric conditions. It is based on the DSM and includes a PTSD scale. As such, it is possible to make a DSM-IV diagnosis of PTSD. The DICA-R is available in child (DICA-C-R, age range six to twelve), adolescent (DICA-A-R, age range thirteen to seventeen) and parent versions (DICA-P-R). The PTSD module comprises seventeen questions, which address six criteria (traumatic experience, reexperiencing, numbing/avoidance, arousal, duration, intensity). This measure has acceptable sensitivity, reliability, validity (De la Osa, Ezpelera, Oomenech, Navarro, & Losilla, 1997; Reich, 2000), and has been translated into Spanish and Arabic.

Child/Adolescent Interview

Clinician Administered PTSD Scale for Children
and Adolescents (CAPS-CA; Newman et al., 2004)

The CAPS-CA is a thirty-six-item semistructured clinical interview designed to assess PTSD symptomatology in children and adolescents aged eight to fifteen years. It is a modified version of the adult measure, the Clinician-Administered PTSD Scale (Blake et al., 1990), and provides a scalar and categorical assessment of both PTSD and PTSD-related psychopathology such as school problems and hostility (Nader, Blake, Kriegler, & Pynoos, 1994). It also measures the impact of symptoms on aspects of functioning such as coping skills, overall distress, and impairment. In a recent review of the frequency in which clinicians use trauma exposure and assessment measures, the CAPS-CA was found to be the most commonly used child and adolescent interview, being used by 7 percent of the clinicians in the sample ($n = 227$; Elhai, Gray, Kashdan, & Franklin, 2005). However, the interview is not based on DSM criteria, and as such it is not possible to make a DSM-IV diagnosis. Test-retest reliability is not available and there is no published normative data. Therefore, although this newly developed measure appears promising, further information on its psychometric properties is required.

UCLA PTSD Reaction Index-Revised for DSM-IV (PTSD-RI; Pynoos, Goenjian, & Steinberg, 1998)

This twenty-item instrument is one of the oldest and best-studied semistructured interviews for PTSD. Used when a traumatic event is known to have occurred, the PTSD-RI is a revised version of the widely used and researched Child Post-Traumatic Stress Disorder Reaction Index (CPTS-RI; Frederick, Pynoos, & Nader, 1992). It can be used with children aged eight years or older, and is sometimes used as a self-report measure. The interview takes approximately ninety minutes to administer. The items are based on an adult measure of PTSD, and only assess reactions to a specific trauma. The interview emphasizes projective techniques such as play and drawings to explore the child's trauma reactions, rather than direct inquiry. There is no normative data available for this measure, and no interrater reliability, internal consistency reliability scores, or validity scores have been published. As such, the confidence with which clinicians can draw conclusions about the implications of their findings is severely diminished.

The PTSD-RI is reported to relate well to clinical judgment of PTSD severity (Yule & Udwin, 1991), however not all of the DSM-IV

symptoms are covered. As such, it is not possible to make a DSM diagnosis of PTSD using this measure. The PTSD-RI has been used to
assess children who have experienced a diverse range of traumatic
events including earthquakes (Asarnow et al., 1999; Goenjian et al.,
1995), sniper attack (Nader, Pynoos, Fairbanksm, & Frederick, 1990),
war (Laor, Wolmer, & Cohen, 2001; Thabet & Vostanis, 2000), and
hurricane (Chemtob, Nakishima, & Carlson, 2002). The measure has
also been translated into Armenian, Cambodian, Arabic, Croatian, and
Norwegian. However, normative data for these multiethnic populations is not available.

Children's PTSD Inventory (Saigh, 2002)

This clinician-administered structured interview can be used to assess children and adolescents aged seven to eighteen years. The items
were designed based on DSM-IV criteria, although minor modification of items was done on the basis of the feedback from youths regarding clarity, comprehension, and developmental relevance. The
child or adolescent is first assessed for potential exposure to a traumatic event. If they do not meet criteria for a significantly traumatic
event then the interview is terminated. If the child does have a trauma
history then the interview takes approximately twenty minutes to
complete. This measure has good reliability (Saigh et al., 2000) and
validity (Yasik et al., 2001), and convergent validity between the inventory's scores and the DSM-IV criteria appears to be excellent, although it has only been used in a small number of studies. However,
this is a newly developed scale and preliminary results suggest that
this may be a highly applicable scale.

Parent Interview

Post-Traumatic Stress Disorder Semistructured Interview
and Observation Record (Scheeringa & Zeanah, 1994)

This examinee-based interview of the parent is designed to assess
PTSD symptomatology in children aged zero to six years. Conducted
while the child is present in the room, this interview measures DSM-
IV PTSD symptoms as well as symptoms such as loss of previous
skills, separation anxiety, and aggression. Raters are able to diagnose

the child using the DSM-IV criteria, or by an alternate criterion created by the authors. The child's parent is asked a number of questions, with the parent initially questioned about a series of traumas that the child may have experienced. If the parent endorses any of these events, then they are asked a series of questions about each of the PTSD symptoms, namely the symptom's onset, frequency, and duration. At the same time as questioning the parent, the interviewer must also observe the child to see whether any symptoms are visible. The division of attention that is required by the interviewer can be somewhat problematic, making this quite a difficult measure to use. No test-retest or internal consistency reliabilities have been reported.

Preschool Aged Psychiatric Assessment
(PAPA; Egger, Ascher, & Angold, 1999)

The PAPA is a structured interview of the parent, and is a comprehensive assessment of mental health symptoms in children aged two to five. It is based on the CAPA, which is designed for children aged eight to fifteen. It includes items, which assess those DSM-IV criteria that are relevant to very young children. It also assesses family environment and relationships, psychosocial problems, and life events. The parent is first asked about a series of potentially traumatic life events, and whether the parent would attribute a symptom (e.g., separation anxiety, physical symptoms) to this event. If at least one event and one symptom are endorsed, the interview continues, and the parent is asked a series of questions related to PTSD symptomatology in children. The PAPA is a lengthy assessment of a wide range of psychiatric conditions in children, and as such it is a time-consuming measure to administer. Test-retest scores, and reliability and validity data have not been published for the PAPA. There are not any published studies in which the PTSD module of the PAPA has been used solely for the assessment of PTSD, and psychometric data for the PTSD module alone is unavailable.

The Schedule for Affective Disorders and Schizophrenia
for School-Aged Children (K-SADS; Kaufman et al., 1997)

This semistructured interview was originally designed as a comprehensive assessment of psychopathology in children. The K-SADS contains a PTSD module that reflects DSM-IV criteria, and which assesses for a lifetime and current diagnosis of PTSD. Interviewees are asked whether a series of traumatic events have occurred recently or in the past. If a traumatic event is endorsed then questions assessing PTSD criteria are asked in relation to one specific event. The authors' instructions indicate that the interview should be administered to the child and parent independently and a diagnosis formulated on the basis of these results combined. Reliability and validity has been found to be adequate (Kaufman et al., 1997), with these psychometrics being based on both the child and parent informants.

SELF-REPORT MEASURES

General Assessment Issues

Researchers trying to develop self-report assessment measures appropriate for children of all ages face considerable difficulty. Reading and writing abilities vary depending on developmental stage and so does the comprehension of language. To combat this, several measures have been designed that require the caregiver of the child to report symptoms or behaviors on the child's behalf.

It has been shown that gaining reports from both an abused child and the child's nonoffending caregiver provides the most accurate representation of both the traumatic event and the ensuing problems endured by the child (Jensen et al., 1999). Caregivers tend to have a better perception of the passage of time during the event and since the event, whereas children often cannot accurately perceive the time that has passed since the event. However, children more accurately report their emotions and feelings about the trauma than their parents do (Korol et al., 1999), hence the importance of assessing both the child and their caregiver, particularly when a young child (under ten) is concerned (see Ronen, 2002, for a review of these issues).

There are many psychometrically tested self-report measures available for assessing post-traumatic stress in sexually abused children. Measures discussed here were selected on the basis of those most frequently used and those with psychometric data to support their use. As with the structured interviews, this section is divided into child self-report and parent/caregiver-report.

Children's Self-Report Measures

Trauma Symptom Checklist for Children (TSCC; Briere, 1996)

The TSCC is a fifty-four-item measure that was designed specifically to assess the effects of trauma on children aged eight to sixteen. A wide range of responses can be given and the TSCC is not specific to any one type of trauma. The measure consists of two validity scales (the first to assess underresponsiveness and the second to assess hyperresponsiveness), six clinical scales (to assess anxiety, post-traumatic stress, depression, sexual concerns, dissociation and anger), and six critical items. The six clinical scales are made up of zero to ten items each. In addition, there are two subscales for the sexual concerns scale (sexual preoccupation and sexual distress) and the dissociation scale (fantasy and overt dissociation). This measure is not appropriate as a complete tool for the diagnosis of PTSD and should be used in conjunction with other measures.

The TSCC has been confirmed as a valuable measure for assessing symptoms in sexually abused children (Briere, 1996). It has been tested in samples of hospitalized adolescents and was found to accurately discriminate a group of sexually abused youths from the rest of the group (Sadowski & Friedrich, 2000). Normative data has been obtained from some 3,008 children across three studies (Evans, Briere, Boggiano, & Barrett, 1994; Friedrich, 1995; Singer, Anglen, Song, & Lunghofer, 1995).The TSCC has been consistently reported as being a reliable measure (Elliot & Briere, 1994; Lanktree & Briere, 1995). It has been translated into Cambodian, French, Dutch, Chinese, Japanese, Latvian, Spanish, and Swedish.

Children's Impact of Traumatic Events Scale-Revised (CITES-R; Wolf & Gentile, 1991)

The CITES-R was designed to assess the extent of post-traumatic stress in children, as well as possible mediating factors such as social reactions to disclosure of the trauma and abuse-related attributions. It was not specifically designed to diagnose PTSD and should, therefore, be used in conjunction with other measures. The CITES-R is a revised version of the original CITES, and it has been tested in samples of sexually abused children (Chaffin & Shultz, 2001). Though it was originally intended to be used as a structured interview, it is often used as a self-report measure for children aged twelve and older who have good reading ability. Subscales of the CITES-R assess four aspects: PTSD (including intrusive thoughts, avoidance, hyperarousal, and sexual anxiety), abuse attributions (including self-blame and guilt, empowerment, personal vulnerability, and dangerous world), social reactions (including negative reactions by others and social support), and eroticism. Items of the PTSD subscale were based on those of the adult Impact of Event Scale (IES; Horowitz, Wilner, & Alvarez, 1979).

The reliability and validity of the CITES-R has been well established, with several studies finding high correlations between subscales (Chaffin & Shultz, 2001; Nader, 1997) and high convergent validity with other measures including the TSCC (Crouch, Smith, Ezzell, & Saunders, 1999).

Child PTSD Symptom Scale (CPSS; Foa, Johnson, Feeny, & Treadwell, 2001)

The CPSS is a child version of the Post-Traumatic Diagnostic Scale (PTDS; Foa, Cashman, Jaycox, & Perry, 1997). The language used has been simplified for easier comprehension for children aged eight to eighteen. It allows for a PTSD diagnosis and includes one question from each of the DSM-IV PTSD criteria to assess the frequency of symptoms in the past month. Seven questions assess daily functioning, and another seventeen items form a symptom severity score that ranges from 0 to 51. From these seventeen items, three symptom groups of re-experiencing, avoidance, and arousal are formed. Psychometric data on the CPSS is limited, although initial examination shows good reliability and excellent convergent and divergent validity (Foa et al., 1997).

Other Important Self-Report Measures

When assessing a child's reaction following trauma, it is important to measure more than just PTSD symptoms. A child may not display all PTSD symptoms but may be experiencing problems with anxiety, fear, and depression that may be otherwise undetected unless specifically assessed. Self-report measures such as the Revised Children's

Manifest Anxiety Scale (RCMAS; Reynolds & Richmond, 1978), the Revised Fear Schedule for Children (Ollendick, 1983), and the Children's Depression Inventory (CDI; Kovacs, 1985) are commonly used for this purpose and help to gain a fuller picture of how the child is coping. They are generally quick to administer and can be given to any child with good reading ability to complete privately and in their own time.

Self-Report Measures Completed by Caregivers

Trauma Symptom Checklist for Young Children (TSCYC; Briere et al., 2001)

The TSCYC is a revised version of the TSCC that was specifically designed for caregivers to complete on behalf of their young children aged three to twelve. It has been tested on many trauma populations. The TSCYC is a comprehensive measure that includes two validity scales: the first to assess caregivers tendency to deny what is considered normal or mildly problematic behavior (underresponsiveness) and the second to assess caregivers willingness to report odd or unrelated behaviors (hyperresponsiveness). In contrast to the TSCC, the TSCYC includes eight instead of six clinical scales: intrusion, avoidance, arousal, sexual concerns, dissociation, anxiety, depression, and anger/aggression. A total of ninety items are completed by the caregiver. The TSCYC allows for a diagnosis of PTSD, except in the case of three- and four-year-olds in which further measures should be used (Briere, 2005).

The psychometrics of the TSCYC have been established (Briere et al., 2001; Gilbert, 2004). In one study, the TSCYC was administered to 219 children who consecutively presented at clinics across the United States following abuse or trauma (Briere et al., 2001). Of these children, 56 percent had a history of sexual abuse. Reliability was acceptable for all measures except for "hyperresponsiveness." Children who had a history of sexual abuse scored highly on measures of post-traumatic stress-intrusion, post-traumatic stress-avoidance, post-traumatic total score (sum of intrusion, avoidance, and arousal subscales), and sexual concern. This measure is frequently used for the assessment of children following sexual abuse. Normative trials of the English version have been completed with 750 children, allowing for the calculation of standard scores that are based on age and gender (Stover & Berkowitz, 2005). The TSCYC has been translated into Spanish and Swedish.

Child Sexual Behavior Inventory (CSBI; Friedrich, Grambsch, Damon, & Hewitt, 1992)

Children who have been sexually abused have a tendency to display more sexual behavior than do children with no history of sexual abuse (Gale, Thompson, Moran, & Sack, 1988; Goldsten, Turnquist, & Knutson, 1989). The CSBI is a thirty-eight-item measure designed to allow caregivers to report on sexual behavior observed in the past six months in children aged two to twelve. Behaviors assessed include sexually aggressive behavior, violations of the personal boundaries of others, and self-stimulation. It is commonly administered to sexually abused children as a means of assessing the psychological impact of sexual abuse on the child.

The CSBI has been psychometrically tested with normative, psychiatric, and sexual abuse samples (Friedrich et al., 2001). The CSBI has good validity. This has been indicated by its ability to discriminate between sexually abused and nonabused children on the basis of the number of nonnormative behaviors indicated (Friedrich, Grambsch, Damon, & Hewitt, 1992). The CSBI has been translated into French, Dutch, Spanish, German, and Swedish.

Other Important Caregiver Measures

There are many other common measures that can be completed by caregivers to gain a broader understanding of a child's reaction following sexual assault. For example, the Child Behavior Checklist (CBCL; Achenbach, 1991) is an instrument designed to assess the occurrence of varying behaviors in children. It was not designed to assess the presence of PTSD following trauma, but is a good accompaniment to other PTSD measures. It allows for the monitoring of behavior change over time—both before and after therapy, for example. The Trauma Exposure Symptom Inventory–Parent Report Revised (TESI-PRR; Ghosh-Ippen et al., 2002) is another useful measure designed to assess post-traumatic stress in children from birth through to age six, an age group often excluded by other measures.

PSYCHOPHYSIOLOGICAL ASSESSMENT

The measurement of psychophysiological variables in studies of post-traumatic stress is becoming more common. Several key papers have highlighted the potential for psychophysiological measures to aid in the diagnosis of PTSD, assessment of treatment outcomes, and even to help differentiate "true" cases of PTSD from "false" ones. Although progress is still in the early stages, results are encouraging. Such measures may aid in the comprehensive assessment of sexually abused children both following trauma and after treatment.

Several studies have examined the physical manifestation of PTSD symptoms. For instance, to examine the startle response (described in DSM-IV), Ornitz and Pynoos (1989) compared responses to an auditory stimuli in children who had developed PTSD after witnessing sniper fire and those who had not. The children who had witnessed sniper fire showed problems inhibiting startle responses in comparison to those children without PTSD. The startle responses of those with PTSD also tend to be much larger than those without PTSD. Heart rate responses are frequently reported as being much higher and skin conductance responses tend to decline more slowly in those with PTSD than those without (Orr, Lasko, Shalev, & Pitman, 1995).

Those with PTSD also seem to experience a permanently heightened sense of arousal, as indicated by increased resting heart rate and blood pressure, than those without PTSD (Gerardi, Keane, Cahoon, & Klauminzer, 1994). Several studies have looked at physiological markers both before and after treatment and have observed that as PTSD symptoms wane, heart rate and skin conductance start to appear more normal (Hyer, Woods, Summers, & Boudewyns, 1990; Keane & Kaloupek, 1982). Readers particularly interested in this line of research are directed to Wilson and Keane's excellent book (2004).

Several studies have also highlighted differences between those with and without PTSD, in their ability to complete certain tasks. PTSD patients show a tendency to have increased occurrence of memory deficits (Bremner et al., 1995; Bremner, Scott, Delaney, & Southwick, 1993; Hannay & Levin, 1985), and have longer response latencies to trauma-related words in an emotional Stroop task (Dubner & Motta, 1999).

Studies have shown electrophysiological differences between those with and without a history of trauma. Teicher and colleagues (1997) demonstrated significant neural connectivity differences in sexually/ physically abused children in comparison to nonabused controls. This demonstrated that neural development appears to be impeded in abused children and that these differences may be easily observed by use of EEG. In a similar study of adults with and without a history of trauma, very similar neural connectivity patterns were again observed between those with and without a history of childhood trauma (Cook, Ciorciari, Varker, & Devilly, submitted for publication). This suggests that electrophysiological assessment could differentiate those with and those without a trauma history. It may prove, with further exploration, to be a useful tool in the diagnosis of PTSD and in the monitoring of recovery.

CONCLUSION

It should be stressed that this chapter has focused predominantly on the assessment of PTSD following child trauma (and specifically sexual abuse), and in no way reflects all possible assessment strategies and needs that may occur following such harrowing events. We wish to stress the need for individualized case formulations and referral questions being the driving forces behind the selection of assessment methods. Hypothesis testing remains the bedrock of responsible assessment strategies when conducted in an objective yet sensitive manner, and we hope that we have outlined the need, and some options for, forensically defensible approaches in the assessment of child trauma and sexual assault cases.

REFERENCES

Achenbach, T. M. (1991). *Manual for the child behavior checklist/4-18.* Burlington, VT: University of Vermont Department of Psychiatry.

Ainsworth, F. (2002). Mandatory reporting of child abuse and neglect: Does it really make a difference? *Child & Family Social Work, 7,* 57-63.

American Psychiatric Association (1994). *Diagnostic and statistical manual of mental disorders,* Fourth edition. Washington, DC: American Psychiatric Association.

Angold, A., Prendergast, M., Cox, A., Harrington, R., Simonoff, E., & Rutter, M. (1995). The Child and Adolescent Psychiatric Assessment (CAPA-C). *Psychological Medicine, 25*(7), 739-753.

Asarnow, J., Glynn, S., Pynoos, R. S., Nahum, J., Guthrie, D., Cantwell, D. P., et al. (1999). When the earth stops shaking: Earthquake sequelae among children diagnosed for pre-earthquake psychopathology. *Journal of the American Academy of Child & Adolescent Psychiatry, 38,* 1016-1023.

Balaban, V. (2006). Psychological assessment of children in disasters and emergencies. *Disasters, 30*(2), 178-198.

Blake, D. D., Weathers, F. W., Nagy, L. M., Kaloupek, D. G., Klauminzer, G., Charney, D. S., et al. (1990). A clinician rating scale for assessing current and lifetime PTSD. The CAPS-1. *Behavior Therapist, 13,* 187-188.

Brainerd, C. J., Reyna, V. F., & Brandse, E. (1995). Are children's false memories more persistent than their true memories? *Psychological Science, 6,* 359-364.

Brand, E. F., King, C. A., Olson, E., Ghaziuddin, N., & Naylor, M. (1996). Depressed adolescents with a history of sexual abuse: Diagnostic comorbidity and suicidality. *Journal of the American Academy of Child & Adolescent Psychiatry, 35*(1), 34-41.

Bremner, J. D., Randall, P., Scott, T. W., Capelli, S., Delaney, R., McCarthy, G., et al. (1995). Deficits in short-term memory in adult survivors of childhood abuse. *Psychiatry Research, 59,* 97-107.

Bremner, J. D., Scott, T. M., Delaney, R. C., & Southwick, S. M. (1993). Deficits in short-term memory in posttraumatic stress disorder. *American Journal of Psychiatry, 150,* 1015-1019.

Briere, J. (1992). *Child abuse trauma: Theory and treatment of the lasting effects.* Newbury Park, CA: Sage.

Briere, J. (1996). *Trauma Symptom Checklist for Children (TSCC).* Odessa, FL: Psychological Assessment Resources.

Briere, J. (2005). *Trauma Symptom Checklist for Young Children (TSCYC).* Odessa, FL: Psychological Assessment Resources.

Briere, J., & Elliott, D. M. (1997). Psychological assessment of interpersonal victimization effects in adults and children. *Psychotherapy 34*(4), 353-364.

Briere, J., Johnson, K., Bissada, A., Damon, L., Crouch, J., Gil, E., et al. (2001). The Trauma Symptom Checklist for Young Children (TSCYC): Reliability and association with abuse exposure in a multi-site study. *Child Abuse & Neglect, 25,* 1001-1014.

Chaffin, M., & Shultz, S. K. (2001). Psychometric evaluation of the Children's Impact of Traumatic Events Scale–Revised. *Child Abuse & Neglect, 25,* 401-411.

Chemtob, C. M., Nakishima, J., & Carlson, J. G. (2002). Brief treatment for elementary school children with disaster-related posttraumatic stress disorder: A field study. *Journal of Clinical Psychology, 58*(1), 99-112.

Conte, J., & Schuerman, J. (1987). Factors associated with an increased impact of child sexual abuse. *Child Abuse & Neglect, 11,* 201-211.

Cook, F. J., Ciorciari, J., Varker, T., & Devilly, G. J. (Submitted). Changes in long term neural connectivity following psychological trauma.

Cosentino, C. E., Meyerbahlburg, H. F. L., Alpert, J. L., Weinberg, S. L., & Gaines, R. (1995). Sexual-behavior problems and psychopathology symptoms in sexually abused girls. *Journal of the American Academy of Child & Adolescent Psychiatry, 34*(8), 1033-1042.

Costello, E. J., Angold, A., March, J., & Fairbank, J. (1998). Life events and post-traumatic stress: The development of a new measure for children and adolescents. *Psychological Medicine, 28,* 1275-1288.

Crouch, J. L., Smith, D. W., Ezzell, C. E., & Saunders, B. E. (1999). Measuring reactions to sexual trauma among children: Comparing the children's impact of traumatic events scale and the trauma symptom checklist for children. *Child Maltreatment, 4*(3), 225-263.

Dauvergne, M., & Johnson, H. (2001). Children witnessing family violence. *Juristat (Statistics Canada Catalogue no. 85-002-XPE). Ottawa: Statistics Canada, 21,* 6.

De Bellis, M. D., Keshavan, M. S., Clark, D. B., Casey, B. J., Giedd, J. N., Boring, A. M., et al. (1999). Developmental traumatology Part II: Brain development. *Biological Psychiatry, 45*(10), 1271-1284.

De la Osa, N., Ezpelera, L., Oomenech, J. M., Navarro, J. B., & Losilla, J. M. (1997). Convergent and discriminate validity of the structured diagnostic interview for children and adolescents (DICA-R). *Psychology in Spain, 1*(1), 37-44.

Denov, M. S. (2001). A culture of denial: Exploring professional perspectives on female sex offending. *Canadian Journal of Criminology, 43*(3), 303-329.

Denov, M. S. (2004). The long-term effects of child sexual abuse by female perpetrators: A qualitative study of male and female victims. *Journal of Interpersonal Violence, 19*(10), 1137-1156.

Devilly, G. J., Varker, T., Hansen, K., & Gist, R. (2007). An analogue study of the effects of psychological debriefing on eyewitness memory. *Behaviour Research & Therapy, 45*(6), 1245-1254.

Dubner, A. E., & Motta, R. W. (1999). Sexually and physically abused foster care children and posttraumatic stress disorder. *Journal of Consulting and Clinical Psychology, 67*(3), 367-373.

Earls, R., Smith, E., Reich, W., & Jung, K. G. (1988). Investigating psycho-pathological consequences of disaster in children: A pilot study incorporating a structured diagnostic interview. *Journal of the American Academy of Child & Adolescent Psychiatry, 27,* 90-95.

Egger, H., Ascher, B., & Angold, A. (1999). *Preschool Aged Psychiatric Assessment-Parent Interview.* Unpublished manuscript, Center for Developmental Epidemiology, Department of Psychiatry and Behavioral Sciences, Duke University Medical Center at Durham, NC.

Elhai, J. D., Gray, M. J., Kashdan, T. B., & Franklin, C. L. (2005). Which traumatic instruments are most commonly used to assess traumatic event exposure and posttraumatic event?: A survey of traumatic stress professionals. *Journal of Traumatic Stress, 18*(5), 541-545.

Elliott, D., & Briere, J. (1994). *The Trauma Symptom Checklist for Children: Validation data from a child abuse evaluation centre.* Unpublished Manuscript, Los Angeles, CA.

Evans, J. J., Briere, J., Boggiano, A. K., & Barrett, M. (1994). Reliability and validity of the Trauma Symptom Checklist for Children in a normative sample. Paper presented at the San Diego conference on responding to child maltreatment. Cited in Briere, J. (1996). *Trauma Symptom Checklist for Children: Professional manual*. Florida: Psychological Assessment Resources Inc.

Everson, M. D., Hunter, W. M., Runyon, D. K., Edelsohn, G. A., & Coulter, M. L. (1989). Maternal support following disclosure of incest. *American Journal of Orthopsychiatry, 59*, 197-207.

Fergusson, D., Lynskey, M., & Horwood, L. (1996). Childhood sexual abuse and psychiatric disorder in young adulthood, I: Prevalence of sexual abuse and factors associated with sexual abuse. *Journal of the American Academy of Child & Adolescent Psychiatry, 35*, 1355-1364.

Finkelhor, D., & Berliner, L. (1995). Research on the treatment of sexually abused children—A review and recommendations. *Journal of the American Academy of Child & Adolescent Psychiatry, 34*(11), 1408-1423.

Fletcher, K. E. (1996). *Measuring school-aged children's PTSD: Preliminary psychometrics of four new measures*. Paper presented at the 12th annual meeting of the International Society for Traumatic Stress Studies, San Francisco, CA.

Foa, E. B., Cashman, L., Jaycox, L., & Perry, K. (1997). The validation of a self-report measure of posttraumatic stress disorder: The Posttraumatic Diagnostic Scale. *Psychological Assessment, 9*, 445-451.

Foa, E. B., Johnson, K. M., Feeny, N. C., & Treadwell, K. R. H. (2001). The Child PTSD Symptom Scale: A preliminary examination of its psychometric properties. *Journal of Clinical Child Psychology, 30*(3), 376-384.

Frederick, C. J., Pynoos, R. S., & Nader, K. (1992). Child Post-Traumatic Stress Reaction Index. Unpublished Instrument.

Friedrich, W. N. (1995). Unpublished dataset. Mayo Clinic, Rochester, MN. Cited in Briere, J. (1996), *Trauma Symptom Checklist for Children: Professional manual*. Florida: Psychological Assessment Resources Inc.

Friedrich, W. N., Fisher, J. L., Dittner, C. A., Acton, R., Berliner, L., Butler, J., et al. (2001). Child Sexual Behavior Inventory: Normative, psychiatric, and sexual abuse comparisons. *Child Maltreatment, 6*(1), 37-49.

Friedrich, W. N., Grambsch, P., Damon, L., & Hewitt, S. K. (1992). Child Sexual Behavior Inventory: Normative and clinical comparisons. *Psychological Assessment, 4*(3), 303-311.

Gale, J., Thompson, R. J., Moran, T., & Sack, W. H. (1988). Sexual abuse in young children: Its clinical presentation and characteristic patterns. *Child Abuse & Neglect, 12*, 163-170.

Garven, S., Wood, J. M., & Malpass, R. S. (2000). Allegations of wrongdoing: The effects of reinforcement on children's mundane and fantastic claims. *Journal of Applied Psychology, 85*, 38-49.

Garven, S., Wood, J. M., Malpass, R. S., & Shaw, J. S. (1998). More than suggestion: The effect of interviewing techniques from the McMartin preschool case. *Journal of Applied Psychology, 83*, 347-359.

Gerardi, R. J., Keane, T. M., Cahoon, B. J., & Klauminzer, G. W. (1994). An in vivo assessment of physiological arousal in posttraumatic stress disorder. *Journal of Abnormal Psychology, 103,* 825-827.

Ghosh-Ippen, C., Ford, J., Racusin, R., Acker, M., Bosquet, K., Rogers, C., et al. (2002). *Trauma Events Screening Inventory–Parent Report Revised.* San Francisco, The Child Trauma Research Project of the Early Trauma Network and The National Centre for PTSD Dartmouth Child Trauma Research Group.

Gilbert, A. M. (2004). Psychometric properties of the Trauma Symptom Checklist for Young Children (TSCYC). *Dissertation Abstracts International, 65*(1-B), 478.

Goenjian, A. K., Pynoos, R. S., Steinberg, A. M., Najarian, L. M., Asarnow, J. R., Karayan, I., Ghurabi, M., & Fairbanks, L. A. (1995). Psychiatric comorbidity in children after the 1988 earthquake in Armenia. *Journal of the American Academy of Child & Adolescent Psychiatry, 34,* 1174-1184.

Goldston, D. B., Turnquist, D. C., & Knutson, J. F. (1989). Presenting problems of sexually abused girls receiving psychiatric services. *Journal of Abnormal Psychology, 98,* 314-317.

Gomes-Schwartz, B., Horowitz, J. M., Cardarelli, A. P., & Sauzier, M. (1990). The aftermath of child sexual abuse: 18 months later. In B. Gomes-Schwartz, J. M. Horowitz, & A. P. Cardarelli (Eds.), *Child sexual abuse: The initial effects* (pp. 132-152). Thousand Oaks, CA: Sage Publications, Inc.

Handford, H. A., Mayes, S. D., Mattison, R. E., Humphrey, F. J., Bagnato, S., Bixler, E. O., et al. (1986). Child and parent reactions to the Three Mile Island nuclear accident. *Journal of the American Academy of Child & Adolescent Psychiatry, 25*(3), 346-356.

Hannay, H. J., & Levin, H. S. (1985). Selective reminding test: An examination of the equivalence of four forms. *Journal of Clinical and Experimental Neuropsychology, 7,* 251-263.

Hawkins, S. S., & Radcliffe, J. (2006). Current measures of PTSD for children and adolescents. *Journal of Pediatric Psychology, 31*(4), 420-430.

Hetherton, J., & Beardsall, L. (1998). Decisions and attitudes concerning child sexual abuse: Does the gender of the perpetrator make a difference to child protection professionals? *Child Abuse & Neglect, 22*(12), 1265-1283.

Horowitz, M. J., Wilner, N., & Alvarez, W. (1979). Impact of event scale: A measure of subjective stress. *Psychosomatic Medicine, 41,* 209-218.

Hyer, L., Woods, M. G., Summers, M. N., & Boudewyns, P. (1990). Alexithymia among Vietnam veterans with posttraumatic stress disorder. *Journal of Clinical Psychiatry, 51*(6), 243-247.

Hyman, I. E., & Loftus, E. F. (2002). False childhood memories and eyewitness memory errors. In M. L. Eisen, J. A. Quas, & G. S. Goodman (Eds.), *Memory and suggestibility in the forensic interview* (pp. 63-84). Mahwah, NJ: Lawrence Erlbaum Associates.

Jensen, P. S., Rubio-Stipec, M., Canino, G., Bird, H. R., Dulcan, M. K., Schwab-Stone, M. E., et al. (1999). Parent and child contributions to diagnosis of mental disorder: Are both informants always necessary? *Journal of the American Academy of Child & Adolescent Psychiatry, 38*(12), 1569-1579.

Kaplow, J. B., Dodge, K. A., Amaya-Jackson, L., & Saxe, G. N. (2005). Pathways to PTSD, Part II: Sexually abused children. *American Journal of Psychiatry, 162*(7), 1305-1310.

Kaufman, J., Birmaher, B., Brent, D., Rao, U., Flynn, C., Moreci, P., et al. (1997). Schedule for Affective Disorders and Schizophrenia for School-Age Children-Present and Lifetime Version (K-SADS-PL): Initial reliability and validity data. *Journal of the American Academy of Child & Adolescent Psychiatry, 36*(7), 980-988.

Keane, T. M., & Kaloupek, D. G. (1982). Imaginal flooding in the treatment of a posttraumatic stress disorder. *Journal of Consulting and Clinical Psychology, 50,* 138-140.

Kendall-Tackett, K. A., Williams, L. M., & Finkelhor, D. (1993). Impact of sexual abuse on children—A review and synthesis of recent empirical studies. *Psychological Bulletin, 113*(1), 164-180.

Kilpatrick, K. L., & Williams, L. M. (1997). Post-traumatic stress disorder in child witnesses to domestic violence. *American Journal of Orthopsychiatry, 67,* 639-644.

Korol, M., Green, B. L., & Gleser, G. L. (1999). Children's responses to a nuclear waste disaster: PTSD symptoms and outcome prediction. *Journal of the American Academy of Child & Adolescent Psychiatry, 38,* 368-375.

Kovacs, M. (1985). The Children's Depression Inventory (CDI). *Psychopharmacology Bulletin, 21,* 995-998.

Landolt, M. A., Vollrath, M., & Timm, K. (2005). Predicting posttraumatic stress symptoms in children after road traffic accidents. *Journal of the American Academy of Child & Adolescent Psychiatry, 44,* 1276-1283.

Lanktree, C. B., & Briere, J. (1995). Outcome of therapy for sexually abused children: A repeated measures study. *Child Abuse & Neglect, 19,* 1145-1155.

Laor, N., Wolmer, L., & Cohen, D. J. (2001). Mothers' functioning and children's symptoms 5 years after a SCUD missile attack. *American Journal of Psychiatry, 158,* 1020-1026.

Levitan, R. D., Parikh, S. V., Lesage, A. D., Hegadoren, K. M., Adams, M., Kennedy, S. H., et al. (1998). Major depression in individuals with a history of childhood physical or sexual abuse: Relationship to neurovegetative features, mania, and gender. *American Journal of Psychiatry, 155*(12), 1746-1752.

Mannarino, A. P., Cohen, J. A., Smith, J. A., & Mooremotily, S. (1991). 6-Month and 12-month follow-up of sexually abused girls. *Journal of Interpersonal Violence, 6*(4), 494-511.

McClellan, J., McCurry, C., Ronnei, M., Adams, J., Eisner, A., & Storck, M. (1996). Age of onset of sexual abuse: Relationship to sexually inappropriate behaviors. *Journal of the American Academy of Child & Adolescent Psychiatry, 35*(10), 1375-1383.

McNally, R. J., Clancy, S. A., Barrett, H. M., & Parker, H. A. (2004). Inhibiting retrieval of trauma cues in adults reporting histories of childhood sexual abuse. *Cognition and Emotion, 15,* 479-493.

McNally, R. J., Clancy, S. A., & Schacter, D. L. (2001). Directed forgetting of trauma cues in adults reporting repressed or recovered memories of childhood sexual abuse. *Journal of Abnormal Psychology, 110,* 151-156.

Mennen, F. (1995). The relationship of race/ethnicity to symptoms in child sexual abuse. *Child Abuse & Neglect, 19,* 115-124.

Nader, K. O. (1997). Assessing traumatic experiences in children. In J. P. Wilson & T. M. Keane (Eds.), *Assessing psychological trauma and PTSD* (pp. 291-348). New York: Guilford Press.

Nader, K., Blake, D. D., Kriegler, J. A., & Pynoos, R. S. (1994). *Clinician-Administered PTSD Scale for Children (CAPS-C).* UCLA Neuropsychiatric Institute and Hospital/National Center for PTSD.

Nader, K., Pynoos, R., Fairbanks, L., & Frederick, C. (1990). Children's PTSD reactions one year after a sniper attack at their school. *American Journal of Psychiatry, 147,* 1526-1530.

Nagel, D. E., Putnam, F. W., Noll, J. G., & Trickett, P. K. (1997). Disclosure patterns of sexual abuse and psychological functioning at a 1-year follow-up. *Child Abuse & Neglect, 21,* 137-147.

Nelson, E. C., Heath, A. C., Madden, P. A. F., Cooper, M. L., Dinwiddie, S. H., Bucholz, K. K., et al. (2002). Association between self-reported childhood sexual abuse and adverse psychosocial outcomes: Results from a twin study. *Archives of General Psychiatry, 59,* 139-146.

Newberger, C. M., Gremy, I. M., Waternaux, C. M., & Newberger, E. H. (1993). Mothers of sexually abused children: Trauma and repair in longitudinal perspective. *American Journal of Orthopsychiatry, 63,* 92-102.

Newman, E., Weathers, F. W., Nader, K., Kaloupek, D. G., Pynoos, R. S., Blake, D. D., et al. (2004). *Clinician-Administered PTSD Scale for Children and Adolescents (CAPS-CA).* Los Angeles, CA: Western Psychological Services.

Nourkova, V. V., Bernstein, B. M., & Loftus, E. F. (2004). Altering traumatic memory. *Cognition and Emotion, 18,* 575-585.

NSPCC Library and Information Service. (2006). *An introduction to the child protection system in the UK.* Retrieved 20th October 2006, from http://www.nspcc.org.uk/Inform/OnlineResources/InformationBriefings/CPSystem_ifega30118.html.

Ollendick, T. H. (1983). Reliability and validity of the Revised Fear Survey Schedule for Children (FSSC-R). *Behaviour Research and Therapy, 21,* 685-692.

Ornitz, E. M., & Pynoos, R. S. (1989). Startle modulation in children with posttraumatic stress disorder. *American Journal of Psychiatry, 146*(7), 866-870.

Orr, S. P., Lasko, N. B., Shalev, A. Y., & Pitman, R. K. (1995). Physiologic responses to loud tones in Vietnam veterans with posttraumatic stress disorder. *Journal of Abnormal Psychology, 104,* 75-82.

Palmer, S. E., Brown, R. A., Rae-Grant, N. I., & Loughlin, M. J. (1999). Responding to children's disclosure of familial abuse: What survivors tell us. *Child Welfare, 78,* 259-282.

Paolucci, E. O., Genuis, M. L., & Violato, C. (2001). A meta-analysis of the published research on the effects of child sexual abuse. *Journal of Psychology, 135*(1), 17-36.

Putnam, F. W. (2003). Ten-year research update review: Child sexual abuse. Research update review. *Journal of the American Academy of Child & Adolescent Psychiatry, 42*(3), 269-278.

Pynoos, R. S., Goenjian, A. K., & Steinberg, A. M. (1998). A public mental health approach to the post-disaster treatment of children and adolescents. *Child and Adolescent Psychiatric Clinics of North America, 7,* 195-210.

Reich, W. (2000). Diagnostic Interview for Children and Adolescents (DICA). *Journal of the American Academy of Child & Adolescent Psychiatry, 39,* 59-67.

Reynolds, C. R., & Richmond, B. O. (1978). What I think and feel: A revised measure of children's manifest anxiety. *Journal of Abnormal Child Psychology, 6*(2), 271-280.

Ronen, T. (2002). Difficulties in assessing traumatic reactions in children. *Journal of Loss and Trauma, 7,* 87-106.

Sadowski, C. M., & Friedrich, W. N. (2000). Psychometric properties of the Trauma Symptom Checklist for Children (TSCC) with psychiatrically hospitalized adolescents. *Child Maltreatment, 5*(4), 364-372.

Saigh, P. A. (2002). *The Children's Post Traumatic Stress Disorder Inventory (CPTSDI).* Available from Phillip A. Saigh, PhD, Department of Educational Psychology: Graduate Centre, City University, New York.

Saigh, P. A., Yasik, A. E., Oberfield, R. A., Green, B., Halamadaris, P. V., Rubenstein, et al. (2000). The children's PTSD inventory: Development and reliability. *Journal of Traumatic Stress, 13,* 369-380.

Sansonnet-Hayden, H., Haley, G., Marriage, K., & Fine, S. (1987). Sexual abuse and psychopathology in hospitalized adolescents. *Journal of the American Academy of Child & Adolescent Psychiatry, 26*(5), 753-757.

Scheeringa, M. S., & Zeanah, C. H. (1994) Semi-structured interview and observation record for infants and young children. New Orleans, LA: Department of Psychiatry and Neurology, Tulane University Health Sciences Center.

Schooler, J. W., Bendiksen, M., & Ambadar, Z. (1997). Taking the middle line: Can we accommodate both fabricated and recovered memories of sexual abuse? In M. Conway (Ed.), *False and recovered memories* (pp. 251-292). Oxford: Oxford University Press.

Scottish Executive. (2002). *"It's everyone's job to make sure I'm alright." Report of the child protection audit and review.* Retrieved October 27, 2006, from http://www.scotland.gov.uk/Publications/2002/11/15820/14009.

Seng, J. S., Graham-Bermann, S. A., Clark, M. K., McCarthy, A. M., & Ronis, D. L. (2005). Posttraumatic stress disorder and physical comorbidity among female children and adolescents: Results from service-use data. *Pediatrics, 116*(6), 1532-1533.

Shaw, J., Lewis, J., Loeb, A., Rosado, J., & Rodrieguez, R. (2001). A comparison of Hispanic and African-American sexually abused girls and their families. *Child Abuse & Neglect, 25,* 1363-1379.

Singer, M. I., Anglen, T. M., Song, L. Y., & Lunghofer, L. (1995). Adolescents' exposure to violence and associated symptoms of psychological trauma. *Journal of the American Medical Association, 273*(6), 477-482.

Stover, C. S., & Berkowitz, S. (2005). Assessing violence exposure and trauma symptoms in young children: A critical review of measures. *Journal of Traumatic Stress, 18*(6), 707-717.

Tebbutt, J., Swanston, H., Oates, R. K., & O'Toole, B. I. (1997). Five years after child sexual abuse: Persisting dysfunction and problems of prediction. *Journal of the American Academy of Child & Adolescent Psychiatry, 36*(3), 330-339.

Teicher, M. H., Ito, Y., Glod, C. A., Andersen, S. L., Dumont, N., & Ackerman, E. (1997). Preliminary evidence for abnormal cortical development in physically and sexually abused children using EEG coherence and MRI. In E. R. Yehuda, & A. McFarlane (Eds.), *Psychobiology of posttraumatic stress disorder* (pp. 160-175). New York: New York Academy of Sciences.

Thabet, A. A., & Vostanis, P. (2000). Posttraumatic stress reactions in children of war: A longitudinal study. *Child Abuse & Neglect, 24*(2), 291-298.

U.S. Department of Health and Human Services. (1999). *Blending perspectives and building common ground: A report to congress on substance abuse and child protection.* Washington, DC: U.S. Department of Health and Human Services.

Urquiza, A. J., & Goodlin-Jones, B. L. (1994). Child sexual abuse and adult victimization with women of color. *Violence and Victims, 9*(3), 223-232.

Victorian Government Department of Human Services. (1999). *Reporting child abuse.* Retrieved 20th October 2006, from http://www.office-for children.vic. gov.au/children/ccdnav.nsf/childdocs/-56B837B371C7D279CA256E180064 DCC8-A6A3F518B54D122C4A25675300226C00?open.

Waterman, J. (1993). Mediators of effects on children: What enhances optimal functioning and promotes healing? In J. Waterman, R. J. Kell, J. McCord, & M. K. Oliveri (Eds.), *Behind the playground walls: Sexual abuse in preschools.* New York: Guilford Press.

Webb, M. B., & Harden, B. J. (2003). Beyond child protection: Promoting mental health for children and families in the child welfare system. *Journal of Emotional and Behavioral Disorders, 11*(1), 49-58.

Welner, Z., & Reich, W. (1997). *Diagnostic Interview for Children and Adolescents–Revised (Parent Version).* St Louis, MO: Washington University.

Wells, G. L., Wright, E. F., & Bradfield, A. L. (1999). Witnesses to crime: Social and cognitive factors governing the validity of people's reports. In R. Roesch, S. D. Hart, & J. R. P. Ogloff (Eds.), *Psychology and law: The state of the discipline* (pp. 54-89). New York: Kluwer/Plenum.

Wilson, J. P., & Keane, T. M. (2004). *Assessing psychological trauma and PTSD* (2nd ed.). New York: The Guilford Press.

Wolfe, J., & Kimerling, R. (1997). Gender issues in the assessment of posttraumatic stress disorder. In J. P. Wilson & T. M. Keane (Eds.), *Assessing psychological trauma and PTSD* (pp. 192-238). New York: Guilford Press.

Wolfe, V., & Gentile, C. (1991). *Children's impact of traumatic events scale– Revised.* Unpublished assessment instrument, Department of Psychology, London Health Sciences Centre, London, Ontario.

Wolmer, L., Laor, N., Gershon, A., Mayes, L. C., & Cohen, D. J. (2000). The mother-child dyad facing trauma: A developmental outlook. *Journal of Nervous and Mental Disease, 188,* 409-415.

Wonderlich, S. A., Brewerton, T. D., Jocic, Z., Dansky, B. S., & Abbott, D. W. (1997). Relationship of childhood sexual abuse and eating disorders. *Journal of the American Academy of Child & Adolescent Psychiatry, 36*(8), 1107-1115.

World Health Organization (WHO) (1992). *International classification of diseases and related health problems,* Tenth revision, Geneva: World Health Organization.

Yasik, A. E., Saigh, P. A., Oberfield, R. A., Green, B., Halamandaris, P., & McHugh, M. (2001). The validity of the children's PTSD Inventory. *Journal of Traumatic Stress, 14,* 81-94.

Yule, W., & Udwin, O. (1991). Screening child survivors for post-traumatic stress disorders: Experiences from the "Jupiter" sinking. *British Journal of Clinical Psychology, 30,* 131-138.

Zoellner, L. A., Foa, E. B., & Brigidi, B. D. (2000). Are trauma victims susceptible to "false memories?" *Journal of Abnormal Psychology, 109,* 517-524.

Chapter 7

Treatment for the Sexually Abused Child

Barry Nurcombe

ADULT OUTCOME

Briere and Elliott (1994) have reviewed the extensive research linking child sexual abuse (CSA) with adult psychopathology. Despite the potential flaws in retrospective research (Briere, 1992), there is a general consensus that CSA is related to serious problems in adulthood, for example:

1. Depreciated self-concept
2. Unstable personal relationships
3. Self-harm and dangerous lifestyles (e.g., prostitution)
4. Chronic emotional distress and suicidal behavior
5. Substance abuse and addiction
6. Dissociation, conversion, and somatization
7. Sexual dysfunction
8. Revictimization and sexual offending

However, sexual abuse commonly occurs in a matrix of psychosocial adversity involving parental psychopathology, parental substance use, marital discord, domestic violence, parental separation, physical abuse, neglect, and lack of family cohesion. Does sexual abuse increase the risk of psychopathology over and above the risk conveyed by adverse family environment? In the Christchurch

Handbook of Social Work in Child and Adolescent Sexual Abuse
© 2008 by The Haworth Press, Taylor & Francis Group. All rights reserved.
doi:10.1300/5804_07

longitudinal study, Fergusson, Horwood, and Lynskey (1996a,b) found that it does.

THE IMMEDIATE EFFECTS OF CSA

Kendall-Tackett, Williams, and Finkelhor (1993) and Fergusson and Mullen (1999) have reviewed research into the impact of sexual abuse during childhood and adolescence. The classified effects are as follows:

1. Post-traumatic stress disorder
2. Impulsive or poorly controlled behavior
3. Emotional distress
4. Distorted attitudes to the self and to others
5. Dissociation and conversion
6. No symptoms

Post-traumatic symptomatology (intrusive traumatic imagery, emotional numbing, phobic and avoidant behavior, autonomic hyperarousal) occurs in 20 to 70 percent of sexually abused children, and subclinical traumatic symptomatology is often found. Impulsive behavior (e.g., aggressive outbursts, hyperactivity, running away from home, developmentally inappropriate sexual behavior) is common. Emotional distress (fear, anxiety, depression, withdrawal, sleep disturbance, somatic complaints) and distorted attitudes (e.g., guilt, self-hatred, self-blame, distrust of others, and a sense of powerlessness) occur in up to 60 percent of victims. Dissociation and conversion syndromes (e.g., vagueness, excessive fantasy, "blackouts," hallucinosis, pseudoseizures) are less common but dramatic effects of sexual abuse. Some researchers have found that up to 50 percent of victims of serious abuse are asymptomatic, a figure probably inflated by inadequate assessment and by dissociation in the early aftermath of abuse (Gomes-Schwartz, Horowitz, & Cardarelli, 1990).

There is continuity between the post-traumatic, disruptive, impulsive, emotional, self-derogatory, or dissociative behavior characteristic of abused children and adolescents and the depressive, suicidal, self-injurious behavior characteristic of adult borderline personality. Sexual dysfunction and unstable personal relationships are likely.

The dramatic but uncommon conversion and dissociative disorders of adulthood often stem from earlier physical or emotional abuse. Dangerous lifestyles such as substance abuse and prostitution may evolve from earlier maltreatment. A significant minority of sexually abused males eventually become sex offenders themselves (Skuse et al., 1998).

RISK FACTORS

Spaccarelli and Kim (1995) have reviewed the factors that predict an adverse outcome of sexual abuse. A child from a cohesive family who was psychologically well before being sexually fondled on one occasion by a stranger, and whose parents were supportive after she disclosed having been molested, is less likely to exhibit adverse psychological effects than a child from a dysfunctional family, already disturbed before the abuse, who has been repeatedly and coercively genitally penetrated, with threats, by a member of the family, and who chooses not to disclose the abuse or is disbelieved and rejected when she does. Risk factors can be divided into *moderating* and *mediating,* as follows.

Moderating Factors

Predisposing factors antedate abuse (e.g., the child's prior psychological adjustment, poor family cohesion, disrupted attachment experiences, parental psychopathology). There has been an insufficient number of studies of male victims, but it is possible that males are at greater risk of psychopathology following abuse (Glasser et al., 2001; Merry & Andrews, 1994).

Abuse stressors known to affect outcome are as follows: penetrative abuse, repeated abuse, long duration of abuse, abuse accompanied by coercion or threat, and abuse perpetrated by a family member.

Stressors occurring after the abuse are as follows: parental disbelief, lack of parental support, parental failure to protect, parental rejection, parental psychopathology and family dysfunction, and the experience of giving testimony (Quas et al., 2005).

Mediating Factors

The effect of moderating stressors is mediated through the child's self-concept, attitude to others, and method of coping with traumatic anxiety. Adverse coping techniques include failure to disclose, denial, suppression, detachment, dissociation, conversion, externalization, escape via substance use or running away, and repetition-compulsion. Disclosure is effective if support is received and the child is helped to assimilate distressing memories, diffuse traumatic anxiety, and "work through" and cognitively restructure his or her memories of the abuse, reappraise the self-concept, and find some meaning in an adverse experience. This is, of course, the aim of psychotherapy.

TREATMENT RESEARCH

Since 1986, there have been sixteen controlled, random-assignment studies in which the effectiveness of an index sexual abuse treatment was compared with that of a no-treatment control group or a comparison treatment.

Between 1986 and 1994, there were five experimental studies of the effectiveness of group therapy. Burke (1988) and Verleur, Hughes, and Dobkin-de Rios (1986) found that group therapy was more effective than no treatment. Baker (1987) found that group therapy was more effective than individual psychotherapy. Perez (1988) found that group therapy and individual therapy had equivalent outcomes, and that both were more effective than no treatment. Monck et al. (1994) found that both group therapy alone and group therapy combined with family therapy yielded significant improvement, but to a similar degree. These early studies should be interpreted cautiously because they are characterized by small sample size, limited outcome evaluation, brief follow-up, treatment that was poorly standardized, lack of clarity concerning clinician training, and failure to monitor the fidelity of treatment implementation. In the past decade, the focus of research has shifted predominantly to cognitive-behavioral therapy (CBT), with studies that have attempted to address these methodological deficiencies.

Berliner and Saunders (1996) compared the outcome of two ten-week interventions: group therapy and group therapy combined with

CBT. The sample was large, the assessment comprehensive, and the follow-up extended for two years. Both programs yielded equivalent significant changes; but there was no evidence that treatment efficacy was boosted by adding CBT to group therapy.

In two small studies (Celano, Hazzard, Webb, & McCall, 1996; Dominguez, 2002), CBT was found to be no more effective than non-specific therapy. The very small numbers in these two studies militated against the finding of any statistically significant differences.

Deblinger, Steer, and Lippmann (1999) compared three twelve-week treatment conditions with standard community care: CBT for the child only, CBT for the mother only, and CBT for both child and mother. CBT for child and parent exceeded in efficacy of CBT to either parent or child alone, and all three CBT conditions exceeded standard community treatment in efficacy. These results were sustained over two years. The abuse-specific evaluation, follow-up, control design, and fidelity of this study were excellent.

Cohen and Mannarino (1996) compared two twelve-week programs for three- to six-year-old children: CBT and nonspecific therapy (NST). CBT exceeded NST in its effect on general psychopathology and internalizing symptoms. NST effected no significant change in the targeted domains. The training of clinicians, treatment manualization, fidelity checks, and follow-up in this study were exemplary. Cohen and Mannarino (1998) attempted to repeat this study in children aged seven to thirteen years. The results of treatment with older children were much less impressive, possibly due to a high dropout rate (40 percent), especially in the NST group. In a third (multisite) study, Cohen, Deblinger, Mannarino, and Steer (2004) compared CBT with NST for a large group of children aged seven to thirteen years, and found CBT to be clearly superior.

King et al. (2000) compared three twenty-week treatment conditions for abused children aged five to seventeen years: CBT for the child alone, CBT for child and parent, and waiting list controls. The two CBT groups improved significantly more than the controls in relation to fear, anxiety, post-traumatic symptoms, and global functioning; but there was no evidence that the inclusion of a parent in therapy improved outcome.

Trowell et al. (2002) studied two forms of therapy for abused girls aged six to fourteen years: psychoanalytically oriented, individual psychotherapy (up to thirty sessions), and group therapy (up to eighteen sessions). In both forms of treatment, the parents received supportive therapy. Treatment was delivered by supervised, trained therapists, using manuals, but without fidelity checks. Both treatments yielded significant improvement in global functioning and post-traumatic symptoms, but to a similar degree.

Wooding et al. (submitted for publication) compared the effectiveness of two manualized, eighteen-week interventions—CBT and family therapy—to which participants aged six to sixteen years were randomly allocated. Community clinicians were trained in workshops to deliver the two treatment programs. Children and mothers were psychologically tested at baseline, eighteen weeks and twelve months. At eighteen weeks and twelve months, both kinds of treatment (CBT and family therapy) produced clinically significant improvement in child behavior problems, anxiety, anger, depression, post-traumatic stress, dissociation, and avoidant coping. The two treatments proved to be equally effective; however, neither treatment had beneficial effects on maternal mental health or the quality of family relationships. The attrition (self-termination) rate was a serious problem. Families were more likely to fail to appear for treatment, or to drop out before it was completed, if the child was male, if the therapist was male, or if the therapist's basic training had not included experience with children and adolescents (Nurcombe, Bickman, DeAndrade, submitted for publication).

In summary, there is evidence that CBT and group therapy are more effective than no treatment or nonspecific treatment. However, neither kind of therapy has demonstrated superiority to a competing treatment designed specifically for abused children. Nonspecific counseling is ineffective or, at best, only weakly effective. The status of family therapy is unclear, and only one study has examined the effectiveness of psychodynamic psychotherapy. Much of this research has been conducted in somewhat artificial laboratory settings, which lack ecological validity. Despite treatment, some children deteriorate. Other problems relate to variations in the definition of sexual abuse, the sample size needed to produce clear results, the universally problematic dropout rate, the appropriate duration of treatment, the uncertainty of whether to treat asymptomatic children, the vexed question of whether and how to involve the nonoffending caregiver, clinician training, the standardization of treatment, the fidelity of treatment implementation, and the appropriateness and comprehensiveness of the evaluation of treatment effectiveness.

MODULAR, GOAL-DIRECTED TREATMENT

The methodology of treatment research requires the delivery of "one-size-fits-all" techniques; otherwise, it would be impossible to determine which part of a complex treatment is effective. However, sexual abuse is a varied and complex phenomenon, often embedded in a matrix of other psychosocial problems. It is unreasonable to expect that a single kind of treatment will suit all families. The method of intervention should be tailored to suit individual systems. A modular program is required, based on a comprehensive evaluation.

Diagnostic Evaluation

As soon as possible after referral or ascertainment, the child and family should be assessed. Information is gathered from the parent or caregiver concerning the child's medical history, family background, developmental history, social adjustment, educational progress, mental health history, and current behavior problems. If the parent is able to provide it without excessive distress, information is elicited concerning the nature of the abuse (timing, frequency, duration, the nature of the abuse, the relationship of perpetration to the child, whether the perpetrator is in treatment, whether the perpetrator is still in contact with the child, and whether a criminal trial is anticipated at which the child is expected to testify). The parent's stress level, mental health history and status, burden of practical problems (e.g., accommodation, income, transport), and motivation for treatment are assessed, with particular concern for whether the family are ready for focused treatment, or whether a period of preparation is required. The parent's own history of abuse, if any, should be noted.

The child is assessed according to age and maturity, using standard interviewing techniques. Psychological testing can be helpful but should not be allowed to become too burdensome. Diagnostic psychological tests also form part of the outcome evaluation. The following tests are recommended:

- An omnibus test of child psychopathology such as the Child Behavior Checklist, CBCL (1-5; 6-17) (Achenbach & Rescorla, 2001)
- A test for post-traumatic symptomatology such as the Trauma Symptom Checklist for Children (TSCC) (for ages twelve to sixteen) or Trauma Symptom Inventory (TSI) (for children under twelve years) (Briere, 1995, 1996)
- A test of parental adjustment such as the General Health Questionnaire (GHQ-28) (Goldberg & Williams, 1988)
- A test of family cohesion such as the Family Assessment Device (Epstein, Baldwin, & Bishop, 1983)

It is important not to burden the child and family with too many tests. A comprehensive diagnostic formulation is prepared (Nurcombe, 2000).

Potential Foci for Goal-Directed Treatment Planning

Depending on the diagnostic formulation, the therapist selects some or all of the following foci for therapeutic intervention. The foci are then rewritten as goals and objectives (Nurcombe, 2000).

- Practical problems
- Lack of motivation for treatment
- Caregiver psychopathology
- Traumatic anxiety/depression
- Adverse attitudes to the self and to others
- Oppositional/disruptive behavior
- Developmentally inappropriate sexual behavior
- Dissociative and conversion symptoms
- Lack of family cohesion
- Self-protection
- The promotion of potentials

Practical Problems

Before focused treatment can begin, the family's immediate needs for safe accommodation, income, food, and transport must be addressed.

Lack of Motivation for Treatment

The attrition rate from experimental programs has been high. It is probably even higher in community clinics (Nurcombe, Bickman, DeAndrade, submitted for publication). Many family members are reluctant to enter treatment for the fear of invasion of privacy, the exposure of family secrets, being blamed, or being regarded as abnormal. The more family members rely upon suppression, denial, avoidance or dissociation, the less likely are they to enter or continue with therapy. Adolescent boys are particularly resistant to treatment. Parents are more likely to accept treatment if they perceive a child's problems as serious and psychological in origin, and regard professional help as accessible and likely to help. Demoralized parents may have little expectation that treatment will be effective. Other factors potentially associated with the therapeutic alliance are the clarity of the treatment plan and its negotiation with the family. Corcoran (2002) combines a stages-of-change model with motivational interviewing to counter parental ambivalence to treatment. Santisteban et al. (1996) have introduced Strategic Structural Systems Engagement, a technique in which the therapist joins the family in the first interview, establishes alliances, and negotiates and reframes problems.

The importance of the clinician's behavior should not be underestimated. Haste, coldness, rigidity, sociocultural misunderstanding, and ineptness with children are likely to provoke or aggravate resistance (Ackerman & Hilsenroth, 2001).

Caregiver Psychopathology

Many parents have psychological symptoms at the time of referral. Reactive anxiety, depression, and anger can usually be dealt with in the course of parental or family counseling. However, serious conditions such as major depression, borderline personality disorder, substance abuse, or dissociative disorder require specialized attention.

If the clinician works in a multidisciplinary clinic, it is preferable to refer the affected parent to a psychiatrist or clinical psychologist colleague who will collaborate closely in the treatment plan. Outside referral can be problematic but may be necessary.

Traumatic Anxiety and Depression

With regard to the treatment of child post-traumatic symptoms, CBT has the most impressive evidence base. The manualized programs described by Cohen and Mannarino (1996, 1998) and Deblinger, Steer, and Lippmann (1999) involve the techniques of relaxation, stress management, reframing, thought monitoring, thought stopping, and problem solving. There is less evidence for the effectiveness of psychodynamic psychotherapy. However, dynamic psychotherapies provide a method of allowing the child to reenter, explore, and assimilate suppressed or dissociated memories of abuse, via play therapy in younger children and verbal psychotherapy in adolescents (Fonagy, Roth, & Higgitt, 2005).

The question of whether it is necessary for the child to deal directly with traumatic memories is controversial. For many clinicians, this is an article of faith; however, there is no clear scientific evidence on this matter. Furthermore, it is possible that some very disturbed children in families with little resilience will be harmed by exploratory therapy. Caution is required. A gradual approach via support and the promotion of family cohesion may be preferable for highly vulnerable families, or for those with limited verbal capacity (Appelman, 2000).

Adverse Attitudes to the Self and to Others

Low self-esteem, self-blame, and self-stigmatization are highly prevalent in abused children. Among adolescent victims, group therapy can be very helpful in counteracting such problems. CBT promotes beneficial cognitive restructuring, as does the promotion of compensatory abilities.

Oppositional and Disruptive Behavior

Behavioral therapies such as Triple-P (Sanders, 1999) and parent training (e.g., Dishion & Andrews, 1995) have demonstrated effectiveness in counteracting difficult behavior that persists after traumatic anxiety has been addressed. Oppositional-defiant behavior sometimes stems from resentment of the child toward the nonoffending parent perceived failure to protect. Disruptive behavior (e.g., stealing, running away) often stems from a coping style aimed to distract the child from traumatic anxiety.

Developmentally Inappropriate Sexual Behavior

Sexually seductive or sexually aggressive behavior stems from precocious eroticization, sometimes in combination with repetition-compulsion and distractive defenses. If traumatic anxiety has been resolved, problematic sexual behavior usually dissipates, particularly if the parent is assisted to provide sexual psychoeducation to the child. However, sexual perpetration in male adolescents requires special attention, and is usually provided in a group context in association with the criminal justice system. Relapse prevention is stressed (e.g., Burton, Smith-Darden, & Frankel, 2006).

Dissociative and Conversion Symptoms

Major psychiatric problems such as dissociative identity disorder are uncommon. However, vagueness, detachment, depersonalization, and dissociative hallucinations are commonly encountered as part of post-traumatic anxiety. Self-injury (e.g., wrist cutting, self-burning, wall punching) represents an attempt to numb discordant traumatic affect. Sometimes these behaviors are so acute as to warrant brief hospitalization in an adolescent psychiatric unit. Extended hospitalization is inadvisable, as is admission to an adult psychiatric inpatient unit.

Conversion syndromes (e.g., pseudoseizures, paralysis, aphonia of nonorganic origin) are usually encountered in pediatric settings. Treatment requires close pediatric-psychiatric collaboration.

Lack of Family Cohesion

Without good parental support, focused treatment for the child may be ineffective. Family cohesion can be promoted by parental counseling and family therapy that aims to promote clear communication, interpersonal sensitivity, the sharing of emotion, family problem solving, and calm behavior control. Parent management training (e.g., Dishion & Andrews, 1995) incorporates these approaches.

Self-Protection

A meta-analysis (Berrick & Barth, 1992) of the findings of more than thirty prevention interventions found a small but significant improvement in knowledge following group-based universal psycho-educational programs. Young children learned less than older children. All had difficulty appreciating that a molester could be a member or friend of the family. Although it is unclear whether CSA victims can benefit from intervention that promotes body ownership, self-assertion, and the ability to distinguish "good" from "bad" touch, it would be imprudent not to incorporate such techniques in a comprehensive treatment plan for children under twelve years of age.

The Promotion of Potentials

All treatment plans should include a goal or goals relevant to the child's potentials. The realization of athletic, artistic, academic, or social abilities through athletic training, artistic tutoring, and well-chosen social experiences enhances self-esteem, prevents self-stigmatization, and potentially counteracts the passivity associated with victimhood.

The Sex of the Therapist

Generally speaking, female therapists are less threatening to abused children and their parents, and less likely to evoke obstructive transference reactions (Nurcombe, Bickman, & De Andrade, submitted for publication).

Negotiating the Diagnosis and Treatment Plan

The clinician should carefully explain to the family the diagnostic formulation, goals of treatment, and rationale for selected treatment strategies. The parent and adolescent should be asked to contribute to the diagnosis and plan, and the plan should be modified in accordance with their information, if it is desirable to do so. The frequency and likely duration of therapy should be discussed, along with the cost and method of payment, if relevant. The need for outcome evaluation and follow-up is explained. Clinician and family should jointly sign the final treatment plan. Subsequent changes in the plan, if any, should be negotiated and re-signed by clinician and family.

Clinician Morale

Families subject to child maltreatment are highly vulnerable and difficult to recruit to or retain in treatment. The clinician may feel overwhelmed and discouraged by the complexity of such problems and the inevitable treatment failures. It is probably advisable not to deal exclusively with sexually abused children, and to set a limit to how many of such cases one can treat at the same time. Peer group training, supervision, and support are desirable, though sometimes difficult to access. The importance of having a satisfying life outside of work cannot be overemphasized.

The Duration of Treatment

Children exposed to minor extrafamilial abuse who have well-functioning families usually require no more than one or two parental counseling sessions. More complex or serious problems involving composite modular treatment aimed at multiple goals are likely to require up to twenty sessions of weekly treatment, with the option of later, booster sessions. Few families have the financial, temporal, and emotional resources to sustain longer periods of treatment.

Medication

Generally speaking, psychotropic medication plays only a minor and adjunctive role in the treatment of sexually abused children. Although there is no empirical evidence for their effectiveness in children or adolescents with post-traumatic symptomatology, specific serotonin reuptake inhibitors (SSRIs) are often prescribed to counter the intrusive symptoms, autonomic hyperarousal, and insomnia of post-traumatic stress disorder. Antipsychotic medication is sometimes prescribed to ameliorate dissociative hallucinations by analogy to (or confusion with) schizophrenia. Antipsychotics should be avoided because their side effect of cognitive dulling interferes with education and psychotherapy.

Testifying in Court

Some children benefit by asserting themselves in court against those who have wronged them. Many do not, particularly if the alleged offender escapes punishment (Quas et al., 2005). A further complication is the desire of prosecuting attorneys to delay treatment until the criminal case is concluded, for fear that intervention will contaminate the evidence. Delays of this kind can last for months or years, allowing acute symptomatology to become chronic and indurated. If the child's best interests are considered, it must be concluded that early treatment is required.

CONCLUSION

As there is no specific sexual abuse syndrome and sexual abuse usually occurs in a complex matrix of family and social problems, there can be no universal remedy. Treatment must be a composite of strategies derived from a comprehensive diagnostic evaluation, and directed to specified goals and objectives. Treatment outcome should be evaluated clinically and by a reapplication of the psychological tests involved in the initial assessment.

Thus far, treatment research has examined the effectiveness of no more than one or two kinds of treatment at a time, applied to heterogeneous groups of sexually abused children. Because behavioral techniques lend themselves to empirical treatment outcome studies, most of the evidence for efficacy is associated with cognitive-behavioral therapy. Group therapy seems to have fallen out of favor with researchers and psychodynamic psychotherapy and family therapy are in danger of being superseded on the basis that "absence of evidence equals evidence of absence."

The clinician who works in the community rather than the research laboratory must rely upon elective composite treatment methods, even though empirical evidence is lacking that composite treatment is more effective than a unitary approach.

REFERENCES

Achenbach, T. M., & Rescorla, L. A. (2001). *Manual for the ASEBA school-age forms and profiles*. Burlington, VT: Research Center for Children, Youth, and Families.

Ackerman, S., & Hilsenroth, M. (2001). A review of therapist characteristics and techniques negatively impacting the therapeutic alliance. *Psychotherapy, 38*(2), 171-185.

Appelman, E. (2000). Attachment experiences transformed into language. *American Journal of Orthopsychiatry, 70*(2), 192-202.

Baker, C. R. (1987). A comparison of individual and group therapy as treatment of sexually abused adolescent females. *Dissertation Abstracts International, 47,* 4319-4320.

Berliner, L., & Saunders, B. E. (1996). Treating fear and anxiety in sexually abused children: Results of a controlled 2-year follow-up study. *Child Maltreatment, 1,* 294-309.

Berrick, J., & Barth, R. (1992). Child sexual abuse prevention: Research review and recommendations. *Social Work Research & Abstracts, 28,* 6-15.

Briere, J. (1992). Methodological issues in the study of sexual abuse effects. *Journal of Consulting and Clinical Psychology, 60,* 196-203.

Briere, J. (1995). *Manual for the Trauma Symptom Inventory (TSI)*. Lutz, FL: Psychological Assessment Resources.

Briere, J. (1996). *Manual for the Trauma Symptom Checklist for Children (TSCC)*. Lutz, FL: Psychological Assessment Resources.

Briere, J. N., & Elliott, D. M. (1994). Immediate and long-term impacts of child sexual abuse. *Sexual Abuse of Children, 4*(2), 54-69.

Burke, M. M. (1988). Short-term group therapy for sexually abused girls: A learning theory based treatment for negative affect (Doctoral dissertation, University of Georgia, Athens, November, 1988). *Dissertation Abstracts International,* 49(5-B), 1935.

Burton, D. L., Smith-Darden, J., & Frankel, S. J. (2006). Research on adolescent sexual abuser treatment programs. In H. E. Barbaree & W. L. Marshall (Eds.), *The juvenile sex offender* (2nd ed.) (pp. 291-312). New York: Guilford.

Celano, N., Hazzard, A., Webb, C., & McCall, C. (1996). Treatment of traumagenic beliefs among sexually abused girls and their mothers: An evaluation study. *American Journal of Child Psychology, 24,* 1-17.

Cohen, J. A., Deblinger, E., Mannarino, A. P., & Steer, A. P. (2004). A multisite randomized controlled trial for children with sexual abuse-related PTSD symptoms. *Journal of the American Academy of Child & Adolescent Psychiatry, 43,* 393-402.

Cohen, J. A., & Mannarino, A. P. (1996). A treatment outcome study for sexually abused preschool children: Initial findings. *Journal of the American Academy of Child & Adolescent Psychiatry, 35,* 42-50.

Cohen, J. A., & Mannarino, A. P. (1998). Interventions for sexually abused children: Initial treatment findings. *Child Maltreatment, 3,* 17-26.

Corcoran, J. (2002). The transtheoretical stages of change model and motivational interviewing for building maternal supportiveness in cases of sexual abuse. *Journal of Child Sexual Abuse, 11,* 1-10.

Deblinger, E., Steer, R., & Lippmann, J. (1999). Two-year follow-up study of cognitive behavior therapy for sexually abused children suffering post-traumatic stress symptoms. *Child Abuse & Neglect, 23,* 1371-1378.

Dishion, T. J., & Andrews, D. W. (1995). Preventing escalation in problem behaviors with high-risk young adolescents: Immediate and 1-year outcomes. *Journal of Clinical & Consulting Psychology, 63,* 538-548.

Dominguez, R. Z. (2002). Evaluation of cognitive-behavioral and supportive treatments for sexually abused children: Analyzing the process of change using individual growth curve analyses. *Dissertations Abstracts International, 62,* 5370.

Epstein, N. B., Baldwin, L. M., & Bishop, D. S. (1983). The McMaster family assessment device. *Journal of Marital & Family Therapy, 9,* 171-180.

Fergusson, D. M., Horwood, L. J., & Lynskey, M. T. (1996b). Childhood sexual abuse and psychiatric disorder in young adulthood: II. Psychiatric outcomes of child sexual abuse. *Journal of the American Academy of Child & Adolescent Psychiatry, 35,* 1365-1374.

Fergusson, D. M., Lynskey, M. T., & Horwood, L. J. (1996a). Childhood sexual abuse and psychiatric disorder in young adulthood: I. Prevalence of sexual abuse and factors associated with sexual abuse. *Journal of the American Academy of Child & Adolescent Psychiatry, 35,* 1355-1364.

Fergusson, D. M., & Mullen, P. E. (1999). *Childhood sexual abuse: An evidence based perspective.* Vol. 40. *Developmental clinical psychology and psychiatry.* Thousand Oaks, CA: Sage.

Fonagy, P., Roth, A., & Higgitt, A. (2005). Psychodynamic psychotherapies: Evidence based practice and clinical wisdom. *Bulletin of the Menninger Clinic, 69,* 1-58.

Glasser, M., Kolvin, I., Campbell, D., Glasser, A., Leitch, I., & Farrelly, S. (2001). Cycle of child sexual abuse: Links between being a victim and becoming a perpetrator. *British Journal of Psychiatry, 179,* 482-494.

Goldberg, D., & Williams, P. (1988). *A user's guide to the general health questionnaire.* Windsor, UK: NFER-Nelson.

Gomes-Schwartz, B., Horowitz, J. M., & Cardarelli, A. P. (Eds.). (1990). *Child sexual abuse: The initial effects.* Newbury Park, CA: Sage.

Kendall-Tackett, K. A., Williams, L. M., & Finkelhor, D. (1993). Impact of sexual abuse on children: A review and synthesis of recent empirical studies. *Psychological Bulletin, 113,* 164-180.

King, N. J., Tonge, B. J., Mullen, P., Myerson, N., Heyne, D., Rollings, et al. (2001). Treating sexually abused children with posttraumatic stress symptoms: A randomized clinical trial. *Journal of the American Academy of Child & Adolescent Psychiatry, 39,* 1347-1355.

Merry, S. N., & Andrews, L. K. (1994). Psychiatric states of sexually abused children 12 months after disclosure of abuse. *Journal of the American Academy of Child & Adolescent Psychiatry, 33,* 939-944.

Monck, E., Bentovim, A., Goodall, G., Hyde, C., Lewin, B., & Sharland, E. (1994). *Child sexual abuse: A descriptive and treatment outcome study.* London: Her Majesty's Stationery Office (HMSO).

Nurcombe, B. (2000). Diagnostic formulation, treatment planning, and modes of treatment. In M. H. Ebert, P. T. Loosen, & B. Nurcombe (Eds.), *Current diagnosis and treatment in psychiatry* (pp. 520-532). New York: Lange/McGraw Hill.

Nurcombe, B., Bickman, L., & De Andrade, A. (submitted). Attrition from a community-based treatment program for child sexual abuse. *Journal of the American Academy of Child & Adolescent Psychiatry.*

Perez, C. L. (1988). A comparison of group play therapy and individual therapy for sexually abused children. *Dissertation Abstracts International, 48,* 3079.

Quas, J. A., Goodman, G. S., Ghetti, S., Alexander, K. W., Edelstein, R., Redlich, A. D., et al. (2005). Childhood sexual assault victims: Long-term outcomes after testifying in criminal court. *Monographs of the Society for Research in Child Development, 70,* vii-1-128.

Sanders, M. R. (1999). The Triple P-Positive Parenting Program: Toward an empirically validated multilevel parenting and family support strategy for the prevention of behavior and emotional problems in children. In T. H. Ollendick R. J. Prinz (Eds.), *Advances in clinical child psychology* (Vol. 18, pp. 283-330). New York: Plenum.

Santisteban, D. A., Szapocznik, J., Prez-Vidal, A., Murray, E. J., Kurtines, W. M., & LaPerriere, A. (1996). Efficacy of intervention of engaging youth and families into treatment and some variables that may contribute to differential effectiveness. *Journal of Family Psychotherapy, 10,* 35-44.

Skuse, D., Bentovim, A., Hodges, J., Stevenson, J., Andreou, C., Lanyado, M., et al. (1998). Risk factors for development of sexually abusive behavior in sexually victimized adolescent boys: Cross sectional study. *British Medical Journal, 317,* 175-179.

Spaccarelli, S., & Kim, S. (1995). Resilience criteria and factors associated with resilience in sexually abused girls. *Child Abuse & Neglect, 19,* 1-11.

Trowell, J., Kolvin, I., Weeramanthi, T., Sadowski, H., Berelowitz, M., Glasser, D., et al. (2002). Psychotherapy for sexually abused girls: Psychopathological outcome findings and patterns of change. *British Journal of Psychiatry, 180,* 234-247.

Verleur, D., Hughes, R.E., & Dobkin-de Rios, M. (1986). Enhancement of self-esteem among female incest victims: A controlled comparison. *Adolescence, 21,* 843-854.

Wooding, S., Nurcombe, B., De Andrade. A., Marrington, P., Roberts, G., Lilley, P.-R., et al. (submitted). The Queensland child sexual abuse treatment study: The relative effectiveness of cognitive behavior therapy and family therapy. *Journal of the American Academy of Child & Adolescent Psychiatry.*

Chapter 8

Treatment for Sexually
Abused Adolescents

Debra Nelson-Gardell

INTRODUCTION

Social workers see clients embedded in context. When considering the provision of treatment by social workers for adolescents affected by sexual victimization, many contextual issues come to mind. What type of abuse, perpetrated by whom, with what effect? When did it happen, recently or when the teen was much younger? What was the teen's life before the abuse? What coping skills were already available? What was the disclosure process like? Was she or he believed? Who is providing emotional support? These are the issues of assessment.

For the problem-solving social worker, after assessment comes intervention. In 1967, Gordon Paul, a psychologist, posed the question that now comes to mind: "*What* treatment, by *whom,* is most effective for *this* individual with *that* specific problem, and under *which* set of circumstances?" (p. 111, italics in original). Close consideration of this seemingly straightforward question reveals the incredible complexity of the task. The helping professions are, at this moment in time, at the very early stages of understanding when it comes to knowing what works best for whom under which circumstances. The good news is that we have begun the process. At a minimum, we know that, in general, psychotherapy for youth has shown positive effects (Weisz, Weiss, Hann, Granger, & Morton, 1995). We also know specifically, at least for some clients, that trauma-focused cognitive-behavioral

Handbook of Social Work in Child and Adolescent Sexual Abuse
© 2008 by The Haworth Press, Taylor & Francis Group. All rights reserved.
doi:10.1300/5804_08

therapy (TF-CBT) has shown positive effects (Dalgleish, Meiser-Stedman, & Smith, 2005). Randomized clinical trials and longitudinal research are still in their infancy in this topical area. In the literature, much of the information regarding treatment for adolescents is presented in combination with treatment for children. As such, information specific to adolescents and not children, and vice versa, may be difficult to differentiate. This chapter tries to be specific, when specificity is possible. Further, the chapter focuses on treatment for adolescent victims of sexual maltreatment and does not focus on treating adolescents whose primary problem is compulsive or addictive sexual behavior problems, although it is acknowledged that sexual behavior problems can certainly be one of the outcomes of victimization. The chapter is not intended to serve as a primary source of information for this type of problem. This chapter provides an overview, along with suggestions for additional reading (directly and through citation), of topics and issues social workers need to understand and/or appreciate as they provide treatment for adolescents affected by sexual victimization. The ever-increasing speed with which new information becomes available increases the amount of knowledge available (and necessary) at what seems like an exponential rate. This chapter may best be viewed as a series of signposts suggesting directions for your continued professional development.

ADOLESCENCE: WHAT IS IT?

It is necessary to be mindful of the meaning of the concept of adolescence before addressing the specifics of how sexual abuse might affect an adolescent and how one might address those effects. Walsh (2004) in a delightful book written for parents of adolescents (but also incredibly useful to nonmedical human service professionals) that demystifies adolescent brain development defines adolescence as a time of transition, an "in-between stage" that "begins at puberty, and ends . . . sometime" (p. 1). Although adolescence is the continuation of a path of development begun in infancy and childhood, it is also a time of biological, social, and psychological transition (Novak & Pelaez, 2004). It is historically (Hall, 1904) and familiarly perceived as a time of difficulty and challenge. Although not all adolescents experience turmoil or present problems for their families (Gil, 1996; Hecht,

Chaffin, Bonner, Worley, & Lawson, 2002), there are significant changes and adjustments that individuals face at this time of their lives. The uniqueness of this developmental period when it comes to sexual abuse has to do with the notion that sexuality takes on a particular salience for adolescents because of these life transitions. The life stage is actually heralded by physical changes that prepare us for our sexual and reproductive functions as humans. Sexual victimization and traumatization present an additional huge challenge during a time that developmental changes may already be presenting challenges. Paired with the ambivalence many adults (parents and professionals, alike) feel in relation to adolescents, addressing sexual abuse at this life stage takes on an even greater complexity. As a teen might be quick to point out, she or he is not a child any longer, but as an adult caregiver would also be quick to point out, that teen is not an adult either. Realizing the circumstances of "not a child, not an adult," with a brain that is still "under construction," so to speak (Walsh, 2004, p. 38), and a body undergoing major developmental modifications (Hughes, 2001), we can begin to appreciate the developmental challenges and barriers facing the victimized teen we want to help.

NEUROLOGICAL EFFECTS OF TRAUMA

Social workers working with sexually traumatized youth need to try to understand how current dysfunctional behaviors or problems help them to cope with perceived stress (Ziegler, 2002). Humans react to perceived danger in a variety of ways. "Fight or flight" is the most commonly reported, but there are others. For example, Perry, Pollard, Blakley, Baker, and Vigilante (1995) suggest the "freeze or surrender" reaction or, in other words, dissociation. Dissociation can seem like "day dreaming," in its most benign form, and thus an adolescent may be blamed for not attending, purposefully, to some task. This "skill" of psychologically absenting themselves from a situation allows the child to survive the trauma and so serves as an important coping skill. However, when used in other contexts, such as school, it clearly becomes dysfunctional.

Our brains have evolved in ways that support our survival, as individuals and as a species. We are born with a multitude of neurons, but the simple presence of the neuron does not mean our brain is fully developed. The neurons are not yet fully connected to each other when we are born. We are not ready, yet, for thinking at the most advanced, abstract levels. That process of connecting takes place during infancy, childhood, and *through adolescence* (Walsh, 2004). It is the interaction between our brain and our environment that results in how we develop (Cicchetti & Toth, 2005). There are periods in our development that are "windows" when we are more ready to learn certain things. If we miss those "windows," it is harder to learn those things later. Those "windows" do not occur only in infancy and childhood, but also during adolescence (Walsh, 2004).

Child maltreatment, including sexual abuse, can result in a type of deprivation of opportunity during development (Perry et al., 1995). If our brain is busy trying to survive a trauma, it may not have the resources to attend to the developmental tasks that would have customarily been completed at that point in time. Professionals working in this area use a phrase that is quite descriptive, "neurons that fire together, wire together" (Stirling, 2006). Essentially, the implication for working with adolescents who have experienced a trauma is that if certain patterns of neural firing become established because of traumatic experiences during development, it is difficult to change those patterns. A teen with a history of abuse may develop a brain that is "over-prepared to seek, find and avoid threats" (Ford, 2005, p. 417). One example is sensitivity to stimuli associated with the original trauma, but that also occurs in cases in which danger is not imminent. Perhaps the offender had a beard, and the sight and feel of that facial hair became associated with the original trauma. When the victim sees someone with a beard, her or his brain may react as if the trauma is happening again because the stimuli of seeing a beard has become paired, from a behaviorally conditioned point of view, with her or his body's reaction to imminent harm, even though the teen is intellectually aware that the individual is not the offender.

De Bellis et al. (2001) cautions that trauma during childhood and adolescence may have more detrimental effects than during later life stages because brain structures can be changed by traumatic experiences that take place during this time. To summarize, the development of the brain supports survival. If the environment during development is one of trauma, then the brain develops to cope with the conditions of trauma, resulting in it being less able to function under other conditions. However, De Bellis et al. (2001) also remind us to have hope. Although the adverse neurological effects resulting from traumatic stress are real and serious, they are amenable to intervention. He reported on research that supports this hope, but bemoans the lack of funding for intervention research for maltreated children and their families.

Perry (2006) provides an excellent summary of brain development with regard to traumatized children, summarizing principles and making application connections to clinical work. He called for a more "developmentally sensitive, biologically respectful approach" (p. 47). This material is crucial to appreciate. On the basis of his principle of sequential neurodevelopment, if neurodevelopment was delayed because of early trauma, the neurodevelopmental level of a teen may not match their chronological age; the trauma may have resulted in the adolescent being "stuck" at a neurodevelopmental stage "normally" associated with an earlier chronological age. Understanding when trauma occurred and assessing the effects of that trauma on a teen client can help the clinician to know as to which therapeutic approaches need to be applied first and which later, what Perry (2006) called a "neurosequential approach" (p. 47).

Full explanations of brain structure, brain development, and the neurobiological consequences of child maltreatment are obviously not possible in a single book chapter, so the reader is encouraged to seek additional knowledge through other means. This area of knowledge is one of the most rapidly expanding areas of inquiry because of technological advances enabling researchers to actually see brain function using technology such as functional magnetic resonance imaging (MRI) and positron-emissions tomography (PET) (Ziegler, 2002). The implications for intervention and treatment are profound. The more thoroughly we understand the causes of how sexual maltreatment results in problems for adolescents, the better able we are to identify and implement appropriate and effective interventions. Gil (1996) stated that she believed understanding adolescents' current symptomatic behaviors in the context of their abuse enables therapists to see more clearly which issues need to be part of the therapeutic process. At some level, many people, including adolescents and their families, often see psychological problems through a lens of stigma. Understanding how to reframe the psychological problems arising from trauma through a physiological lens (which has less stigma attached) and then making the connection between how psychosocial intervention can affect, both physiologically and psychologically, an individual's ability to cope can be a powerful tool for clinicians.

THE EFFECTS OF SEXUAL VICTIMIZATION

How sexual victimization affects any particular adolescent depends on many factors, including gender and culture. A detailed focus on the impact of sexual victimization can be found elsewhere in this volume. Research has shown that following disclosure of sexual abuse, adolescents, in comparison with younger children, appear to react with more depression, possess lower self-worth, and perceive less social support, and increased negative reactions from others (Feiring, Taska, & Lewis, 1999). To set the stage for discussing treatment issues, however, a few points need to be emphasized. A term increasingly entering the lexicon of professionals interested in helping traumatized adolescents is "complex trauma" (Cook et al., 2005). This term refers to the circumstance often faced by social workers of clients who are not only affected by the trauma of sexual abuse, but also by other traumas that have occurred during the course of their lives. Turner, Finkelhor, and Ormrod (2006) studied youth affected by multiple types of victimization in conjunction with other types of adversities, such as poverty or parental marital discord. Families with children who have been multiply traumatized and/or affected by multiple adverse circumstances are among those most often comprising the caseloads of social workers and among those presenting the biggest intervention challenges. Turner et al. (2006) provided research support that children and adolescents who experience one type of victimization have also likely experienced others and that the effects were cumulative. Each type of victimization and adversity added its own contribution to the rate of reported harmful mental health consequences. Clinicians should be careful to avoid overestimating the effects of a single trauma and underestimating the effects of multiple, cumulative traumas, emphasizing the need for individualized assessment. Keeping in mind the complexity introduced by these two sources, a useful conceptual framework, termed traumagenic dynamics, can be used to think about the unique effects of sexual victimization (Finkelhor & Browne, 1985). Finkelhor and Browne (1985) identified four traumagenic dynamics unique to the trauma of sexual victimization: traumatic sexualization, betrayal, stigmatization, and powerlessness. This conceptual framework can be a useful tool for the clinician to use to organize her or his thinking as the treatment process progresses.

Culture

Culturally sensitive practice requires practitioners to continually acquire new understanding of various cultural groups and resist stereotyping. Learning about cultural differences helps clinicians to know what kinds of questions to ask and what clinical issues may be of greater salience, depending on the clients' cultural background. However, to allow that knowledge to result in "pigeon-holing" would be to bastardize the notion of cultural competence (Fontes, 2005). Two characteristics of culture, one that culture is not static and the other that culture is multifaceted (Fontes, 2005), must be kept in mind when reading about various cultures. In addition, as with every area of consideration when it comes to sexual abuse, the reactions of teens and their families to sexual abuse will be unique and individualized, to include responses based in culture, but also to include many other aspects of their lives. While not focused solely on adolescents, an excellent resource to lay the groundwork for a clinician to appreciate how sexual abuse affects peoples of different cultures is Fontes' (1995) *Sexual Abuse in Nine North American Cultures: Treatment and Prevention*. This edited volume provides an overview of various cultural groups in relation to the phenomenon of sexual abuse, including African Americans, Puerto Ricans, Asians, Pacific Islanders, Filipino Americans, Cambodians, Jews, Anglo Americans, Seventh Day Adventists, gay males, and lesbian females. Following up on her 1995 publication, Fontes (2005) described a multicultural orientation to child maltreatment work that can be a basis for clinicians providing treatment for sexually abused adolescents. She encouraged the use of an ecosystemic framework, both for the client(s) and for the clinician reminding us that we need to understand our own culture and that our professional identity is a type of culture, as well. She reminds us to work diligently to recognize our own biases in an effort to avoid them affecting our clients. Perhaps one of the most crucial aspects she points out was the need to recognize that help seeking may be prescribed culturally. Though it may look like caregivers are "doing nothing," "they may be engaged in an elaborate process to help a child recover that is invisible to us because it does not conform to the usual practices of our culture" (Fontes, 2005, p. 16).

Gender

For many reasons, the sexual abuse of males has been under-recognized and underresearched. We know much more about females and sexual abuse than we do about males. Much of the research that focuses on teen males relies on small, nonrandom samples. Because of these circumstances, one must be cautious in using the findings of the research (Feiring et al., 1999). Because of limited research, we know even less about how gender and age interact in the expression of the effects of sexual abuse. Widespread homophobia in the U.S. culture combined with a gender double standard regarding sexuality are likely to contribute to this circumstance. Males perpetrate most sexual abuse, so much of the abuse of males is by other males (Snyder, 2000). Homophobia is perhaps even more likely to inhibit teen males from reporting or facing their victimization than younger boys because of the developmental salience of identity formation during adolescence. Due to the gender double standard regarding sexuality, when teen males are sexually maltreated by older women, there seems to be wider social acceptance of that behavior as less objectionable than the abuse of teen females by older men, to the detriment of male victims.

Friedrich (1995) cautioned that the response to sexual victimization is unique to each individual, but summarized some of the potential differences between males and females. Statistically, physical abuse is more often an accompaniment to sexual abuse for boys than girls. Coupled with a cultural tendency for males to associate sexuality and aggression, this may exacerbate boys' tendency in this area. Perhaps because of socialization, perhaps because of biological differences, boys tend to show aggressive or oppositional behaviors (in what is called externalizing) in response to trauma more often than females, who more often show signs of depression and anxiety (or what is called internalizing). This response pattern is not unique to sexual abuse (Feiring et al., 1999). It is important to remember that existence of patterns does not mean that boys only engage in externalizing and girls in internalizing, but that each individual will uniquely express the effects of child sexual abuse. At least one study found little difference in sexual effects between male and female sexual abuse survivors who had been incarcerated (Gover, 2004), and another found greater problems among sexually abused boys than either sexually abused girls or a matched comparison group of non–sexually abused boys and girls (Garnefski & Diekstra, 1997). Sexual behavior also seems to be differentially affected by sexual victimization with boys showing greater levels of aggressive sexual acting out behaviors than girls. Knowledge about sexual abuse and males is increasing and professionals need to watch for new resources and take advantage of them as they arise.

ASSESSMENT

All teenagers who have experienced sexual abuse should have the opportunity of being evaluated for mental health intervention, but not all teenagers who are sexually abused will require mental health treatment (Hecht et al., 2002). The difficulty lies in discerning who needs treatment and who does not. There is no particular "syndrome" resulting from sexual abuse victimization (Kendall-Tackett, Williams, & Finkelhor, 1993; Paolucci, Genius, & Violato, 2001). The effects of sexual abuse are varied, and depend on what happened, when it occurred, and the psychosocial history and current circumstances of the teen. Some teens use avoidance or denial to cope with the effects of their victimization and may not report any dysfunction or symptoms (Hecht et al., 2002). Deblinger et al. (2006) in the context of discussing when completion of a trauma narrative is indicated in TF-CBT suggested that if the teen could comfortably discuss details of their trauma, then avoidance did not seem to be an issue. In the absence of dysfunction and avoidance, at that point in the TF-CBT treatment progress, further intervention in terms of the construction and processing of the trauma narrative may not be necessary. I would suggest a similar standard for discerning at assessment who may need treatment and who may not. Those teens who are reporting little discomfort and/or dysfunction and are able to relate the details associated with their trauma easily may not require further intervention, beyond instruction of how to respond to future discomfort or dysfunction. Even when more intense intervention is not indicated, offering psychoeducation about sexual abuse could be helpful to prevent future problems (Saywitz, Mannarino, Berliner, & Cohen, 2000).

Social workers are accustomed to the completion of full biopsychosocial assessments for clients coming into treatment. Assessment forms the basis for individualized treatment planning, with interventions specifically geared to the problems identified as a result of assessment. Adolescents will be differentially and uniquely affected by their sexual victimization and a thorough assessment is the only way to know what is needed. Therefore, in working with teens affected by sexual victimization, some additional specialized assessment, beyond the "standard" psychosocial assessment, is in order. Some pertinent questions, already suggested in the introduction to this chapter, include What type of abuse, perpetrated by whom, with what effect? When did it happen, recently or when the teen was much younger? What was the teen's life like before the abuse? What coping skills were already available? What was the disclosure process like? Was she or he believed? Who is providing emotional support?

When thinking about assessment of sexual abuse, two types of assessment come to mind, assessments of the validity of the sexual abuse allegations and assessments of the psychosocial needs of those affected by sexual abuse. This chapter does not address the assessment of the validity of the sexual abuse allegation. The role of professionals engaged in these types of assessments is very different from those of the treating clinician, with differing "clients" and differing goals (Mannarino & Cohen, 2001). The forensic investigator is serving the needs of the child protection system, whether child welfare or legal. The outcomes of their assessments are provided to their clients—the child welfare or legal/judicial authorities. The therapist is in a very different role, serving the needs of the victim with the goal of healing. The child and family comprise their client system. Forensic investigators are not free to come into an alliance with the adolescent taking a believing stance regarding the reported victimization. In fact, it is their job to reserve judgment on the validity of sexual abuse allegations. They must take a neutral stance in order to do their job effectively.

Therapists however can and should enter the alliance with the victim (and family) with a believing stance. That is, the therapist should be ready to convey to the victim (and their family) their belief in the reports of sexual victimization. Teens have voiced this need to be believed as one of the core aspects of what has helped them following the sexual abuse disclosure (Nelson-Gardell, 2001).

Another very important point to explore during assessment has to do with the issue of safety. If the teen is in a situation where the abuse is still going on, or where there is a risk, in the perception of the adolescent, of further abuse, progress in treatment will be difficult if not impossible. There are various circumstances under which this can occur, for example, it might happen when the identity of the offender has not been disclosed (perhaps because of fear) and the teen is still living in a situation where access by that offender is ongoing. Another example includes cases of abuse by partners of nonoffending caregivers, where the nonoffending caregivers fail to provide adequate protection. This lack of protection can include allowing the offender back into the home either on a temporary or full-time basis. It is difficult to know what to do if these circumstances arise. On the one hand, one does not wish to refuse treatment to a victimized adolescent, yet on the other providing treatment when one has little hope of success also presents ethical considerations. As is often the case in clinical work, there may not be a "right" answer to this question.

A special issue of assessment identified by Saunders, Berliner, and Hanson (2004) has to do with the perception of caregivers to the issue of sexual maltreatment and their teen. It is important to know whether caregivers believe that their teen has been sexually abused (Elliott & Carnes, 2001). In addition, assessment should be made of how supportive caregivers were to their teen at the time of disclosure and after with regard to the issues of sexual abuse. It is also important to know to what extent the abuse of their teen has affected their own psychosocial well-being. Caregivers struggling with their own trauma reactions may be unable or unwilling to provide support for their adolescent. Nonoffending caregiver belief and support has been demonstrated to be crucial in the level of the teen's distress and recovery (Elliott & Carnes, 2001; Spaccarelli, 1995). A more in-depth focus on nonoffending caregivers may be found elsewhere in this volume.

Sexual abuse, as has already been pointed out, is not a syndrome. It is an event or series of events that take place within the context of a victim's life, having the potential for producing deleterious effects for the victim. As such, the clinician should assess the various specific areas in which one might expect dysfunction. Mannarino and Cohen (2006) categorized general areas in which symptoms resulting from trauma might be displayed as affective trauma symptoms (including fear, sadness, anger, anxiety, and especially, affective regulation), behavioral trauma symptoms (including avoidance, sexualized behaviors, violent behaviors, bullying, traumatic bonding, anger, substance abuse, and self-injury), and cognitive trauma symptoms (including irrational beliefs, distrust, distorted self-image, loss/betrayal of social contract, and accurate, but unhelpful, cognitions).

As is usually the case in assessing clients for treatment, clinicians use a variety of methods for assessment including interview with the adolescent and with caregivers, observation, contact with significant collateral sources of information, such as teachers, and the review of other assessments, including any forensic assessments that have been completed. Suicide assessment should be a standard part of any assessment of traumatized adolescents (De Bellis et al., 2001). As has already been pointed out, a history of multiple traumas is likely and clinicians should assess other areas of potential trauma in addition to the sexual trauma. Both the sexual trauma for which treatment is currently being sought and previous sexual traumas should be assessed, including the witnessing of violence, both family and community, physical abuse by caregivers or other family members, and physical assault by individuals outside the family. Two interview schedules, Clinical Assessment Interview for Children (Saunders, Williams, Hanson, & Smith, 2003a) and Event History Interview for Children (Saunders, Williams, Hanson, & Smith, 2003b), can be helpful tools in this endeavor. Recall here material discussed earlier in this chapter on neurodevelopment. Assessing earlier traumas and appreciating their effects on a teen's neurodevelopmental level will help the clinician to have a sense of whether the client can successfully manage, emotionally and cognitively, various interventions (Perry, 2006).

Standardized Measures

The clinician may decide to incorporate the results of standardized assessment tools, especially in the specific areas potentially affected by a history of sexual victimization, including trauma, depression, anxiety, or acting out behaviors. Strand, Sarmiento, and Pasquale (2005) categorized and described trauma assessment tools for children and adolescents. They provided a table giving an overview of twenty-four instruments that one can use to compare instruments along various categories, including the construct measured, time needed to administer, psychometric status, and cost. Ohan, Myers, and Collett (2002) did a similar review and comparison with some overlap with the Strand et al. (2005) publication, but included scales measuring dissociation. Diseth and Christie (2005) provided an overview of assessment instruments for trauma-related dissociative disorders (along with treatment recommendations). Another significant resource in this area is *Psychological Assessment of Sexually Abused Children and Their Families* by Friedrich (2002). Although written specifically for psychologists, the volume holds excellent educational value for social workers. It is a very thorough overview of psychological assessment of issues pertinent to sexual traumatization. Some of the instruments, that is, self-report instruments, described by Friedrich can be appropriate for use by master's level social work clinicians.

One of the most widely used and well-validated measures (including clinical cutoff scores) suitable for use with adolescents with a history of sexual abuse is the Trauma Symptom Checklist for Children (TSCC) (Briere, 1996). Social workers are well prepared by their education to use this type of instrument. The TSCC is a fifty-four-item self-report measure of post-traumatic stress and related psychological symptoms in children of ages eight to sixteen years who have experienced events such as physical or sexual abuse, major loss, natural disaster, or have witnessed violence. The TSCC has eight subscales that include two validity scales of underresponse and hyperresponse and six clinical scales: anxiety, depression, anger, post-traumatic stress, dissociation, and sexual concerns. There are also eight critical items. The TSCC was standardized on a group of more than 3,000 children and adolescents from diverse population groups, both racially and economically. Scoring is facilitated using specialized administration forms that include carbonless transfer of responses to a scoring worksheet. Although there is a cost involved in purchase of the instruments, the quality of the measure combined with the ease of administration makes it a very attractive alternative.

Another widely used and valid measure (across very diverse population groups) for assessing problems in a broad-based way is the Child Behavior Checklist (CBCL) (Achenbach, 1991). Although this instrument is intended for clinical use, it has been widely used in research focusing on child abuse and neglect, supporting its appropriateness for this population. The CBCL is a 118-item instrument that assesses competencies and problems of children and adolescents of ages four to eighteen as reported by youth themselves, parents, or other primary caregivers (it is available in multiple formats). The CBCL consists of three subscales: Competence Scale, Syndrome Scale, and Total Problem Scale. Scoring can be done by hand using scoring templates or by computer using specialized software designed for that purpose. Total competence and problem's scores can be generated. From grouping certain problem-oriented items, syndrome (withdrawn, somatic complaints, anxious/depressed, social problems, thought problems, attention problems, delinquent behavior, aggressive behavior) scores can be obtained. Subscale scores called "internalizing" and "externalizing" are obtained by grouping certain syndrome scores.

Finally, a resource for use in ongoing assessment, or practice evaluation, was described by Sawyer, Tsao, Hansen, and Flood (2006). They reported on research testing the use of Weekly Problem Scales to monitor treatment progress for sexually abused children, adolescents, and their families. Acceptable psychometric characteristics were identified given that this was an initial evaluation of the measure with a small sample ($n = 64$ children and adolescents with a mean age of twelve years).

Comorbidity

Comorbidity is defined by the *Social Work Dictionary* (Barker, 2003) as follows:

> The simultaneous existence of two or more diseases or dysfunctions within an individual. Each disease may or may not exacerbate the severity, duration, or prognosis of the other but

frequently leads the diagnostician to overlook one or the other disease. (p. 193)

It is impossible to generalize expected comorbid conditions in most adolescents who have been sexually victimized. Individualized assessment is the only way to ascertain comorbid conditions as the histories and responses of adolescents will be unique to individual life circumstances. Multiple types of dysfunction are likely to coexist; however, whether they do and which ones may or may not coexist depends on individual history and circumstances. Gender differences in comorbidity are apparent in the literature, but patterns are not clear and vary by type of dysfunction. Whether the existence of these problems predates the sexual abuse experience or arises after the sexual abuse is a matter of individual assessment given that research does not give us a clear picture at this time (Kaminer, Seedat, Lockhat, & Stein, 2000). Dysfunctions associated with adolescents who have been sexually victimized include traumatic stress (Ackerman, Newton, McPherson, Jones, & Dykman, 1998), anxiety (De Bellis et al., 2001; Pillay & Schoubben-Hesk, 2001), dissociation (Diseth, 2005), depression (Brown, Cohen, Johnson, & Smailes, 1999; Romano, Zoccolillo, & Paquette, 2006), delinquency (Stuewig & McCloskey, 2005), suicide (Dube et al., 2001), self-mutilation (Brown, Houck, Hadley, & Lescano, 2005), substance abuse (Harrison, Fulkerson, & Beebe, 1997), sexual problems (including physiological, sexual functioning, and high-risk sexual behaviors) (Loeb et al., 2002), and intellectual impairment (Jones, Trudinger, & Crawford, 2004).

Post-traumatic stress disorder (American Psychiatric Association, 2000) is a commonly used diagnosis for adolescents affected by sexual traumatization, but it is far from universally applied and knowledge about comorbid diagnoses is limited (Lipschitz, Winegar, Harnick, Foote, & Southwick, 1999). Saywitz et al. (2000) in summarizing research on sexual abuse and post-traumatic stress disorder (PTSD) reported that more than 50 percent of child and adolescents affected by sexual abuse are diagnosed with PTSD. Research seems to support, although not consistently, a greater tendency for rates of PTSD occurrence among females to exceed that of males (Walker, Carey, Mohr, Stein, & Seedat, 2004). Other diagnoses would be those associated with the observed dysfunctions listed earlier (e.g., mood disorders, anxiety disorders). One should be cautious about applying multiple diagnoses in the initial aftermath of a traumatic experience. There are normal reactions to trauma that subside on their own with minimal or no intervention (Briere & Scott, 2006). A diagnosis of PTSD is made only with a persistence of symptoms for longer than a month, with the diagnosis of acute stress disorder available for those experiencing significant dysfunction as a result of exposure to a traumatic stressor, but with symptom persistence of shorter than a month (but at least two days) (APA, 2000).

In summary, assessment needs to consider how the abuse may have disrupted development (including attachment), how the trauma affected the individual, how the individual survived the trauma using both what might be termed psychological defenses (e.g., dissociation) and/or resiliency factors (e.g., intelligence) along with other factors of their psychosocial history (e.g., additional adversities—other traumas, poverty, racial discrimination, etc.), and current family and social support (Gil, 1996).

TREATMENT PLANNING

A treatment plan has several functions. First, it serves as a list of the individualized goals on which treatment will be focused in order to ameliorate the difficulties identified through the assessment process. Second, it can serve as a contract between the clinician and the client(s) so that each is aware of the others' responsibilities and tasks. Sometimes laypeople think therapy is something that is "done to" an individual, rather than as a process through which clients work, with guidance from a therapist, to help them overcome problems. The treatment plan can help clarify the therapy process. Third, it can help the clinician and the client(s) sort through and prioritize the most pressing concerns to give hope that the issues that bring someone to therapy are manageable and treatable. An excellent resource for help in articulating treatment goals in a behaviorally specific manner is Budrionis and Jongsma (2003), *The Sexual Abuse Victim and Sexual Offender Treatment Planner*. It is structured to mirror diagnoses that are based on the DSM-IV-TR (2000). Unfortunately, the volume lacks a focus on the work that is necessary with nonoffending caregivers. However, it does provide, especially for novice clinicians, useful verbiage, which is utilitarian and necessary in an environment where third party payments are of concern. Another, more generic volume, *The Child and Adolescent Psychotherapy Planner* (Jongsma, Peterson, & McInnis, 1996), is also useful.

TREATMENT

The Context of Treatment

Clinicians not only need to understand the context of individual clients, but they also need to appreciate the context of their own practice. Treatment for sexual abuse does not take place in a vacuum. Although the therapist's role is separate from that of a forensic investigator, the fact is that this type of treatment can have forensic implications. Adolescents who are sexually victimized may be part of a case that seeks to prosecute their offender through the criminal justice system. They may also be part of a civil case seeking to assure their protection through the child protection system. In addition, social workers providing clinical intervention work within a web of service providers that surrounds their clients. When we hear the term "juvenile justice," most of us think about the system that deals with juvenile offenders. Finkelhor, Cross, and Cantor (2005), however, describe a model for understanding this web through description of what they call the "Juvenile Victim Justice System." Finkelhor et al. (2005) graphically depict where victim services, including therapeutic services, fit into the overall web. Therapeutic services sit *between* the child protection and criminal justice systems, not really a part of either system, but simultaneously a part of both systems.

Engagement of Families

Even with adolescents who have more independence and resources than younger children, effective treatment depends on cooperative caregivers who agree to treatment, support and encourage treatment participation for their teen, and provide necessary transportation. In addition, a central consideration in providing treatment to adolescents affected by sexual abuse is the inclusion of nonoffending caregivers themselves in the treatment process. This issue of engagement is one of the most challenging aspects of the entire treatment process and deserves more attention than it currently gets. Often the families on the caseloads of social workers include those with more complex problem histories and comparatively fewer resources. McKay and Bannon (2004) reported in a review of research that examined treatment engagement strategies that both logistical and perceptual barriers interfered with both initial and ongoing engagement. Logistical barriers include insufficient time, transportation problems, and agency waiting lists. Perceptual barriers include parental expectations about the value of therapy, beliefs about the therapeutic process, and therapeutic relationship factors. McKay, in an earlier publication (McKay, Nudelman, McCadam, & Gonzales, 1996), described a social work intervention that research demonstrated increased engagement. The intervention included clarification of the helping process, the need to develop a collaborative relationship right from the initial contact with the family (training that included clerical staff was described), helping with concrete concerns on the part of the parents including crises and practical issues, and problem solving around barriers that could prevent attendance at treatment, such as transportation or cost of treatment. McKay and Bannon (2004) provided a very practical summary of these interventions along with the training that is necessary to implement them. Very striking results that are based on this and other similar interventions have been achieved (McKay & Bannon, 2004; McKay et al., 2004).

Therapeutic Alliance

No matter what approach to therapy one uses, all therapies begin with establishment of a solid therapeutic alliance. At the most basic level, the quality of the therapeutic relationship affects whether individuals stay in treatment (McKay & Bannon, 2004). Mannarino and Cohen (2006) in describing TF-CBT emphasized that a solid therapeutic relationship was a necessary basis for TF-CBT, acknowledging that though the existence of the relationship alone was not enough, a solid relationship was a necessary condition to pursuit of therapeutic change. Little research has specifically investigated therapeutic alliances between adolescents and their therapists (Martin, Romas, Medford, Leffert, & Hatcher, 2006), much less adolescents affected by sexual victimization. Building trust, the basis of the alliance, may be even more of a challenge with adolescents who have had their trust in other humans and in a safe world shattered by sexual trauma. In addition, adolescents are at a life stage when independence from adults is sought. Patience and genuineness are essential qualities. The use of therapeutic games and expressive therapies may be of particular use at this stage of treatment. There are many useful resources available, for example, Ollier and Hobday (2004). These authors offer a number of creative alternatives for building rapport, as well as other aspects of the therapeutic process.

Disclosure and Therapy

In many ways, therapy can be viewed as part of a potentially life-long disclosure process for a teen survivor. Public disclosure of sexual abuse is preceded by an internal awareness and acceptance that one has been victimized. Disclosure of the experience to another person may be done purposively or accidentally. Report of the incident(s) to authorities may or may not take place. When it does, it may feel as if "ownership" of the story has been taken from the teen (Staller & Nelson-Gardell, 2005). Investigation by public authorities and what the adolescent says during that process is customarily what is referred to when someone uses the term "disclosure." However, therapy itself is concerned with disclosure. A trusting relationship between the adolescent and the therapist is what enables the adolescent to face and process the trauma she or he has experienced. As part of every therapeutic approach of which this author is aware, there is some level of processing of the trauma itself. Victims of sexual abuse face the decision of who needs to know about their sexual victimization throughout their lives. They may need to decide whether (and when) they will tell intimate partners, especially since a history of victimization is often associated with sexual dysfunction (Loeb et al., 2002). They may need to decide whether to tell medical doctors; increased rates of physical ailments have been associated with a history of child sexual abuse (Felitti et al., 1998). They may face unresolved issues associated with developmental stages they have not yet reached, and they will need to decide to tell another mental health professional. Some may need to decide whether to tell their own children, since it is statistically certain that a percentage of adult survivors who have a family will themselves have to face the victimization of their own children. Treatment is concerned with disclosure and can help the teen resolve issues associated with past disclosure and prepare the individual for future disclosure.

Evidence-Supported Interventions for Sexual Abuse Trauma

This chapter began with comments about the state of our field regarding knowing what works. Currently there is a trend toward approaching practice from an "evidence-based practice" perspective. This approach had its origins in medicine and has been defined as "the integration of best research evidence with clinical expertise and patient values" (Sackett, Straus, Richardson, Rosenberg, & Haynes, 2000, p. 1). It is important to notice that "clinical expertise" and "patient values" are considered in this definition, along with "best research evidence." I would argue that, as social workers, we have an ethical responsibility to our clients to practice from an "evidence-based" perspective.

At the time of writing of this chapter, we had some of the most outstanding evidence available for the efficacy of TF-CBT for children and adolescents affected by sexual abuse (Berliner, 2005). This is some of the best quality evidence currently available for a psychosocial intervention in the field of child mental health for any type of problem. We actually have replicated "gold standard" evidence, the outcome of a series of randomized clinical trials, supporting the use of TF-CBT for sexually abused youth. Mannarino and Cohen (2006) reported that in their review across these studies, 80 percent of the youth got better. Moreover, research supported the efficacy of TF-CBT across diverse samples of children and adolescents with regard to race, ethnicity, gender, and socioeconomic class (Cohen, Deblinger, Mannarino, & Steer, 2004). Does this mean we know all we need to know about how to help sexually abused adolescents? Of course not. Nevertheless, given the level of evidence for TF-CBT, one should consider TF-CBT as a first-line intervention. Clinicians may react negatively to what they perceive as a cold "manualized" approach, devoid of "practice wisdom." I urge you to put aside any preconceived notions you may have about TF-CBT and investigate the approach. Mannarino and Cohen (2006) described TF-CBT as "not rigid, lock-step, inflexible," as many clinicians seem to assume. Like every other therapeutic intervention, it can only work with a solid therapeutic relationship. Within the various TF-CBT components, the implementation of many of the techniques that you, as a clinician, may already practice can be appropriate (e.g., activities drawn from Crisci, Lay, & Lowenstein, 1998, or from Hindman, 1991). The intervention is intended to be delivered to both adolescents (or children) and their caregivers using individual sessions and conjoint sessions. Clinicians use their professional training and expertise to adapt the model to the developmental level of their clients (Deblinger & Heflin, 1996). Clients experiencing *internalizing* symptoms of traumatic stress, including depression and anxiety along with others, respond best to this intervention. There are other empirically supported interventions for *externalizing* symptoms, for example, abuse-focused cognitive-behavioral therapy (Kolko & Swenson, 2002) and multisystemic therapy (Swenson, Henggler, Taylor, & Addison, 2005). Comorbid substance abuse problems have been successfully treated using TF-CBT (Cohen, Mannarino, Zhitova, & Capone, 2003). Goals of TF-CBT include teaching skills and changing cognitions with the knowledge that behavior change will follow, along with a processing of the sexual abuse and helping the youth and adolescent see how the experience fits into their lives rather than defining their lives (Berliner, 2006). Components of the model (Cohen et al., 2004) include the following:

1. Skills in expressing feelings
2. Training in coping skills
3. Recognizing the relationship between thoughts, feelings, and behaviors
4. Gradual exposure (also referred to as creating the child's trauma narrative)
5. Cognitive processing of the abuse experience(s)
6. Joint child-parent sessions
7. Psychoeducation about child sexual abuse and body safety
8. Parent management skills

Excellent resources for self-education on this approach include the TF-CBT Web (Medical University of South Carolina), Deblinger and Heflin's (1996) book, and another book, brand new at the time of the writing of this book chapter, *Treating Trauma and Traumatic Grief in*

Children and Adolescents by Cohen, Mannarino, and Deblinger (2006). In addition, training and updates on the model are available through the Web site for the National Child Traumatic Stress Network (http://www.nctsnet.org/nccts/nav.do?pid=hom_main).

There are, of course, many other types of interventions for trauma described in the literature, including eye movement desensitization and reprocessing (EMDR) and pharmacology. EMDR is a specialized technique that requires intensive training to implement. Saunders, Berliner, and Hanson (2004) regard it as a supportable and acceptable treatment. See Saunders et al. (2004) for a description of this technique (as well as other miscellaneous treatment approaches used with children affected by child abuse and neglect). In general, because of lack of research, the tendency to worry about the effects of psychotropic medication on developing brains, and family preferences for psychosocial over drug treatment for young people (Vitiello, 2006), pharmacological intervention for trauma has been limited (Cohen, Berliner, & Mannarino, 2003). There is some use of selective serotonin reuptake inhibitors (Donnelly, Amaya-Jackson, & March, 1999); however with the recent concern about the increase in suicidal behaviors associated with their use (Vitiello, 2006), there is reason for caution.

A discussion of treatment for adolescents would be incomplete without an acknowledgment of group interventions. Adolescents, because of their developmental stage, identify strongly with peer groups. A particular strength of group intervention is the opportunity for peer interaction with those who have shared a similar life-changing event. There is research evidence supporting efficacy of group interventions (Foy, Eriksson, & Trice, 2001; Reeker, Ensing, & Elliott, 1997; Thun, Sims, Adams, & Webb, 2002), although the evidence is not based on random clinical trials (the so-called "gold standard"). One might assume on the basis of the available evidence for group treatment efficacy combined with evidence for the efficacy of cognitive-behavioral interventions that a cognitive-behavioral group intervention would hold excellent promise and would enjoy at least an acceptable level of support.

Two additional resources that merit special mention include those that focus specifically on sexual abuse of males, although neither is specifically aimed to meet the therapeutic needs of adolescents. Both resources are theoretically based, but both lack specific research support for their efficacy. That does not mean they are not effective, it just means we do not have empirical support for their effectiveness. Friedrich's book *Psychotherapy with Sexually Abused Boys* (1995) was groundbreaking when it was published, employing a sophisticated integrated theoretical approach relying on attachment, disregulation, and self-theories. Friedrich (1995) described applications of his theoretically based intervention techniques across individual, group, and family therapy modalities. Spiegel (2003) described a model developed specifically for sexually abused boys on the basis of the practice and research of the author using an eclectic theoretical approach.

Documentation

The sophisticated clinician documents treatment with sexually abused youth; walking a fine line between enough detail and too much. Although not likely, it is possible, because of the forensic implications when working with sexually abused adolescents, that one's records could be subpoenaed. Details that the client thought would remain private could be disclosed in the public forum of a courtroom. At worst, details disclosed in therapy could potentially be used against the client's best interests if an offender's attorney presented them to a jury. Reamer (2005) wrote about the currently emerging view of documentation as part of risk management, in addition to the customary uses of assessment and planning, service delivery, continuity and coordination of services, supervision, service evaluation, and accountability. Standards he provided are particularly pertinent to apply to documenting the treatment with sexually abused adolescents in order to do everything possible to preserve the confidentiality and therefore the trust and confidence of the adolescent. This trust is basic to maintenance of the therapeutic relationship, and therefore essential to the therapy process.

BIBLIOTHERAPY RESOURCES

I would like to close this chapter on treatment of sexually abused adolescents by providing an annotated list of several books that can be used in a self-help fashion by adolescents themselves, or as an adjunct to the treatment process. The first three resources are what one might perceive as true "self-help" books (Angelica, 2002; Feuereisen, 2005; Mather & Debye, 2004). The next two are books that are meant to be used as adjunct to therapy (Carter, 2002; Munson & Riskin, 1995), and the final two are not focused specifically on sexual abuse, but are of particular help to those affected by traumatic stress (Davis, Eshelman, & McKay, 1995; Williams & Poijula, 2002).

We Are Not Alone: A Guidebook for Helping Professionals and Parents Supporting Adolescent Victims of Sexual Abuse by Jade Christine Angelica (2002). This volume provides a guide to the court system as it relates to child sexual abuse, the only book to do so for adolescents. It also includes sections that provide an insight into the issues of sexual abuse from the perspective of adolescent survivors, both male and female.

Invisible Girls: The Truth About Sexual Abuse—A Book for Teen Girls, Young Women, and Everyone Who Cares About Them by Patti Feuereisen with Caroline Pincus (2005). This volume covers a wide array of sexually abusive experiences including caregiver incest, sibling incest, sexual abuse by teachers or coaches, acquaintance and stranger rape. It relies on the stories of young women who have survived abuse.

How Long Does It Hurt? A Guide to Recovering from Incest and Sexual Abuse for Teenagers, Their Friends, and Their Families by Cynthia Mather with Kristina E. Debye (2004). The book's main audience is teenage girls. Explanations are offered of the phenomenon of sexual abuse, what it is like to tell, and how to move beyond the abuse. It describes the dynamics of the experience along with empowering teens through knowledge and encouragement.

It Happened to Me: A Teen's Guide to Overcoming Sexual Abuse by William Lee Carter (2002) and *In Their Own Words: A Sexual Abuse Workbook for Teenage Girls* by Lulie Munson and Karen Riskin (1995). Both of these publications are workbooks intended to accompany therapy sessions conducted by a professional. They provide structured reading and writing activities to help teens process the issues associated with sexual victimization.

The Relaxation and Stress Reduction Workbook Fourth Edition by Martha Davis, Elizabeth Eshelman, and Matthew McKay (1995) and *The PTSD Workbook* by Mary Beth Williams and Soili Poijula

(2002). Both these publications are intended for an adult audience, but are likely to be suitable for adolescents with reasonable reading abilities. Both are best used as supplemental to therapy with a professional. They deal respectively with basic relaxation techniques, and specialized knowledge for dealing with symptoms of PTSD.

CONCLUSION

This chapter could be likened to a window allowing a glimpse into a vast landscape of knowledge and the literature describing it. Areas to which practitioners need to pay special attention, because they are all in an active state of development with regard to knowledge expansion, include culture, gender, neurobiological effects, pharmacology, and research on additional approaches to treatment. TF-CBT had the best level of research support for efficacy with adolescents affected by sexual abuse at the time of writing of this chapter, but that should not be taken to imply that other types of treatment may not be useful. Readers are urged to watch for publication of research providing support for an ever-increasing array of interventions for sexually abused adolescents, especially approaches like Perry's (2006) neurosequential approach that relies on the latest research in the neurobiology of trauma and a sensitivity to developmental stages.

REFERENCES

Achenbach, T. (1991). *Manual for the Child Behavior Checklist/4-18 and 1991 profile.* Burlington: University of Vermont, Department of Psychiatry.

Ackerman, P., Newton, J., McPherson, W., Jones, J., & Dykman, R. (1998). Prevalence of post traumatic stress disorder and other psychiatric diagnoses in three groups of abused children (sexual, physical, and both). *Child Abuse & Neglect, 22*(8), 759-774.

American Psychiatric Association. (2000). *Diagnostic and statistical manual of mental disorders* (4th ed., Text Revision). Washington, DC: American Psychiatric Association.

Angelica, J. (2002). *We are not alone: A guidebook for helping professionals and parents supporting adolescent victims of sexual abuse.* Binghamton, NY: The Haworth Maltreatment and Trauma Press.

Barker, R. L. (2003). *Social work dictionary* (5th ed.). Washington, DC: NASW Press.

Berliner, L. (2005). The results of randomized clinical trails move the field forward. *Child Abuse & Neglect, 29,* 103-105.

Berliner, L. (2006, June). *When an EBI isn't available or isn't enough, then what?* Presentation at the 14th Annual Colloquium of the American Professional Society on the Abuse of Children, Nashville, TN.

Briere, J. (1996). *Trauma Symptom Checklist for Children (TSCC): Professional manual.* Lutz, FL: Psychological Assessment Resources.

Briere, J., & Scott, C. (2006). *Principles of trauma therapy: A guide to symptoms, evaluation, and treatment.* Thousand Oaks, CA: Sage Publications.

Brown, J., Cohen, P., Johnson, J., & Smailes, E. (1999). Childhood abuse and neglect: Specificity and effects on adolescent and young adult depression and suicidality. *Journal of the American Academy of Child & Adolescent Psychiatry, 38*(12), 1490-1496.

Brown, L., Houck, C., Hadley, W., & Lescano, C. (2005). Self-cutting and sexual risk among adolescents in intensive psychiatric treatment. *Psychiatric Services, 56*(2), 216-218.

Budrionis, R., & Jongsma, A. (2003). *The sexual abuse victim and sexual offender treatment planner.* Hoboken, NJ: John Wiley & Sons, Inc.

Carter, W. (2002). *It happened to me: A teen's guide to overcoming sexual abuse.* Oakland, CA: New Harbinger Publications.

Cicchetti, D., & Toth, S. (2005). Child maltreatment. *Annual Review of Clinical Psychology, 1*(1), 409-438.

Cohen, J. A., Deblinger, E., Mannarino, A. P., & Steer, R. A. (2004). A multisite, randomized controlled trial for children with sexual abuse-related PTSD symptoms. *Journal of the American Academy of Child & Adolescent Psychiatry, 43*(4), 393-402.

Cohen, J., Berliner, L., & Mannarino, A. (2003). Psychosocial and pharmacological interventions for child crime victims. *Journal of Traumatic Stress, 16*(2), 175-186.

Cohen, J., Mannarino, A., & Deblinger, E. (2006). *Treating trauma and traumatic grief in children and adolescents.* New York: Guilford.

Cohen, J., Mannarino, A., Zhitova, A., & Capone, M. (2003). Treating child abuse-related posttraumatic stress and comorbid substance abuse in adolescents. *Child Abuse & Neglect, 27,* 1345-1365.

Cook, A., Spinazzola, J., Ford, J., Lanktree, C., Blaustein, M., Cloitre, R., et al. (2005). Complex trauma in children and adolescents. *Psychiatric Annals, 35*(5), 390-398.

Crisci, G., Lay, M., & Lowenstein, L. (1998). *Paper dolls and paper airplanes: Therapeutic exercises for sexually traumatized children.* Indianapolis, IN: KIDSRIGHTS.

Dalgleish, T., Meiser-Stedman, R., & Smith, P. (2005). Cognitive aspects of post-traumatic stress reactions and their treatment in children and adolescents: An empirical review and some recommendations. *Behavioral and Cognitive Psychotherapy, 33,* 459-486.

Davis, M., Eshelman, E., & McKay, M. (1995). *The relaxation & stress reduction workbook* (4th ed.). Oakland, CA: New Harbinger Publications.

De Bellis, M., Broussard, E., Herring, D., Wexler, S., Moritz, G., & Benitez, J. (2001). Psychiatric co-morbidity in caregivers and children involved in maltreatment: A pilot research study with policy implications. *Child Abuse & Neglect, 25,* 923-944.

Deblinger, E., & Heflin, A. (1996). *Treating sexually abused children and their nonoffending families: A cognitive behavioral approach.* Thousand Oaks, CA: Sage Publications.

Deblinger, E., Mannarino, A. P., Cohen, J. A., & Steer, R. A. (2006). A follow-up study of a multisite, randomized, controlled trial for children with sexual abuse-related PTSD symptoms. *Journal of the American Academy of Child & Adolescent Psychiatry, 45*(12), 1474-1484.

Diseth, T. (2005). Dissociation in children and adolescents as reaction to trauma—An overview of conceptual issues and neurobiological factors. *Nordic Journal of Psychiatry, 59*(2), 79-91.

Diseth, T., & Christie, H. (2005). Trauma-related dissociative (conversion) disorders in children and adolescents—An overview of assessment tools and treatment principles. *Nordic Journal of Psychiatry, 59*(4), 278-292.

Donnelly, C., Amaya-Jackson, L., & March, J. (1999). Psychopharmacology of pediatric posttraumatic stress disorder. *Journal of Child and Adolescent Psychopharmacology, 9*(3), 203-220.

Dube, S., Anda, R., Felitti, V., Chapman, D., Williamson, D., & Giles, W. (2001). Childhood abuse, household dysfunction, and the risk of attempted suicide throughout the lifespan: Findings from the Adverse Childhood Experiences Study. *JAMA, 286,* 3089-3096.

Elliott, A., & Carnes, C. (2001). Reactions of nonoffending parents to the sexual abuse of their child: A review of the literature. *Child Maltreatment, 6*(4), 314-331.

Feiring, C., Taska, L., & Lewis, M. (1999). Age and gender differences in children's and adolescents' adaptation to sexual abuse. *Child Abuse & Neglect, 23*(2), 115-128.

Felitti, V., Anda, R., Nordenberg, D., Williamson, D., Spitz, A., Edwards, V., et al. (1998). Relationship of childhood abuse and household dysfunction to many of the leading causes of death in adults. *American Journal of Preventive Medicine, 14*(4), 245-258.

Feuereisen, P. (2005). *Invisible girls: The truth about sexual abuse—A book for teen girls, young women, and everyone who cares about them.* Emeryville, CA: Seal Press.

Finkelhor, D., & Browne, A. (1985). The traumatic impact of child sexual abuse: A conceptualization. *American Journal of Orthopsychiatry, 55,* 530-541.

Finkelhor, D., Cross, T. P., & Cantor, E. N. (2005). The justice system for juvenile victims: A comprehensive model of case flow. *Trauma, Violence, & Abuse, 6*(2), 83-102.

Fontes, A. (1995). *Sexual abuse in nine North American cultures: Treatment and prevention.* Thousand Oaks, CA: Sage.

Fontes, L. (2005). *Child abuse and culture: Working with diverse families.* New York: Guilford Press.

Ford, J. (2005). Treatment implications of altered affect regulation and information processing following child maltreatment. *Psychiatric Annals, 35*(5), 410-419.

Foy, D., Eriksson, C., & Trice, G. (2001). Introduction to group interventions for trauma survivors. *Group Dynamics: Theory, Research, and Practice, 5*(4), 246-251.

Friedrich, W. (1995). *Psychotherapy with sexually abused boys: An integrated approach.* Thousand Oaks, CA: Sage Publications.

Friedrich, W. (2002). *Psychological assessment of sexually abused children and their families.* Thousand Oaks, CA: Sage Publications.

Garnefski, N., & Diekstra, R. (1997). Child sexual abuse and emotional and behavioral problems in adolescence: Gender differences. *Journal of the American Academy of Child & Adolescent Psychiatry, 36*(3), 323-329.

Gil, E. (1996). *Treating abused adolescents.* New York: Guilford Press.

Gover, A. (2004). Childhood sexual abuse, gender, and depression among incarcerated youth. *International Journal of Offender Therapy and Comparative Criminology, 48*(6), 683-696.

Hall, G. (1904). *Adolescence.* Englewood Cliffs, NJ: Prentice Hall.

Harrison, P., Fulkerson, J., & Beebe, T. (1997). Multiple substance use among adolescent physical and sexual abuse victims. *Child Abuse & Neglect, 21*(6), 529-539.

Hecht, D., Chaffin, M., Bonner, B., Worley, K., & Lawson, L. (2002). Treating sexually abused adolescents. In J. Myers, L. Berliner, C. Hendrix, C. Jenny, & T. Reid (Eds.), *The APSAC handbook of child maltreatment* (pp. 159-174). Thousand Oaks, CA: Sage.

Hindman, J. (1991). *The mourning breaks: 101 proactive treatment strategies breaking the bonds of trauma for victims of sexual abuse.* Ontario, OR: Alexandria Associates.

Hughes, L. (2001). *Paving pathways: Child and adolescent development.* Belmont, CA: Wadsworth Publishing.

Jones, D., Trudinger, P., & Crawford, M. (2004). Intelligence and achievement of children referred following sexual abuse. *Journal of Paediatric Child Health, 40,* 455-460.

Jongsma, A., Peterson, L., & McInnis, W. (1996). *The child and adolescent psychotherapy treatment planner.* New York: John Wiley & Sons, Inc.

Kaminer, D., Seedat, S., Lockhat, R., & Stein, D. (2000). Violent trauma among child and adolescent girls: Current knowledge and implications for clinicians. *International Clinical Psychopharmacology, 15,* S51-S59.

Kendall-Tackett, K., Williams, L., & Finkelhor, D. (1993). Impact of sexual abuse on children: A review and synthesis of recent empirical studies. *Psychological Bulletin, 113*(1), 164-180.

Kolko, D., & Swenson, C. (2002). *Assessing and treating physically abused children and their families.* Thousand Oaks, CA: Sage Publications.

Lipschitz, F., Winegar, R., Hartnick, E., Foote, B., & Southwick, S. (1999). Posttraumatic stress disorder in hospitalized adolescents: Psychiatric comorbidity and clinical correlates. *Journal of the Academy of Child & Adolescent Psychiatry, 38*(4), 385-392.

Loeb, T., Williams, J., Carmona, J., Rivkin, I., Wyatt, G., Chin, D., et al. (2002). Child sexual abuse: Associations with the sexual functioning of adolescents and adults. *Annual Review of Sex Research, 13,* 307-345.

Mannarino, A., & Cohen, J. (2001). Treating sexually abused children and their families: Identifying and avoiding professional role conflicts. *Trauma, Violence, & Abuse, 2*(4), 331-342.

Mannarino, A., & Cohen, J. (2006, June). *Trauma-focused cognitive behavioral treatment for traumatized children and their families.* Presentation at the 14th annual colloquium of the American Professional Society on the Abuse of Children, Nashville, TN.

Martin, J., Romas, M., Medford, M., Leffert, N., & Hatcher, S. (2006). Adult helping qualities preferred by adolescents. *Adolescence, 41,* 127-140.

Mather, C., & Debye, K. (2004). *How long does it hurt? A guide to recovering from incest and sexual abuse for teenagers, their friends, and their families.* San Francisco: Jossey-Bass.

McKay, M., & Bannon, W. (2004). Engaging families in child mental health services. *Child and Adolescent Psychiatric Clinics of North America, 13,* 905-921.

McKay, M., Hibbert, R., Hoagwood, K., Rodriguez, J., Murray, L., Legerski, J., et al. (2004). Integrating evidence-based engagement interventions into "real world" child mental health settings. *Brief Treatment and Intervention, 4*(2), 177-186.

McKay, M., Nudelman, R., McCadam, K., & Gonzales, J. (1996). Evaluating a social work engagement approach to involving inner-city children and their families in mental health care. *Research on Social Work Practice, 6*(4), 462-472.

Medical University of South Carolina (2005). *TF-CBT Web: A Web-based learning course for trauma-focused cognitive-behavioral therapy.* Retrieved July 10, 2006 from http://tfcbt.musc.edu/.

Munson, L., & Riskin, K. (1995). *In their own words: A sexual abuse workbook for teen girls.* Washington, DC: Child Welfare League of America.

National Child Traumatic Stress Network (2006). *National child traumatic stress network.* Retrieved July 10, 2006 from http://www.nctsnet.org/nccts/nav.do?pid=hom_main.

Nelson-Gardell, D. (2001). The voices of victims: Surviving child sexual abuse. *Child and Adolescent Social Work Journal, 18,* 401-416.

Novak, G., & Peláez, M. (2004). *Child and adolescent development: A behavioral systems approach.* Thousand Oaks, CA: Sage Publications.

Ohan, J., Myers, K., & Collett, B. (2002). Ten-year review of rating scales. IV: Scales assessing trauma and its effects (Research Update Review). *Journal of the American Academy of Child & Adolescent Psychiatry, 41,* 1401-1422.

Ollier, K., & Hobday, A. (2004). *Creative therapy: Adolescents overcoming sexual abuse.* Camberwell, Melbourne: ACER Press.

Paolucci, E., Genius, M., & Violato, C. (2001). A meta-analysis of the published research on the effects of child sexual abuse. *The Journal of Psychology, 135*(1), 17-36.

Paul, G. (1967). Strategy of outcome research in psychotherapy. *Journal of Consulting Psychology, 31*(2), 109-118.

Perry, B. (2006). Applying principles of neurodevelopment to clinical work with maltreated and traumatized children. In N. Webb (Ed.), *Working with traumatized youth in child welfare* (pp. 27-52). New York: Guilford Press.

Perry, B., Pollard, R., Blakley, T., Baker, W., & Vigilante, D. (1995). Childhood trauma, the neurobiology of adaptation, and "Use-dependent" development of the brain: How "states" become "traits." *Infant Mental Health Journal, 16*(4), 271-291.

Pillay, A., & Schoubben-Hesk, S. (2001). Depression, anxiety, and hopelessness in sexually abused adolescent girls. *Psychological Reports, 88*(3), 727-733.

Reamer, F. (2005). Documentation in social work: Evolving ethical and risk-management standards. *Social Work, 50*(4), 325-334.

Reeker, J., Ensing, D., & Elliott, R. (1997). A meta-analytic investigation of group treatment outcomes for sexually abused children. *Child Abuse & Neglect, 21*(7), 669-680.

Romano, E., Zoccolillo, M., & Paquette, D. (2006). Histories of child maltreatment and psychiatric disorder in pregnant adolescents. *Journal of the American Academy of Child & Adolescent Psychiatry, 45*(3), 329-336.

Sackett, D., Straus, S., Richardson, W., Rosenberg, W., & Haynes, B. (2000). *Evidence-based medicine: How to practice and teach EBM.* Philadelphia, PA: Churchill Livingstone.

Saunders, B., Berliner, L., & Hanson, R. (Eds.). (2004). *Child physical and sexual abuse: Guidelines for treatment (Revised Report, April 26, 2004).* Charleston, SC: National Crime Victims Research and Treatment Center.

Saunders, B., Williams, L., Hanson, R., & Smith, D. (2003a). *Clinical assessment interview for children.* Charleston, SC: Authors.

Saunders, B., Williams, L., Hanson, R., & Smith, D. (2003b). *Event history interview for children.* Charleston, SC: Authors.

Sawyer, G., Tsao, E., Hansen, D., & Flood, M. (2006). Weekly problem scales: Instruments for sexually abused youth and their nonoffending parents in treatment. *Child Maltreatment, 11*(1), 34-48.

Saywitz, I. K., Mannarino, A., Berliner, L., & Cohen, J. (2000). Treatment for sexually abused children and adolescents. *American Psychologist, 55*(9), 1040-1049.

Snyder, H. (2000). *Sexual assault of young children as reported to law enforcement: Victim, incident, and offender characteristics: A statistical report using data from the National Incident-Based Reporting System (NCJ 182990).* Washington, DC: U.S. Department of Justice Office of Justice Programs.

Spaccarelli, S. (1995). Resilience criteria and factors associated with resilience in sexually abused girls. *Child Abuse & Neglect, 19*(9), 1171-1182.

Spiegel, J. (2003). *Sexual abuse of males: The SAM model of theory and practice.* New York: Brunner-Routledge.

Staller, K., & Nelson-Gardell, D. (2005). "A burden in your heart": Lessons of disclosure from female preadolescent and adolescent survivors of sexual abuse. *Child Abuse & Neglect, 29,* 1415-1432.

Stirling, J. (2006, June). *Reframing abuse: New directions for child protection.* Presentation at the 14th annual colloquium of the American Professional Society on the Abuse of Children, Nashville, TN.

Strand, V., Sarmiento, T., & Pasquale, L. (2005). Assessment and screening tools for trauma in adolescents: A review. *Trauma, Violence, and Abuse, 6*(1), 55-78.

Stuewig, J., & McCloskey, L. (2005). *Child Maltreatment: Journal of the American Professional Society on the Abuse of Children, 10*(4), 324-336.

Swenson, C., Henggler, S., Taylor, I., & Addison, O. (2005). *Multisystemic therapy and neighborhood partnerships: Reducing adolescent violence and substance abuse.* New York: Guilford.

Thun, D., Sims, P., Adams, M., & Webb, T. (2002). Effects of group therapy on female adolescent survivors of sexual abuse: A pilot study. *Journal of Child Sexual Abuse, 11*(4), 1-16.

Turner, H., Finkelhor, D., & Ormrod, R. (2006). The effect of lifetime victimization on the mental health of children and adolescents. *Social Science & Medicine, 62, 13-27.*

Vitiello, B. (2006). Research in child and adolescent psychopharmacology: Recent accomplishments and new challenges, *Psychopharmacology,* January 2006, pp. 1-9, DOI 10.1007/s00213-006-0414-3, URL http://dx.doi.org/10.1007/s00213-006-0414-3.

Walker, J., Carey, P., Mohr, N., Stein, D., & Seedat, S. (2004). Gender differences in the prevalence of childhood sexual abuse and the development of pediatric PTSD. *Archives of Women's Mental Health, 7,* 111-121.

Walsh, D. (2004). *Why do they act that way? A survival guide to the adolescent brain for you and your teen.* New York: Free Press.

Weisz, J., Weiss, B., Hann, S., Granger, D., & Morton, T. (1995). Effects of psycho-therapy with children and adolescents revisited: A meta-analysis of treatment outcome studies. *Psychological Bulletin, 117*(3), 450-468.

Williams, M., & Poijula, S. (2002). *The PTSD workbook.* Oakland, CA: New Harbinger Publications.

Ziegler, D. (2002). *Traumatic experience and the brain.* Phoenix, AZ: Acacia Publishing, Inc.

Chapter 9

Treatment for the Nonoffending Caregiver

Ramona Alaggia
Theresa Knott

INTRODUCTION

A substantial body of evidence indicating that parental support is positively and significantly related to a child's post–sexual abuse functioning (Elliot & Carnes, 2001; Everson, Hunter, Runyan, Edelsohn, & Coulter, 1989) continues to grow. For example, numerous studies have pointed to positive maternal support as critical to mediating the negative effects of child sexual abuse (CSA) (Conte & Schuerman, 1987; Corcoran, 2004; Deblinger, Steer, & Lippmann, 1999; Everson et al., 1989; Heriot, 1996). Spaccarelli (1994) summarized that

> a warm and supportive relationship with a nonoffending parent may protect children from risks associated with abuse by minimizing perceptions of threat associated with the abuse (e.g., loss of family relationships) and by fostering the use of active or emotionally expressive coping strategies. (p. 357)

And, although the literature in this area often refers to parental support, most of the studies conducted report samples in which the vast majority of participants in the parent treatment condition are mothers. Although the authors of this chapter alternately refer to parental, maternal, and caregiver treatment, we recognize that these treatments most often involve participation of the nonoffending mothers of sexually abused children.

Handbook of Social Work in Child and Adolescent Sexual Abuse
© 2008 by The Haworth Press, Taylor & Francis Group. All rights reserved.
doi:10.1300/5804_09   *203*

Sexual abuse influences the psychological, emotional, sexual, cognitive, physical, familial, and academic aspects of a child's life in addition to the developmental life course, often arresting or accelerating various stages, resulting in mental health issues and the need for treatment (Beitchman et al., 1992; Beitchman, Zucker, Hood, DaCosta, & Akman, 1991; Fergusson, Lynsky, & Horwood, 1996; Mian, Marton, & LeBaron, 1996; Tyler, 2002). For those children and adolescents who do develop symptoms these may have long-term negative implications when those who require treatment for problems associated with the sexual trauma do not successfully enter or fail to complete treatment, thus facing increased risk for mental health impairment as adults. When parents support their child's treatment, and are involved in it, children are more likely to successfully enter and complete their therapy that presumably reduces the likelihood of them developing long-term problems (Haskett, Nowlan, Hutcheson, & Whitworth, 1991; Tingus, Heger, Foy, & Leskin, 1996).

NONOFFENDING CAREGIVER TREATMENT ISSUES

Nonoffending caregiver treatment is usually conducted either in parallel groups (one for the caregivers and one for the children) or in individual conjoint sessions (parent-child treatment). At the heart of these approaches is the notion that nonoffending parents and their victimized children will benefit in the short and long term by participation in family-centered treatment (Corcoran, 2004). Parent intervention is recommended for a number of reasons. First is to ensure or secure support for the child victim. Though some children receive adequate support from mothers in the aftermath of CSA, others do not. Studies attempting to pinpoint the degree of maternal support, offered on disclosure, reported wide variability, with between 27 and 80 percent of mothers being supportive of their sexually abused children (Arata, 1998; Faller, 1988; Salt, Myer, Coleman, & Sauzier, 1990; Sirles & Franke, 1989). Most recently, Bolen and Lamb (2004), in their summary of existing reviews, concluded that 25 percent of nonperpetrating caregivers are not supportive, 31 percent are partially supportive or ambivalent, while 44 percent fully supported their victimized child. Pintello and Zuravin (2001) also captured rates of maternal ambivalence and concluded that, among their sample of 437 nonperpetrating mothers, 41.8 percent believed and protected their child, 27.3 percent responded in an ambivalent manner, while 30.8 percent did not believe their children's disclosure and were unable to demonstrate a consistent protective response. In the most serious cases, inadequate maternal support has been associated with child welfare involvement and apprehension of victimized children (Cross, Martell, McDonald, & Ahl, 1999; Leifer, Shapiro, & Kassem, 1993; Pellegrin & Wagner, 1990).

A further rationale for parental intervention is that parents can suffer secondary trauma when their children are abused, making interventions necessary to reduce their distress. In recognition that CSA has an impact on some, work has been done on the effect of parental distress and the ability to cope following disclosure of extrafamilial abuse, but it remains an understudied area. This research suggests that parents of sexually abused children experience significant levels of distress that may manifest as eating and sleeping disorders, tension headaches, anxiety, fatigue, emotional responses of guilt, intrusive thoughts, and ambivalent feelings toward the child (Regehr, 1990). Davies (1995) also found that a significant number of these parents experienced marital stress, preoccupation about their child's sexual development, conflict with their adolescent children, overprotectiveness of their younger children, mistrust of adults, anger toward the perpetrator, and isolation due to loss of friends and family as a consequence of charging the perpetrator. Isolation, general lack of support by service providers, and systems intervention trauma once investigations are completed have also been cited by parents as consequences (Henry, 1994; Rivera, 1988).

Other research reveals that mothers of sexually abused children are more likely to have been sexually abused in their own childhood when compared with mothers of non–sexually abused children (Oates, Tebbutt, Swanston, Lynch, & O'Toole, 1998). As a result, disclosure of their child's CSA is likely to have a profound effect on mothers' parenting practices and parental self-confidence—a fact that has been confirmed through empirical data (Cole, Woolger, Power, & Smith, 1992). However, the level of vicarious trauma experienced by nonperpetrating mothers is unknown.

Secondary or vicarious trauma refers to the manifestation of traumatic symptoms by persons in close contact with a victim of abuse.

Women with a trauma history may be easily "triggered" by their child's disclosure of sexual abuse as a result of their own traumatic histories. For example, mothers who report their own history of CSA occurring at a similar age at which their child has experienced abuse may experience flashbacks, or intrusive thoughts. This process occurs as mothers recognize the vulnerability in their own children and relate this vulnerability to their own experiences of sexual abuse at a similar age. The awareness of the vulnerability of their own child and recollection of their abusive experience may lead to reexperiencing their traumatic event(s).

Cumulative trauma not only refers to mothers' own experiences of CSA, but subsequent trauma in later years, such as intimate partner violence. The available literature suggests that a disproportionate number of families for whom CSA is suspected or substantiated also experience intimate partner violence (Alaggia & Turton, 2005; Bell, 2002; Bowen, 2000; Hiebert-Murphy, 2001; Kellogg & Menard, 2003; Ray, Jackson, & Townsley, 1991). Kellogg and Menard (2003) document that, among 164 cases reviewed by these authors, 58 percent of perpetrators of CSA were also physically violent toward their partners. Given our understanding that 31 percent of women report abuse at some point in their lifetime, it makes sense that cumulative trauma may influence a mother's response to the disclosure of CSA (U.S. Department of Health and Human Services, 2001).

On the basis of this growing evidence, it is imperative to address caregiver issues in treatment in order to increase positive parental support to children through psychoeducational approaches and also to decrease parental distress by normalizing their responses (Winton, 1990) and using cognitive-behavioral therapy (CBT) for symptoms they may experience (Cohen & Mannarino, 1998b, 1996b; Deblinger, McLeer, & Henry, 1990; Deblinger, Stauffer, & Steer, 2001; Stauffer & Deblinger, 1996).

TREATMENT MODELS WITH NONOFFENDING CAREGIVERS

Devastating acts of sexual abuse perpetrated on children remain an unfortunate reality in North American society. Some estimates calculate prevalence rates of CSA in North America at 40 percent

(Bolen & Scannapieco, 1999; Finkelhor, 1994; Polusny & Follette, 1995). Once perpetrated, these acts cannot be undone. However, parental support is one area where an intervention can make a difference. Generally, the parental components are aimed at increasing positive parental support, helping parents support their children's treatment, providing parents with information about what their child may be experiencing (symptoms and behaviors), teaching parenting skills and strategies for recognizing and responding to problematic behaviors and symptoms, and reducing parental secondary trauma and distress.

Theoretical Frameworks

Theoretical orientations for the various treatment approaches in working with the parents of sexually abused children range from non-specific, supportive therapy, to parent skills training and psycho-education, to specific cognitive-behavioral approaches. Often there is an integration of several theoretical applications in these treatments. A less clearly articulated but critical theoretical framework for advancing parent involved treatment rests on systemic family and ecological theories. In child and family treatments, treating one part of the system in the absence of supporting and treating the whole family system will eventually give rise to symptom reoccurrence (Grunebaum, 1988; Hoffman, 1981; Nichols, 2001). In the worst case scenario, the child victim is vulnerable to being scapegoated, especially when problematic symptoms and behaviors disrupt family functioning, potentially creating a destructive dynamic of victim blaming. From an ecological perspective, the importance of including systems significant to the child victim's daily life activities and day-to-day family functioning is emphasized as important in ameliorating the negative effects of CSA. Within an ecological approach, the clinical treatment of child victims and nonoffending caregivers is ideally accompanied by school involvement (at least from the point of sharing information), court support and preparation, other relevant professional support as required such as health care services, and relevant community involvement such as cultural, ethnic, and faith-based support. It is within this broader framework of interrelated systems and the ecology of family life that child-focused treatment occurs with parental involvement (Jack, 2000; Stormshak & Dishion, 2002).

Earlier treatment models relied on nondirective, support-based interventions utilizing reflective listening, empathy, supportive statements, and some parent training (Winton, 1990). Children, through this approach, usually received nondirective play therapy conjointly with their parents' treatment. Eventually, approaches evolved to include specific parent skills training to help parents improve problematic child behavior (Cohen & Mannarino, 1997; Webster-Stratton & Hammond, 1997). As well, psychoeducational interventions have been introduced with the aim of helping parents understand the impact of sexual abuse on their children (symptoms and behaviors), the perpetrators role, and their own reactions as parents (Corcoran, 2004).

One of the more directive approaches for nonoffending parents is the well-established CBT. In light of the growing knowledge base on post-traumatic stress disorder (PTSD) and its related symptoms, the impact on sexually victimized children and the secondary effects that are often felt by those close to the traumatized child, such as the parents, CBT has recently been strongly recommended for both parents and victims. CBT models that employ reframing, positive imagery, attribution retraining, and cognitive coping skills with parents while their children receive CBT conjointly have emerged as one of the most effective treatments (Cohen & Mannarino, 1998b, 1996b; Deblinger et al., 1990, 2001; Stauffer & Deblinger, 1996). This approach is also often combined with parent skills training, which teaches parents to track child behaviors, positively reinforce prosocial actions, and appropriately punish problematic conduct (Cohen & Mannarino, 1996a, 1996b; Webster-Stratton & Hammond, 1997).

Developmental theory suggests that treatment needs will vary at different developmental levels, and interventions should be appropriately targeted to these various stages. The age of onset and duration of sexual abuse determines manifest symptoms and behaviors. Most treatment approaches are developed in three groupings with specific developmental constructs in mind: preschool-aged children (ages two to five); school-aged children (ages six to twelve), and adolescents (ages thirteen to eighteen). For example, sexually abused preschool children show a higher preponderance of sexualized and sexually inappropriate behavior, and are more vulnerable to revictimization (Cohen & Mannarino, 1996a,b; Wolfe & Birt, 1995). These younger children are more likely to be believed by their mothers, and their problematic behavior can be more readily influenced by their parents through skills training (Serketich & Dumas, 1996; Sirles & Franke, 1989).

School-aged children can be expected to experience more issues in their social sphere because of their increased awareness of the implications of the abuse. Being stigmatized is often a significant treatment area. An additional profound condition, for both school-aged and adolescent victims, is being "believed." Increasing parental awareness around these issues in addition to any identified ambivalence is essential to enhance and maintain a supportive system (Heriot, 1996).

Developmentally, adolescents have increased abilities to engage in therapeutic interventions and benefit from treatment (Durlak, Fuhrman, & Lampman, 1991). At the same time, sexually abused adolescents are the most vulnerable group for not receiving maternal belief or support, yet this support is just as important at this stage as with any other developmental stage (Heriot, 1996; Sirles & Franke, 1989). Parental support, especially maternal support if the perpetrator is the mother's intimate partner, has been found to be the strongest mediator of negative effects in adolescents, thus caregiver involvement in treatment is an extremely important component. Adolescents are also more prone to using avoidance strategies in dealing with the trauma by acting out or running away; thus parental support is most important in treatment (Johnson & Kenkel, 1991; Shapiro & Levendosky, 1999; Spaccarelli, 1994).

Finally, although the construct of support is frequently used when referring to family-based CSA treatment models, there is lack of clarity in defining support (Alaggia, 2002). Social support, especially parental support, and its relationship to well-being is rooted in a well-established literature and is an important element of ecological approaches to practice (Beeman, 1997; Hiebert-Murphy, 1998). Yet, the terms maternal *reaction, response,* and *support* are frequently used interchangeably and most often only refers to support by mothers. Definitions of support in relation to CSA are also referred to mostly in relation to response to disclosure—belief of child, emotional support, and action taken toward the perpetrator (Alaggia, 2002; Everson et al., 1989; Heriot, 1996; Sirles & Franke, 1989)—but are less adequately defined in the treatment context.

Treatment Models and Outcomes

The two most rigorously evaluated models of treatment that include nonoffending caregivers have been developed by Cohen and Mannarino (1996a) and Deblinger et al. (1990, 2001). Both are CBT focused but are delivered in slightly different ways. Cohen and Mannarino (1996a) have developed a protocol of twelve sessions for individual families involving both parent and child. Parents are given a CBT curriculum to address supportiveness, ambivalence toward the perpetrator, attributions of fault and responsibility, legal issues, and their histories of abuse if relevant. This model employs reframing, attribution retraining, cognitive coping strategies, and parent skills training.

Deblinger and her colleagues (1990, 2001) have developed eight-session cognitive-behavioral groups for parents and children who attend separately, although they implement weekly fifteen-minute parent-child activities (Deblinger et al., 1990, 2001). Both models have been implemented with preschool-aged children and school-aged children, and close to one dozen studies using an experimental or quasi-experimental design has been conducted. Though results are promising, these studies have been plagued by small samples due to high dropout rates, lack of "no treatment" control groups, and the fact that child and parent treatments are often confounded (see Corcoran, 2004, for full review of outcome studies).

Specifically, research utilizing CBT as an intervention modality has demonstrated efficacy in mitigating symptom distress among children who have experienced CSA and their nonperpetrating caregivers. When compared with supportive therapies, CBT treatment is associated with improvements in the behavioral and affective responses of children and families. Among these improvements have been reductions in children's PTSD symptoms (Deblinger et al., 1990; King et al., 2000), decreased externalizing behaviors (Cohen & Mannarino, 1996a; Deblinger et al., 1990; Deblinger, Lippmann, & Steer, 1996), improvements in children's social competence (Cohen & Mannarino, 1998b), and reductions in depressive symptomology among victimized children (Cohen & Mannarino, 1998b; Deblinger et al., 1990, 1996). CBT interventions contribute to improvement in parenting practices and postdisclosure adjustment of nonperpetrating caregivers

(Stauffer & Deblinger, 1996), as well as reduction in the negative emotional reactions of parents (Deblinger et al., 2001). Several studies have demonstrated that improvements attributed to CBT treatment were maintained at follow-up intervals of two years and three months, respectively (Deblinger et al., 1999; Stauffer & Deblinger, 1996). In examining the varied responses of victimized children and families, CBT treatment has been identified as the strongest predictor of improved outcome (Cohen & Mannarino, 1998b).

In another approach Celano, Hazzard, Webb, and McCall (1996) use Finkelhor and Browne's (1985) traumagenic factor model to guide intervention. Of note, this intervention involved exposure to an educational videotape at the time of CSA investigation. Parents exposed to treatment incorporating this theoretical framework report feeling more optimistic about their children's future, demonstrate increased support to their victimized child, and report less self-blame when compared with parents who receive treatment as usual. Jinich and Litrownik (1999) similarly report that parents demonstrate increased emotional support subsequent to intervention. In this case, however, intervention occurred at the time of CSA investigation and involved exposure to an educational videotape.

Despite these stated gains for various treatment approaches, paradoxical effects of CBT and supportive therapy have also been noted. Winton (1990), who used an open-ended support group for twenty-seven nonoffending parents, reported that supportive group intervention did not contribute to improved management of stress levels. Cohen and Mannarino (1996a) indicate that CBT and treatment-as-usual both resulted in improvements in children's self-report of social competence. King and colleagues (2000) indicate that CBT treatment with a focus on mitigating PTSD symptoms need not involve nonoffending parents. In fact, these authors demonstrate that parent involvement in CBT treatment failed to offer any additional gains over individual intervention among a group of thirty-six preschool children.

It is important to point out the methodological shortcomings of this body of research. These include the continued use of small sample sizes (often fewer than sixty subjects), absence of randomization to treatment conditions, lack of follow-up assessments, high attrition rates (often 50 percent dropout), and confounding of parent and child treatment conditions (Corcoran, 2004). Bearing these methodological limitations in mind, the overall view is that participation in CSA-focused treatment improves outcomes for child victims and their nonoffending parents with CBT intervention being viewed as superior to supportive treatments. Although supportive approaches contribute to some improvement in the functioning of preschool- and school-aged children and their nonperpetrating parents, cognitive-behavioral models generated more favorable results overall.

THE ROLE OF ATTACHMENT

Attachment patterns between the child, nonoffending parent, and with the perpetrator play a central role in the aftermath of disclosure. Attachment theory provides an important conceptual framework for understanding relational issues in the child victim, as well as relational issues for adults in their role as parents. The importance of attachment history and experiences in predicting subsequent social learning and adaptation has been empirically established (Ainsworth, Blehar, Waters, & Wall, 1978; Main, Kaplan, & Cassidy, 1985; Sroufe, 1988). Patterns of attachment are not limited to understanding the early socialization of the infant and are useful in understanding social experiences throughout the life span, and are especially relevant when trauma has occurred.

These notions are particularly relevant when applied to children and adolescents recovering from sexual victimization. Alexander (1992) posited that the degree or type of attachment experienced by people through all stages of the life cycle has significant bearing on the short- and long-term effects of sexual abuse. At the same time, the severity of long-term effects of sexual abuse may be mediated by the support received by the nonabusive parent (Everson et al., 1989; Spaccarelli, 1994). Insecure and fearful attachment has consistently been found to be present in children who have been sexually abused, physically abused, or neglected (Alexander et al., 1998; Carlson, Cicchetti, Barnett, & Braunwald, 1989; Egeland & Sroufe, 1981), thus making assessment of the parent-child relationship in terms of attachment patterns with the nonoffending parent(s) and perpetrator all the more critical in determining targets for intervention.

Attachment patterns of the nonoffending parent impact on caregiver response, and the nature of attachment can put both the victimized child and parent at risk of social isolation. Attachment patterns, particularly insecure attachments, are known to have a bearing on a wide range of dysfunction (Belsky & Nezworsky, 1988). Of notable concern, the nonabusive parent may lack the internal resources to provide supportive responses to their sexually abused child without intervention. For example, parents who are survivors of CSA themselves can be affected in three major areas of functioning: interpersonal relationships, affect regulation, and disturbance of self. This is important to take note of with regard to parenting given that these effects may enter into attachment formation with their children, and will presumably affect their ability to deal with the aftermath of CSA disclosure. An attachment perspective predicts that parents who have experienced insecure attachment as children may manifest with anxiety and distortions in their relationships with their children (Alexander, 1992). Earlier clinical accounts of mothers with an incest history report difficulty in numerous areas of maternal functioning. Difficulties in organizing routines, providing affection and reasonable discipline, inability to derive satisfaction from their maternal role, heightened sense of responsibility, hypervigilance, and an inability to use support systems have been observed (Gelinas, 1983, 1986; Herman & Hirschman, 1981). Of course, not all mothers have a history of abuse and this should be kept in mind, but if they report CSA, or other childhood trauma, these factors should also be considered.

More recent studies examining attachment in cases of CSA now exist; however, results of attachment studies involving childhood trauma such as sexual victimization are in preliminary phases and sometimes have produced contradictory findings. Leifer, Kilbane, and Skolnick (2002) found that children of insecurely attached mothers demonstrated more frequent internalizing and externalizing behavior problems when compared with children of mothers who were securely attached. Interestingly, the mother's adult attachment style did not significantly differ between CSA and non-CSA dyads. As such, this study failed to demonstrate any significant difference in attachment style between mothers of sexually abused children and mothers of non– sexually abused children. In addition, children's perception of maternal support was not associated with the mother's attachment style. In a related study, Leifer, Kilbane, and Grossman (2001) examined attachment as an intergenerational factor affecting current maternal response patterns. Contrary to Leifer and colleagues' (2002) study, Leifer et al. (2001) indicate that disruptions in the mother's attachment style (due to historical attachment relationships) had a negative effect on her child's perception of maternal support. In addition, Lewin and Bergin (2001) report that mothers of sexually abused children demonstrate diminished levels of attachment when compared with mothers of non–sexually abused children. This group, however, included mothers for whom heightened anxiety and depression are also noted.

In examining the relationship between attachment style and coping strategies of victimized adolescents, Shapiro and Levendosky (1999) conclude that diminished attachment negatively affects coping style evidenced in the more frequent use of avoidant coping among insecurely attached victims. Some of these contrary findings might be explained by resilience factors as mentioned previously, when applied to the parents and their reactions to childhood hardships.

Additional issues for sexually abused children in their attachment experience occur as the result of the relationship to their perpetrator. First, if the perpetrator was the mother's partner he may have actively interfered in the child's relationship with the nonoffending parent. This could occur through the grooming process, by creating distortions about the nonoffending parent's role in the abuse, and distortions about the impact of disclosure and negative responses. Depending at what age these distortions get introduced and the duration of the abuse before disclosure or discovery, serious damage can occur in the relationship between the child victim and mother thus directing the degree of reparative work that needs to be done.

Second, traumatic bonding to the perpetrator may cause confusion for child victims. Clinicians have documented trauma bonding between victims and offenders as a disturbing and confusing dynamic that can complicate therapeutic work (Dutton & Painter, 1993; Gelinas, 1986; Herman, 1983, 1992, 1997; Hindman, 1989; Sgroi, 1982). Stated simply, despite the exploitative aspect of the sexual abuse relationship, it is common for child victims to want to remain connected and to have contact with their perpetrator, especially since this is oftentimes a significant person in their life. The concept of traumatic bonding is based on research that uses the Stockholm syndrome to understand the captive-captor relationship (Graham, Rawlings, &

Rimini, 1988; Symonds, 1982). In situations in which a victim is held hostage by a perpetrator, certain psychological mechanisms, motivated primarily by the victim's need to survive, emerge in response to being in captivity. Though the abusive relationship evokes betrayal and powerlessness in the child victim, other developmental issues are subject to cognitive distortions. Moral development is affected, confusion around sexualization and affection can occur, and active undermining of the child's relationship with the nonoffending parent by the perpetrator can potentially result in traumatic bonding between the offending parent and child victim. Therapeutically induced separation of the offender from the child victim has been known to initially exacerbate the child's longing to be with this significant person.

Attachment and Implications for Practice

The implications of attachment should be explored within the clinical context in three ways:

1. The parent-child relationship with the nonoffending mother before the disclosure or discovery of sexual abuse, and post-disclosure response including level of support.
2. The nonoffending mother's attachment history especially if she experienced childhood trauma, including sexual abuse or other forms of maltreatment.
3. The child's relationship with the perpetrator and attachment issues especially if there is traumatic bonding.

The complexities of these relationships have a bearing on the various stages of pretreatment, entry into treatment, and treatment direction, all of which require skilled and sensitive assessment and engagement approaches (Alaggia, 2001, 2002; Strand, 1990).

Since the type of attachment has an effect on response to the child victim, utilizing a systematic framework of assessment may help to better determine strengths, areas of concern, and avenues of intervention. Caregiver response may also change over time and can be assessed in initial phases and over time to determine enduring responses that may differ from initial response especially with supportive interventions (Alaggia, 2002). With mothers who are supportive to the abused child, clinicians need to clearly identify and reinforce supportive responses. In cases in which mothers are less supportive, clinicians need to determine the source of difficulties to foster more supportive responses (Alaggia, 2002). This can apply to both parents if they are to be involved in nonoffender treatment.

CULTURAL AND GENDER ISSUES

Cultural and gender issues are important to consider in nonoffending parent treatment on several levels. Beginning with gender, up until recently a subversive discourse that blamed mothers for the sexual victimization of their children was often reflected in practice with families. Mothers were frequently blamed for reportedly being aware of the abuse at some level of consciousness, being passively complicit, and even colluding with the perpetrator, especially when this was the mother's partner. As well, they were often portrayed as reacting in an "ineffective" manner once disclosure had occurred. These gender biased formulations had little empirical foundation yet dominated theory and practice for several decades. Fortunately these beliefs surrounding the "myth of the collusive mother" (Faller, 1988; Salt et al., 1990) have been challenged and more accurate data on nonoffending mothers have been collected to inform professional practice (Carter, 1993; Corcoran, 1998; Crawford, 1999; Joyce, 1997). Yet, gender role participation in treatment reflects mothers as still being the parent most often involved, while fathers tend not to participate even when the child has experienced extrafamilial abuse. Caring and treatment for the problems of the family and children are still firmly entrenched in the domain of mothers even when fathers are invited and encouraged to participate, and models of treatment are developed and aimed at both parents. Father involvement, when he is not the perpetrator, is an important consideration in light of recent findings. One such study involving adult survivors who retrospectively commented on their perception of paternal support revealed increased rates of self-worth when they perceived positive paternal support (Guelzow, Cornett, & Dougherty, 2002).

Little progress has been made in developing interventions dealing specifically with families from different cultures and with the complications that CSA brings. Parents who are strongly influenced by cultural and religious beliefs place a high value on family preservation and who choose to adhere to traditional religious schemas are often perceived by professionals as compromising their support to the child victim, especially when the perpetrator is a family member. This can unintentionally lead to mothers being marginalized and alienated by helping professionals because they are often asked to break sanctioned cultural and religious traditions (Alaggia, 2001; Maiter, Alaggia, & Trocmé, 2004). These parents are concerned about being isolated from their ethnic community if they break with cultural traditions and religious practices regarding family values and are, therefore, caught in untenable dilemmas. Furthermore, therapeutic alliances are jeopardized if the mother perceives the practitioner as being responsible, in part, for forcing the dissolution of her family. Although most group modalities provide a psychoeducational component (e.g., explaining perpetrator tactics, negative effects of CSA, child protection, court procedures, review of abuse dynamics, helping parents communicate support to victimized children), this may not be sufficient in dealing with complex cultural value conflicts. The group format in itself may hinder the ability of some members to speak freely about these difficult issues especially when parents are in the minority ethnically, racially, and/or in their intent to reunify their families, or have difficulties with language (Alaggia, 2001).

Although contemporary models of cross-cultural clinical practice and cultural competence are being developed and gaining saliency (Dyche & Zayas, 1995; LaFramboise & Foster, 1992; Tsang & George, 1998), these models are understandably generic and do not offer specific clinical strategies used in CSA treatment. As applied to parental response to CSA and openness to treatment, cultural and religious attitudes toward marriage, family cohesion, and divorce are particularly important to probe and to understand the meaning and the implications for treatment. Because in many cases of CSA perpetrators are members of the immediate or extended family, cultural values and belief systems very much influence the actions of caregivers in terms of the loyalty binds they face.

Gender, Culture, and Implications for Practice

Postdisclosure work is crisis work. It is important to bear in mind that on the point of disclosure or discovery of CSA the family is in crisis (Alaggia, 2002). The potential dissolution of the family, strained relations with extended family members, potential cultural conflict, financial stress and hardship, concern for the emotional and psychological well-being of the child victim, ongoing child protection and police investigations, and impending court proceedings all factor into response to the child victim and their entry into treatment. As revealed by Massat and Lundy (1999) in their study, barriers to service include a number of family stressors, such as having to move, losing income, losing a family member, and losing supports. Change in so many areas of family functioning is overwhelming and should be acknowledged as such.

As highlighted in the previous discussion, gender and culture are two critical variables to be mindful of in initial phases of treatment. Inattention to gender and culture can result in lack of treatment engagement and disengagement from treatment. One only needs to turn to the extraordinarily high attrition rates and lack of father involvement in well-established treatment programs to question the role of gender and/or culture in explaining these phenomena. In a number of studies, the dropout rates during the investigation period hovers around 50 percent and samples are comprised mostly of females, who are white and of a lower socioeconomic strata. Moreover, it is unclear who drops out and for what reasons (Celano et al., 1996; Cohen & Mannarino, 1998a, 2000; Stauffer & Deblinger, 1996).

Clinicians cannot be expected to be knowledgeable and literate in all cultures, as this is an unrealistic and overwhelming expectation. It is more appropriate for the practitioner to assume a stance of openness and curiosity with all diverse clients, as suggested in the experiential-phenomenological model (Dyche & Zayas, 1995). The aim of this approach is to acquire an understanding of each client's unique experiences of her culture, race, gender, and class, including issues of discrimination and prejudice. As applied to parental response to CSA, cultural and religious attitudes toward marriage, family cohesion, and divorce are particularly important to probe and understand. It is within this cultural context that the parental responses and actions can be better understood (Alaggia, 2001).

There is some evidence to indicate that some mothers may benefit from individual intervention that takes into consideration these differences in opinions and approaches regarding how to best respond to their children. Key informant interviews with service providers and in-depth interviews with nonoffending mothers in one qualitative exploratory study suggest there are mothers who might benefit from receiving a preparatory stage of one-on-one counseling because their needs are greater, and because they are more difficult to engage in a group context. This period of engagement would be important for listening to, learning about, and understanding culturally based issues facing their client. A relevant area of exploration would include the degree of acculturation experienced by members of families to determine the strength of ties to their ethnic origins, and explore the degree to which they experience cultural conflicts that may interfere with treatment (Alaggia, 2001).

COMORBIDITY AND DOMESTIC VIOLENCE

To aid in the understanding of the etiology of abuse and violence within families, researchers have turned to examining the environmental contexts within which abuse occurs (Hughes, Humphrey, & Weaver, 2005). Research examining the relationship between childhood maltreatment and domestic violence reveals a substantial co-occurrence (Alaggia & Turton, 2005; de Young, 1994; Hiebert-Murphy, 2001; Kellogg & Menard, 2003; Tamaraz, 1996). Kellogg and Menard (2003) cite research that demonstrates a co-occurrence rate of 33 to 77 percent. Ray et al. (1991) reflect on environmental characteristics of homes wherein CSA is reported. These authors concluded that, when compared with nonviolent homes, CSA is more likely to occur in homes where domestic violence is evident and Kellogg and Maynard's (2003) study was in agreement. Among these CSA offenders with a history of domestic violence, 77 percent were involved in concurrent acts of CSA and domestic violence.

Hiebert-Murphy (2001), in her sample of mothers of children who had disclosed CSA, indicates that more than one-third (36 percent) of the respondents reported current domestic violence, and 72 percent of women reported historical experiences of woman abuse. The majority of domestic violence offenders were friends/acquaintances of the nonoffending mothers, while 12 percent were ex-husbands and ex-partners, 5 percent were husbands, and 2 percent were ex-boyfriends. These data are important when examining maternal responses to CSA disclosure in recognizing that current partner abuse may have a substantial impact on the mother's emotional availability and protective capacity. This former study indicates that women in a currently physically abusive relationship employ avoidance coping strategies in response to their children's disclosure of CSA. Alaggia and Turton (2005), in their secondary analysis of two qualitative studies, similarly reported variances in the type of maternal response related to the form of domestic violence experienced by nonoffending mothers. Their study found different results wherein nonoffending mothers experiencing physical abuse demonstrated a more supportive response than those mothers who were emotionally abused. Mothers involved in an emotionally abusive relationship exhibited an avoidant coping style accompanied by an ambivalent response to their child's disclosure of CSA. At the same time, recent research is documenting the negative effects of children who have been exposed to and witness domestic violence, now considered a form of child maltreatment (Edlesohn, 1999; Jaffe, Wilson, & Wolfe, 1988; Wolfe, Crooks, Lee, McIntyre-Smith, & Jaffe, 2003). A number of these effects can manifest in internalizing and externalizing symptoms that would interact and presumably exacerbate CSA effects. Despite etiological investigations documenting the co-occurrence of other forms of domestic violence and CSA, the majority of studies examining these variables and their interactions with CSA have not obtained sufficient information about the role of woman abuse in terms of child effects and implications for disclosure response and treatment (Alaggia & Kirshenbaum, 2005).

The research described earlier in this section demonstrates several factors: (1) CSA and domestic violence co-occur, (2) domestic violence influences mothers' response to disclosure of CSA, and (3) domestic violence may have a direct effect on child outcomes. These factors exist within an ecological framework characterizing the environment and its effects on emotional outcome in cases of CSA, which has implications for treatment.

CONCLUSION

There is a growing body of research supporting postdisclosure intervention for both sexually victimized children and their nonoffending parents. Considering the developmental trajectory of some sexually victimized children, the benefits of supportive caregiver response and treatment involvement are evinced through the mitigation of serious psychological harm. First, though mediated by preexisting attachment dynamics, maternal response is amenable to change through structured intervention. Second, involvement by either nonoffending parents or other significant caregivers is preferred for optimal treatment results. Third, in light of the clinical advantages of utilizing intervention approaches that integrate CBT principles, professionals working with this vulnerable population should consider their use while being mindful of the methodological limitations. Fourth, a call for more rigorous empirical investigation that aims to reduce these limitations and offers a more accurate reflection of the complex interplay between maternal response, parental involvement in treatment, and child outcomes is warranted. Until such time that evidence-based treatment in CSA is firmly established, integrating approaches may make sense for families based on their unique characteristics and needs. Finally, while a range of treatment models are available to nonoffending parents and victimized children, attention must be paid to equally important contextual issues, such as family life stressors, attachment dynamics, cultural identity of the family, gender roles and involvement, and the impact of gender issues such as domestic violence, in treatment.

REFERENCES

Ainsworth, M. D. S., Blehar, M. C., Waters, E., & Wall, S. (1978). *Patterns of attachment: A psychological study of the strange situation.* Hillsdale, NJ: Erlbaum.

Alaggia, R. (2001). Cultural and religious influences in maternal response to intrafamilial child sexual abuse: Charting new territory for research and treatment. *Journal of Child Sexual Abuse, 10*(2), 41-60.

Alaggia, R. (2002). Balancing acts: Re-conceptualizing support in maternal response to intrafamilial child sexual abuse. *Clinical Social Work Journal, 30*(1), 41-56.

Alaggia, R., & Kirshenbaum, S. (2005). Speaking the unspeakable: Exploring the impact of family dynamics on child sexual abuse disclosures. *Families in Society, 86*(2), 227-234.

Alaggia, R., & Turton, J. (2005). Against the odds: The impact of woman abuse on maternal response to disclosure of child sexual abuse. *Journal of Child Sexual Abuse, 14*(4), 95-113.

Alexander, P. C. (1992). Application of attachment theory to the study of sexual abuse. *Journal of Consulting and Clinical Psychology, 60,* 185-195.

Alexander, P. C., Anderson, C. L., Brand, B., Schaeffer, C., Grelling, B. Z., & Kretz, L. (1998). Adult attachment and long-term effects in survivors of incest. *Child Abuse & Neglect, 22,* 45-61.

Arata, C. M. (1998). To tell or not to tell: Current functioning of child sexual abuse Survivors who disclosed their victimization. *Child Maltreatment, 3*(1), 63-71.

Beeman, S. K. (1997). Reconceptualizing social support and its relationship to child neglect. *Social Service Review,* 421-440.

Beitchman, J. H., Zucker, K. J., Hood, J. E., DaCosta, G. A., & Akman, D. (1991). A review of the short-term effects of child sexual abuse. *Child Abuse & Neglect, 15,* 537-556.

Beitchman, J. H., Zucker, K. J., Hood, J. E., DaCosta, G. A., Akman, D., & Cassavia, E. (1992). A review of the long-term effects of child sexual abuse. *Child Abuse & Neglect, 16,* 101-117.

Bell, P. (2002). Factors contributing to a mother's ability to recognize incestuous abuse of her child. *Woman's Studies International Forum, 25*(3), 347-357.

Belsky, J., & Nezworsky, T. (Eds.) (1988). *Clinical implications of attachment.* Hillsdale, NJ: Lawrence Erlbaum Associates.

Bolen, R., & Lamb, J. L. (2004). Ambivalence of non-offending guardians after child sexual abuse disclosure. *Journal of Interpersonal Violence, 19*(2), 185-211.

Bolen, R. M., & Scannapieco, M. (1999). Prevalence of child sexual abuse: A corrective metanalysis. *Social Services Review, 73*(3), 281-313.

Bowen, K. (2000). Child abuse and domestic violence in families of children seen for suspected sexual abuse. *Clinical Pediatric, 39*(1), 33-40.

Carlson, V., Cicchetti, D., Barnett, D., & Braunwald, K. (1989). Disorganized/disoriented attachment relationships in maltreated infants. *Developmental Psychology, 25,* 525-531.

Carter, B. (1993). Child sexual abuse: Impact on mothers. *Affilia, 8*(1), 72-90.

Celano, M., Hazzard, A., Webb, C., & McCall, C. (1996). Treatment of traumagenic beliefs among sexually abused girls and their mothers: An evaluation study. *Journal of Abnormal Child Psychology, 24,* 1-17.

Cohen, J. A., & Mannarino, A. P. (1996a). A treatment outcome study for sexually abused preschool children: Initial findings. *Journal of the American Academy of Child & Adolescent Psychiatry, 35,* 42-50.

Cohen, J. A., & Mannarino, A. P. (1996b). Factors that mediate treatment outcome of sexually abused preschool children. *Journal of the American Academy of Child & Adolescent Psychiatry, 34,* 1402-1410.

Cohen, J. A., & Mannarino, A. P. (1997). A treatment study for sexually abused preschool children: Outcome during a one-year follow-up. *Journal of the American Academy of Child & Adolescent Psychiatry, 36*(9), 1228-1235.

Cohen, J. A., & Mannarino, A. P. (1998a). Factors that mediate treatment outcome of sexually abused preschool children: Six and 12-month follow-up. *Journal of the American Academy of Child & Adolescent Psychiatry, 37,* 44-51.

Cohen, J. A., & Mannarino, A. P. (1998b). Interventions for sexually abused children: Initial treatment outcome findings. *Child Maltreatment, 3,* 17-26.

Cohen, J. A., & Mannarino, A. P. (2000). Predictors of treatment outcome in sexually abused children. *Child Abuse & Neglect, 24,* 983-994.

Cole, P., Woolger, C., Power, T. G., & Smith, K. D. (1992). Parenting difficulties among adult survivors of father-daughter incest. *Child Abuse & Neglect, 16,* 239-249.

Conte, J. R., & Schuerman, J. R. (1987). The effects of sexual abuse on children: A multidimensional view. *Journal of Interpersonal Violence, 2*(4), 380-390.

Corcoran, J. (1998). In defense of mothers of sexual abuse victims. *Families in Society, 79*(4), 358-369.

Corcoran, J. (2004). Treatment outcome research with the non-offending parents of sexually abused children: A critical review. *Journal of Child Sexual Abuse, 13*(2), 59-84.

Cornman, J. B. (1997). Female adolescent response to childhood sexual abuse. *Journal of Child and Adolescent Psychiatric Nursing, 10*(2), 17-28.

Crawford, S. L. (1999). Intra-familial sexual abuse: What we think we know about mothers, and implications for intervention. *Journal of Child Sexual Abuse, 7*(3), 55-72.

Cross, T. P., Martell, D., McDonald, E., & Ahl, M. (1999). The criminal justice system and child placement in child sexual abuse cases. *Child Maltreatment, 4*(1), 32-44.

Cyr, M., McDuff, P., Wright, J., Theriault, C., & Cinq-Mars, C. (2005). Clinical correlates and repetition of self-harming behaviors among female adolescent victims of sexual abuse. *Journal of Child Sexual Abuse, 14*(2), 49-68.

Davies, M. G. (1995). Parental distress and ability to cope following disclosure of extra-familial sexual abuse. *Child Abuse & Neglect, 19*(4), 399-408.

Deblinger, E., Lippmann, J., & Steer, R. (1996). Sexually abused children suffering posttraumatic stress symptoms: Initial treatment outcome findings. *Child Maltreatment, 1,* 310-321.

Deblinger, E., McLeer, S., & Henry, D. (1990). Cognitive-behavioral treatment for sexually abused children suffering post-traumatic stress: Preliminary findings. *Journal of the American Academy of Child & Adolescent Psychiatry, 29,* 747-752.

Deblinger, E., Stauffer, L., & Steer, R. (2001). Comparative efficacies of supportive and cognitive behavioral group therapies for young children who have been sexually abused and their nonoffending mothers. *Child Maltreatment, 6,* 332-343.

Deblinger, E., Steer, R., & Lippmann, J. (1999). Two-year follow-up study of cognitive behavioral therapy for sexually abused children suffering post-traumatic stress symptoms. *Child Abuse & Neglect, 23*(12), 1371-1378.

de Young, M. (1994). Women as mothers and wives in paternally incestuous families: Coping with role conflict. *Child Abuse & Neglect, 18,* 73-83.

DiLillo, D. (2001). Interpersonal functioning among women reporting a history of childhood sexual abuse: Empirical findings and methodological issues. *Clinical Psychology Review, 21,* 553-576.

Durlak, J., Fuhrman, T., & Lampman, C. (1991). Effectiveness of cognitive-behavior therapy for maladapting children: A meta-analysis. *Psychological Bulletin, 110,* 204-214.

Dutton, D. G., & Painter, S. (1993). Emotional attachments in abusive relationships: A test of traumatic bonding theory. *Violence and Victims, 8*(2), 105-120.

Dyche, L., & Zayas, L. H. (1995). The value of curiosity and naiveté for the cross-cultural psychotherapist. *Family Process, 34,* 389-399.

Edleson, J. L. (1999). The overlap between child maltreatment and woman battering. *Violence Against Women, 5*(2), 134-154.

Egeland, B., & Sroufe, L. A. (1981). Attachment and early maltreatment. *Child Development, 52,* 44-52.

Elliott, A. N., & Carnes, C. N. (2001). Reactions of non-offending parents to the sexual abuse of their child: A review of the literature. *Child Maltreatment, 6*(4), 314-331.

Everson, M., Hunter, W. N., Runyon, D. K., Edelsohn, M. D., & Coulter, M. L. (1989). Maternal support following disclosure of incest. *American Journal of Orthopsychiatry, 59*(2), 197-207.

Faller, K. C. (1988). Criteria for judging the credibility of children's statements about their sexual abuse. *Child Welfare, 68,* 389-401.

Fergusson, D., Lynsky, M., & Horwood, L. (1996). Prevalence of sexual abuse and factors associated with sexual abuse. *Journal of the American Academy of Child & Adolescent Psychiatry, 35*(10), 1355-1365.

Finkelhor, D. (1994). Current information on the scope and nature of child sexual abuse. *Future of Children, 4*(2), 31-53.

Finkelhor, D., & Browne, A. (1985). The traumatic impact of child sexual abuse. A conceptualization. *American Journal of Orthopsychiatry, 55,* 530-541.

Gelinas, D. J. (1983). The persisting negative effects of incest. *Psychiatry, 46,* 312-332.

Gelinas, D. J. (1986). Unexpected resources in treating incest families. In M. Karpel (Ed.), *Family resources: The hidden partner in family therapy* (pp. 327-358). New York: The Guilford Press.

Graham, D., Rawlings, E., & Rimini, N. (1988). Survivors of terror: Battered women, hostages and the Stockholm syndrome. In K. Yllo & M. Bograd (Eds.), *Feminist perspectives on wife abuse* (pp. 217-233). Newbury Park, CA: Sage.

Grunebaum, H. (1988). The relationship of family theory to family therapy. *Journal of Marital and Family Therapy, 14*(1), 1-14.

Guelzow, J. W., Cornett, P. F., & Dougherty, T. M. (2002). Child sexual abuse victims' perception of paternal support as a significant predictor of coping style and global self-worth. *Journal of Child Sexual Abuse, 11*(4), 53-72.

Haskett, M. E., Nowlan, N. P., Hutcheson, J. S., & Whitworth, J. M. (1991). Factors associated with successful entry into therapy in sexual abuse cases. *Child Abuse & Neglect, 15*(4), 467-476.

Henry, J. (1994). System intervention trauma to child sexual abuse victims following disclosure. *Journal of Interpersonal Violence, 12,* 499-512.

Heriot, J. K. (1996). Maternal protectiveness following the disclosure of intrafamilial child sexual abuse. *Journal of Interpersonal Violence, 11,* 181-194.

Herman, J. L. (1983). Recognition and treatment of incestuous families. *International Journal of Family Therapy, 5*(2), 81-91.

Herman, J. L. (1992). Complex PTSD: A syndrome in survivors of prolonged and repeated trauma. *Journal of Traumatic Stress, 5,* 377-391.

Herman, J. L. (1997). *Trauma and recovery.* New York: Basic Books.

Herman, J. L., & Hirschman, L. (1981). *Father-daughter incest.* Cambridge, MA: Harvard University Press.

Hiebert-Murphy, D. (1998). Emotional distress among mothers whose children have been sexually abused: The role of a history of child sexual abuse, social support, and coping. *Child Abuse & Neglect, 22*(5), 423-435.

Hiebert-Murphy, D. (2001). Partner abuse among women whose children have been sexually abused: An exploratory study. *Journal of Child Sexual Abuse, 10*(1), 109-118.

Hindman, J. (1989). *Just before dawn: From the shadows of tradition to new reflections in trauma assessment and treatment of sexual victimization.* Ontario, OR: AlexAndria Associates.

Hoffman, L. (1981). *Foundations of family therapy: A conceptual framework for systems change.* New York: Basic Books.

Hughes, H. M., Humphrey, N. N., & Weaver, T. L. (2005). Advances in violence and trauma: Toward comprehensive ecological models. *Journal of Interpersonal Violence, 20*(1), 31-38.

Jack, G. (2000). Ecological influences on parenting and child development. *British Journal of Social Work, 30,* 703-720.

Jaffe, P., Wilson, S. K., & Wolfe, D. (1988). Specific assessment and intervention strategies for children exposed to wife battering: Preliminary empirical investigations. *Canadian Journal of Community Mental Health, 7,* 157-163.

Jinich, S., & Litrownik, A. (1999). Coping with sexual abuse: Development and evaluation of a videotape intervention for nonoffending parents. *Child Abuse & Neglect, 23,* 175-190.

Johnson, B. K., & Kenkel, M. B. (1991). Stress, coping, and adjustment in female adolescent incest victims. *Child Abuse & Neglect, 15,* 293-305.

Joyce, P. (1997). Mothers of sexually abused children and the concept of collusion: A literature review. *Journal of Child Sexual Abuse, 6*(2), 75-92.

Kellogg, N. D., & Menard, S. W. (2003). Violence among family members of children and adolescents evaluated for sexual abuse. *Child Abuse & Neglect, 27,* 1367-1376.

King, N., Tonge, B., Mullen, P., Myerson, N., Heyne, D., Rollings, S., et al. (2000). Treating sexually abused children with posttraumatic stress symptoms: A randomized clinical trial. *Journal of the American Academy of Child & Adolescent Psychiatry, 39,* 1347-1355.

LaFramboise, T. D., & Foster, S. L. (1992). Cross-cultural training: Scientist-practitioner model and methods. *Counseling Psychologist, 20*(3), 472-489.

Leifer, M., Kilbane, T., & Grossman, G. (2001). A three-generational study comparing the families of supportive and unsupportive mothers of sexually abused children. *Child Maltreatment, 6*(4), 353-364.

Leifer, M., Kilbane, T., & Skolnick, L. I. (2002). Relationships between maternal adult attachment security, child perceptions of maternal support, and maternal perceptions of child responses to sexual abuse. *Journal of Child Sexual Abuse, 11*(3), 107-124.

Leifer, M., Shapiro, J. P., & Kassem, L. (1993). The impact of maternal history and behaviour upon foster placement and adjustment in sexually abused girls. *Child Abuse & Neglect, 17*(6), 755-766.

Lewin, L., & Bergin, C. (2001). Attachment behaviors, depression, and anxiety in nonoffending mothers of child sexual abuse victims. *Child Maltreatment, 6*(4), 365-375.

Main, M., Kaplan, N., & Cassidy, J. (1985). Security in infancy, childhood, and adulthood. In I. Bretherton & E. Waters (Eds.), *Growing Points of Attachment Theory and Research Monographs of the Society for Research in Child Development, 50*(1), 66-106.

Maiter, S., Alaggia, R., & Trocmé, N. (2004). Perceptions of child maltreatment by parents from the Indian sub-continent: Challenging myths about culturally based abusive parenting practices. *Child Maltreatment, 9*(3), 309-324.

Massat, C. R., & Lundy, M. (1999). Service and support needs of non-offending parents in cases of intrafamilial sexual abuse. *Journal of Child Sexual Abuse, 8*(2), 41-56.

Mian, M., Marton, P., & LeBaron, D. (1996). The effects of sexual abuse on 3 to 5 year old girls. *Child Abuse & Neglect, 20*(8), 731-745.

Nichols, M. P., & Schwartz, R. C. (2001). The fundamental concepts of family therapy: Basic techniques. In M. P. Nichols & R. C. Schwartz (Eds.), *The essentials of family therapy* (pp. 54-75). Boston, MA: Allyn and Bacon.

Oates, K., Tebbutt, J., Swanston, H., Lynch, D., & O'Toole, B. (1998). Prior childhood sexual abuse in mothers of sexually abused children. *Child Abuse & Neglect, 22*(11), 1113-1118.

Pellegrin, A., & Wagner, W. G. (1990). Child sexual abuse: Factors affecting victims' removal from home. *Child Abuse & Neglect, 14*(1), 53-60.

Pintello, D., & Zuravin, S. (2001). Intrafamilial child sexual abuse: Predictors of postdisclosure maternal belief and protective action. *Child Maltreatment, 6*, 344-352.

Polusny, M. A., & Follette, V. M. (1995). Long-term correlates of child sexual abuse: Theory and review of the empirical literature. *Applied and Preventive Psychology, 4*, 143-166.

Ray, K. C., Jackson, J. L., & Townsley, R. M. (1991). Family environments of victims of intrafamilial and extrafamilial child sexual abuse. *Journal of Family Violence, 6*, 365-374.

Regehr, C. (1990). Parental responses to extra familial child sexual assault. *Child Abuse & Neglect, 14*, 113-120.

Rivera, M. (1988). Social systems' intervention in families of child sexual abuse. *Canadian Journal of Community Mental Health, 7*(1), 35-51.

Salt, P., Myer, M., Coleman, L., & Sauzier, M. (1990). The myth of the mother as 'accomplice' to the child sexual abuse. In B. Gomes-Schwartz, J. Horowitz & A. Cardarelli (Eds.), *Child sexual abuse: The initial effects* (pp. 109-131). Newbury Park, CA: Sage.

Serketich, W. J., & Dumas, J. E. (1996). The effectiveness of behavioural parent training to modify anti-social behaviour in children: A meta-analysis. *Behavior Therapy, 27*, 171-186.

Shapiro, D. L., & Levendosky, A. A. (1999). Adolescent survivors of childhood sexual abuse: The mediating role of attachment style and coping in psychological and interpersonal functioning. *Child Abuse & Neglect, 23*(11), 1175-1191.

Sgroi, S. (1982). *Handbook of clinical intervention in child sexual abuse*. Lexington, MA: D.C. Heath and Co.

Sirles, E. A., & Franke, P. J. (1989). Factors influencing mothers' reaction to intrafamilial child sexual abuse. *Child Abuse & Neglect, 13,* 131-189.

Spaccarelli, S. (1994). Stress, appraisal, and coping in child sexual abuse: A theoretical and empirical review. *Psychological Bulletin, 116,* 340-362.

Sroufe, L. A. (1988). The role of infant-caregiver attachment in adult development. In J. Belsky & T. Nezworski (Eds.), *Clinical implications of attachment* (pp. 18-38). Hillsdale, NJ: Earlbaum.

Stauffer, L. B., & Deblinger, E. (1996). Cognitive behavioral groups for nonoffending mothers and their young sexually abused children: A preliminary treatment outcome study. *Child Maltreatment, 1,* 65-76.

Stormshak, E., & Dishion, T. (2002). An ecological approach to child and family clinical and counseling psychology, *Clinical Child and Family Psychology Review, 5*(3), 197-215.

Strand, V. C. (1990). Treatment of the mother in the incest family: The beginning phase. *Clinical Social Work Journal, 18*(4), 353-366.

Symonds, M. (1982). Victim's responses to terror: Understanding and treatment. In F. Ochberg & D. Soskis (Eds.), *Victims of terrorism* (pp. 95-103). Boulder, CO: Westview.

Tamaraz, D. N. (1996). Non-offending mothers of sexually abused children: Comparison of opinions and research. *Journal of Child Sexual Abuse, 5,* 75-104.

Tingus, K. D., Heger, A. H., Foy, D. W., & Leskin, G. A. (1996). Factors associated with entry into therapy in children evaluated for sexual abuse. *Child Abuse & Neglect, 20*(1), 63-68.

Tsang, A. K. T., & George, U. (1998). An integrated framework for cross-cultural social work. *Canadian Social Work Review, 15*(1), 73-94.

Tyler, K. A. (2002). Social and emotional outcomes of childhood sexual abuse: A review of recent research. *Aggressive and Violent Behavior, 7*(6), 567-589.

U.S. Department of Health and Human Services (2001). *Child maltreatment 1999: Reports from the states to the national child abuse and neglect data system.* Washington, DC: Author.

Webster-Stratton, C., & Hammond, M. (1997). Treating children with early-onset conduct problems: A comparison of child and parent training interventions. *Journal of Consulting and Clinical Psychology, 65,* 93-109.

Winton, M. (1990). An evaluation of a support group for parents who have a sexually abused child. *Child Abuse & Neglect, 14,* 397-405.

Wolfe, D. A., Crooks, C. V., Lee, V., McIntyre-Smith, A., & Jaffe, P. G. (2003). The effects of children's exposure to domestic violence: A meta-analysis and critique. *Clinical Child and Family Psychology Review, 6,* 171-187.

Wolfe, V., & Birt, J. (1995). The psychological sequelae of child sexual abuse. In T. H. Ollendick & R. J. Prinz (Eds.), *Advances in clinical child psychology* (pp. 233-263). New York: Plenum.

Chapter 10

Prevention Endeavors

Kimberly Renk
Elizabeth Baksh
Reesa Donnelly
Angela Roddenberry

INTRODUCTION

Evidence indicates that as many as 20 percent of females and 5 to 10 percent of males have been abused sexually (Finkelhor, 1994). Unfortunately, statistics have suggested that children of all ages, socioeconomic statuses, and ethnic and racial groups may be subject to the experience of sexual abuse (Finkelhor, 1993). As a result of their sexual abuse experiences, children are likely to experience a wide variety of symptoms and problematic behaviors (Kendall-Tackett, Williams, & Finkelhor, 1993). Given these factors, child sexual abuse has been identified as a major public health concern (McMahon, 2000). Recently, treatments addressing the symptoms experienced by abuse survivors and the sexually abusive behaviors of perpetrators have been a focus of interest. In an effort to reduce the high incidence of sexual abuse experienced by children and adolescents, researchers (e.g., Renk, Liljequist, Steinberg, Bosco, & Phares, 2002) have called for an increasing focus on prevention.

Certainly, prevention efforts addressing child sexual abuse are not new. For example, Daro (1994) reported that 85 percent of the 400 school districts that she surveyed in the United States offered a prevention program covering the topic of abuse within the year prior

Handbook of Social Work in Child and Adolescent Sexual Abuse
© 2008 by The Haworth Press, Taylor & Francis Group. All rights reserved.
doi:10.1300/5804_10

to the survey, and 64 percent of these districts had mandated prevention programs. Further, on the basis of telephone interviews with adolescents in the United States, Finkelhor and Dziuba-Leatherman (1995) indicated that 67 percent of adolescents had been exposed to a prevention program. Given the settings of these prevention programs (i.e., schools), it is evident that a main focus of prevention programs thus far has been on educating children in how to protect themselves from sexual assault and on what to do if an adult touches them in an inappropriate or uncomfortable fashion (Daro & McCurdy, 1994).

Renk and colleagues (2002), however, also suggested the importance of expanding prevention efforts. Using Bronfenbrenner's (1977) ecological model, Renk and colleagues (2002) made attempts to identify prevention efforts regarding child sexual abuse in all settings and contexts of the society in which children live. By using a model such as that described by Bronfenbrenner (1977) to define the possible contexts of prevention efforts, it became evident that such efforts should be targeting not only the children, their families, and their schools, but also other societal systems, especially those that could have the potential for widespread influence (e.g., the media, the Internet). This chapter offers a summary of the work that has been done on prevention in a variety of these contexts and makes suggestions for additional work that could further improve prevention efforts for child sexual abuse. In particular, this chapter discusses prevention efforts that have targeted families, schools, community and legal systems, and the Internet.

FAMILIES

Families remain an important focus of prevention efforts. Unfortunately, a majority of the perpetrators of child sexual abuse are individuals who are related to, live with, or are acquainted with their child victims. In such cases, children and their families frequently have established some level of trust with the perpetrators of their abuse (Crosson-Tower, 2002; Levenson & Morin, 2000). Such facts, however, make prevention a daunting undertaking for parents, as they may be reluctant to consider that their children may be at risk for harm from an individual who is close to their family. Given that the majority of perpetrators know their child victims before the incidents of abuse, teaching children only about *stranger danger* in relation to child sexual abuse misses the mark (Crosson-Tower, 2002; Levenson & Morin, 2000). Thus, prevention efforts for families should be refocused on providing children and their parents with accurate and appropriate information.

Certainly, educating children may be one of the most widely used avenues of prevention for child sexual abuse (e.g., Daro, 1994; Roberts & Miltenberger, 1999). As part of such efforts, parents should discuss the specific behaviors and parts of the body involved in sexual abuse. This discussion should include reference to the child's body as well as how the perpetrator's body may be involved in sexually abusive acts (e.g., touching of "private" body parts; Crosson-Tower, 2002). Further, parents and other family members in protective positions should help socialize children to express affection on their own terms (American Psychological Association, 2001). Alertness to increasingly sexualized talk, which perpetrators often use to desensitize children, may improve protection as well (Kaufman, Hilliker, & Daleiden, 1996). Most important, however, children should be made aware that, in addition to strangers, it is inappropriate for adults and other children they know and trust to engage in behaviors such as these (Crosson-Tower, 2002). In a study of parents living in China, however, 40 percent of the parents surveyed had not shared this type information with their children (Chen & Chen, 2005). Similar rates have been found for parents in the United States (e.g., Wurtele, Kvaternick, & Franklin, 1992) and Canada (Laforest & Hébert, unpublished manuscript, as cited in Hébert & Tourigny, 2004). Thus, more work needs to be done in this area.

In many cases, current prevention programs for children appear to successfully teach children to avoid risky situations, to say "no" to perpetrators, and to report any incidents of abuse or inappropriate touching over the short and long term (Daro, 1994; Finkelhor, Asdigian, & Dziuba-Leatherman, 1995a,b; Roberts & Miltenberger, 1999). These strategies also seem to increase children's knowledge about child sexual abuse (Bolen, 2003; Rispens, Aleman, & Goudena, 1997) and moderately increase children's use of self-protective behaviors in compromising situations (Fryer, Kraizer, & Miyoshi, 1987). There has been some controversy, however, as to whether these programs reduce the actual rates of sexual abuse experienced by children. Some studies have suggested that the rates of sexual abuse are not reduced (Davis & Gidycz, 2000; Pelcovitz, Adler, Kaplan, Packman, & Krieger, 1992; Roberts & Miltenberger, 1999), whereas others have found a reduction in the incidence of sexual abuse in children who have participated in such programs (Gibson & Leitenberg, 2000).

Rather than simply educating children, however, the education of parents and other family members is also important. In fact, some have suggested that parents' knowledge of child sexual abuse prevention may influence directly their children's prevention awareness (Chen & Chen, 2005). As part of these education efforts, parents should become familiar with the emotional and behavioral warning signs that are usually exhibited by children who are being abused sexually. Such recognition may allow parents and other family members to potentially aid in the prevention of reoccurrences of abuse (Crosson-Tower, 2002). In addition, it may be helpful to encourage fathers' involvement with child rearing, as physical and psychological distance is related to an increased risk of father-daughter incest (Parker & Parker, 1986). Further, it has been suggested that increasing parent education and involvement (Gilbert, 1989), role-playing, or providing other active learning experiences (e.g., practicing, interactive involvement; Davis & Gidycz, 2000), helping parents put information in developmentally appropriate terms, encouraging children to disclose incidents of abuse to their parents (Daro & McCurdy, 1994), and providing a means of integrating information into the long-term school curriculum (Davis & Gidycz, 2000) may be important components to include in parent programs.

Given the importance of each of these factors, parents who are uncertain about what they should share with their children may benefit from involvement with programs such as "What Do I Say Now?" when discussing child sexual abuse at home (e.g., Burgess & Wurtele, 1998). Such programs provide parents with examples of the structure and developmentally appropriate language that could be used when discussing sexual abuse with children. For example, Burgess and Wurtele (1998) showed parents the *What Do I Say Now?* video, which was developed by the Committee for Children (1996) and which shows actors depicting parents who calmly talk to their children about sexuality and touching safety. Those parents who watched this video reported significantly greater intentions of discussing child sexual abuse with their children than those parents who watched a control video on home safety (Burgess & Wurtele, 1998). Thus, such a program may not only provide education about child sexual abuse but also provide parents with models of how to handle discussion of this sensitive topic with their children.

In addition, good communication and trust between children and their parents and other close family members may be key to ensuring that children feel comfortable disclosing sexual abuse if it is occurring (Crosson-Tower, 2002). In fact, research has suggested that parents' responses to their children when they disclose incidents of sexual abuse may be one of the most important factors in long-term outcomes for these children (Bolen, 2003; Kendall-Tackett et al., 1993). Not only can parents' reactions to children's disclosures reduce their immediate feelings of isolation, anger, and guilt (Barnett, Miller-Perrin, & Perrin, 2005), but they can potentially influence their long-term functioning as well (Kouyoumdjian, Perry, & Hansen, 2004). Further, after supporting and protecting children who have disclosed incidents of child sexual abuse, it is important for adults to tell someone and get their own support (American Academy of Pediatrics, n.d.). Although some child-focused prevention programs have been successful in increasing disclosures of child sexual abuse (Araji, Fenton, & Staugh, 1995), parents, in general, may not be aware of the importance of their response to such disclosures. For example, in a study of parents living in China, only 40.7 percent of parents endorsed that a child who reports sexual abuse can be believed almost all of the time (Chen & Chen, 2005). Through education, knowledge of risk factors, and responding appropriately to children when they disclose abuse, parents and other family members who believe children when they disclose incidents of child sexual abuse are best able to protect them from further abuse and to provide a support system for these children as they begin to deal with their abuse experiences in a therapeutic context (Elliott, Brown, & Kilcoyne, 1995; Hébert, Lavoie, & Parent, 2002). These practices also can assist in the prevention of child sexual abuse.

Although education and the preparation of parents to handle disclosures of child sexual abuse are important, children, regardless of whether they say "no" or try to get away, are still vulnerable when left alone with someone who has intentions of engaging in incidents of child sexual abuse. There are several risk factors within children's families that may contribute to the occurrence of child sexual abuse, of which parents, family members, and others involved in children's lives need to be aware. For example, reported cases of child sexual abuse are three times more likely to occur for girls than for boys and eighteen times more likely to occur in children from families whose income is $15,000 or less per year relative to those whose families earned more than $30,000 per year (Hines & Malley-Morrison, 2005).

In addition, variables indicative of family dysfunction (e.g., violent adult relationships within the home) have been related to the increased likelihood of child sexual abuse (Bowen, 2000; Kellogg & Menard, 2003). Further, several variables related to maternal functioning (e.g., having experienced abuse as child: DeLillo, 2001; Rumstein-McKean & Hensley, 2001; having experienced a poor intergenerational attachment relationship with her own mother: Leifer, Kilbane, Jacobsen, & Grossman, 2004; having higher levels of psychopathology, substance abuse, and involvement in violent relationships, as well as difficulties with functioning effectively as a parent: Deblinger, Hathaway, Lippmann, & Steer, 1993; Lewin & Bergin, 2001; Maker, Kemmelmeir, & Peterson, 1999; McCloskey & Bailey, 2000) have been found to increase children's risk for sexual abuse. In addition, the presence of a stepparent or significant other not related to the children in the family has been associated with child sexual abuse (Finkelhor, 1984; Russell, 1986). This risk may be due to the lack of an incest taboo since the child is not related biologically to the perpetrator (Hines & Malley-Morrison, 2005). Although these factors are not completely predictive of the occurrence of child sexual abuse in families, such information may provide families and researchers with information about who is high risk for incidents of child sexual abuse and, thus, should be targeted for prevention efforts. Parents and other family members may be able to identify these risk factors and intervene to prevent incidents of child sexual abuse if needed.

Certainly, starting with children and their families as a context for prevention efforts is a commonsensical approach to providing information about child sexual abuse. By educating both children and their parents about child sexual abuse, particularly about the potential risk factors and warning signs that may be involved, prevention efforts can be focused on preventing initial instances of child sexual abuse, preventing reoccurrences, and minimizing the deleterious effects experienced by the children themselves and their families. Targeting children and their families, however, should be just the first step in prevention efforts, with further efforts targeting the community in general as well as the Internet and other sources of media.

SCHOOLS

Relative to other prevention endeavors, schools have the opportunity to serve as a powerful influence in children's lives (Massey-Stokes & Lanning, 2004) and have been one of the most popular settings for abuse prevention programs (Hébert & Tourigny, 2004). Schools may have such a strong impact because they can potentially make up for difficulties or problems in the home settings of children and adolescents (Pransky, 2001). Further, given that the primary function of schools is to educate children, schools are able to reach a large number of diverse children in a cost-efficient manner (Wurtele, 2002). Consistently, prevention programs for child sexual abuse are usually conducted in school settings and are focused on altering the knowledge and skills of children regarding personal safety (Wurtele, 2002).

In fact, school-based safety programs have been adopted widely, with 48 to 85 percent of school districts offering such prevention programs (Daro, 1994) and more than 90 percent of teachers viewing such programs as valuable and effective (Abrahams, Casey, & Daro, 1992). Both principals (Romano, Casey, & Daro, 1990) and parents (Wurtele et al., 1992) have provided support for these programs as well. In general, school-based safety programs provide children with educational information on how to protect themselves from sexual abuse and what to do in the event that they experience an incident of actual or potential abuse (Daro & McCurdy, 1994). Given these statistics, it is not surprising that a telephone survey of adolescents indicated that 67 percent of the responding adolescents reported that they participated in a school-based victimization prevention program at some time during their education (Finkelhor & Dziuba-Leatherman, 1995). Thus, such programs are widespread.

In general, research has demonstrated that school-based prevention programs targeting child sexual abuse can have positive effects. For example, a recent meta-analysis examining prevention programs by Davis and Gidycz (2000) reported that the average effect size for children participating in these programs was significantly higher than that for control children. Further, this meta-analysis suggested that there were significant effects for children's level of participation in the program (i.e., active participants had a significantly higher effect size), the number of intervention sessions completed (i.e., programs that included more than three sessions had significantly higher effect sizes than programs with fewer sessions), the outcome measures that were used (i.e., higher effect sizes were derived from behavioral observation measures), the age of the participants (i.e., studies with older children had lower effect sizes), and the inclusion of behavioral skills training (i.e., such training promoted the largest performance changes; Davis & Gidycz, 2000). Overall, these findings suggested that developmentally appropriate prevention programs that provide children an opportunity to participate actively in behaviorally based educational interventions over several sessions should provide the greatest results in protecting children from incidents of sexual abuse.

Similar to the prevention efforts described earlier in this section for children and their families, school-based prevention programs tend to focus on strengthening children's abilities to identify and resist abusive situations, to encourage children to disclose abusive experiences, and to improve adults' responses to these disclosures (Wurtele, 2002). A meta-analysis by Berrick and Barth (1992) indicated that these programs are promoting greater knowledge of potential threats (e.g., appropriate versus inappropriate touching, how to handle encounters with strangers) in child participants. Further, research has shown that such knowledge gains can be maintained over the course of a one-year follow-up (Briggs & Hawkins, 1994). Such programs also have been shown to improve children's resistance and self-protection skills (e.g., children are taught to say "no," to try to get away, and to tell someone about these incidents; Rispens et al., 1997; Wurtele, 2002), with child participants maintaining these skills over the course of a one-year follow-up (Hazzard, Webb, Kleemeier, Angert, & Pohl, 1991). Overall, children's skill acquisition appears to be highest when programs provide active learning opportunities (Wurtele, Marrs, & Miller-Perrin, 1987) over repeated episodes of learning (Rispens et al., 1997).

Researchers have started to identify improvements that could be made to such programs, however. For example, Kaufman, Barber,

Mosher, and Carter (2002) have suggested that school-based programs should include information regarding the usual operating procedures of perpetrators. Such programs may be more appropriate for preadolescents and adolescents in middle and high school, as they may be more prepared to incorporate this information into their knowledge base (Reppucci, Woolard, & Fried, 1999). In addition, Kaufman and colleagues (2002) suggested that information regarding healthy relationships and intimacy should be included so that positive attitudes toward relationships can be shaped, possibly preventing future abusive acts among relationship partners. Including specific points of information, such as those described here, may be particularly important for school-based prevention programs. For example, Ko and Cosden (2001) found that high school students who participated in an elementary school abuse prevention program did not show significant differences in their general knowledge about abuse issues (e.g., how to recognize and respond to sexual abuse) relative to students who did not participate in such a program. In contrast, those participating students held a greater understanding of the subtle, but important, points addressed in the prevention programming (e.g., understanding that sexual abuse happens to both boys and girls and that sexual abuse is never a child's fault) relative to students who did not participate (Ko & Cosden, 2001).

Overall, the effectiveness of school prevention endeavors would be much improved if family and community involvement were integrated into these endeavors (Massey-Stokes & Lanning, 2004; Wurtele & Miller-Perrin, 1992). In fact, researchers have suggested that the identification and involvement of family members (e.g., parents, siblings) from at-risk families may be a necessary component of interventions, even when it is easier to include children in school-based programs (Daro, 1993; Wolfe, 1993). Further, students are more likely to learn successfully and be resilient when schools, families, and communities provide cohesive programming (Carlyon, Carlyon, & McCarthy, 1998). Thus, rather than working as separate entities, families, schools, and other means of community support should be working together to provide a well-rounded approach to prevention endeavors for child sexual abuse.

THE COMMUNITY AND THE LEGAL SYSTEM

As a context for the prevention of child sexual abuse, the community and the legal system provide a broad base relative to family and school interventions. Rather than focusing on the education of children and families, prevention efforts in the community and the legal system often target perpetrators, rather than survivors, in their efforts to reduce child sexual abuse. Certainly, shifting the focus of such interventions to perpetrators is consistent with the view of Renk and colleagues (2002), who suggested that the "appropriate target of prevention programs [are] potential perpetrators and the cultural system in which they operate. . . . Programs that focus on potential victims ignore the need to place responsibility for abuse with the abuser" (p. 78). Other researchers also have emphasized prevention efforts that target all adults, including perpetrators as well as adults who can serve as protectors and who create children's social milieu (Bolen, 2003; Finklehor, 1990; Renk et al., 2002). Although separated in this section, community and legal efforts are related intrinsically and are likely to have an effect on each other.

Because state and federal statutes require that perpetrators commit a sexually abusive act before they are prosecuted, most laws can be considered secondary prevention, as they would identify a perpetrator after abuse occurs and focus on preventing further abuse. The legal system remains important, however, in that it targets perpetrators and places the responsibility for sexually abusive behavior with them. In addition, current state and federal laws provide other means of protecting children. Current laws prohibit the sexual exploitation, sexual abuse, and prostitution of children, but statutes also mandate that certain professionals (e.g., personnel in law enforcement, mental health, school systems, health care, and child care facilities) report abuse when it is suspected (U.S. DOJ, 2005). Finally, federal law requires that sexual perpetrators register with their state of residence, with each state determining who should register and the means for distributing registration listings to members of the community (U.S. DOJ, 2005). For more information, see www.usdoj.gov/criminal/ceos /citizensguide_sexualabuse.html.

The important question regarding these laws and statutes is whether they actually prevent future abuse. Certainly, during incarceration, perpetrators are not able to commit additional incidents of child sexual abuse. Further, laws regarding registration of perpetrators may increase the speed of rearrest when recidivism does occur. They generally do not reduce recidivism itself (Myers, 1996), however, and may promote the marginalization of these individuals in society rather than promoting rehabilitation into the community (Renk et al., 2002). Thus, more efforts must be put into prevention and treatment programs that target perpetrators (Renk et al., 2002) so that they do not return to their sexually abusive behaviors. For example, one residential treatment center found that adolescent perpetrators were less likely to reoffend after participating in their program relative to untreated adolescent perpetrators (Boswell & Wedge, 2003). Programs that decrease recidivism by increasing alternative coping skills may be especially important, as perpetrators of sexual abuse are considered to be resistant to treatment (Boswell & Wedge, 2003).

With a more overarching goal in mind, most researchers have called for pervasive changes in societal attitudes. In particular, Finkelhor (1990) suggested that communities should focus on targeting individuals who are at high risk for perpetrating and deterring perpetrators by increasing the consequences for their behaviors, rather than subscribing to the lax prosecution of perpetrators that has been present in society historically. In addition, communities may promote the prevention of child sexual abuse by changing the male sex role to be less predatory, patriarchal, dominant, and negative toward women as well as by improving socialization by increasing comfort and communication about meeting sexual needs in appropriate relationships (Finkelhor, 1990). More recently, Bolen (2003) further noted that deterrence of sexually abusive behavior is effective only when perpetrators recognize such behaviors as illegal and only if they are prosecutable adults. These may be important considerations, as many perpetrators do not acknowledge their abusive behaviors as being illegal, even when these behaviors may include rape and other "clear" abuses (Bolen, 2003). Further, more than a third of perpetrators are not adults (Russell, 1983), resulting in a need to identify the characteristics of perpetrators who may be underage. Thus, increasing public messages about the legal consequences and personal responsibility for abusive behaviors may discourage such behavior and reduce the distortions that perpetrators have about child sexual abuse (Melton, 1992; Renk et al., 2002).

Corresponding with Finkelhor's (1990) suggestions, high-risk individuals can be identified as being male, having difficulty in adult relationships or distortions in their cognitions surrounding sexual contact with children (e.g., Marziano, Ward, Beech, & Pattison, 2006), and become abusive following high stress (Elliott et al., 1995). Thus, teaching coping skills and sex education may better socialize men who are at risk for becoming perpetrators and, thus, prevent child sexual abuse. Such interventions may include psychoeducational information for fathers that informs them how increased involvement in child rearing is related to less risk of sexual abuse for their daughters (Parker & Parker, 1986). Mental health professionals may then help fathers to practice skills of effective parenting, brainstorm about ways to increase fathers' child-rearing activity in the home, and problem solve about the obstacles that impede their involvement (e.g., scheduling difficulties or gender role conflicts). Increasing explicit messages in society that child sexual abuse is harmful and never the fault of the child also may help reduce myths that are prevalent among perpetrators (Melton, 1992; Tang & Yan, 2004). By reducing shame around sexuality, communication about sexuality is fostered, and detection of those with sexual difficulties may be increased (Cohn, Finkelhor, & Holmes, 1985). Further, Bolen (2003) noted that improved socialization and sex roles may reduce sexually abusive behavior by promoting health rather than targeting dysfunction.

Some studies of community programs that target adults in particular and communities in general have found positive outcomes. For example, *Stop It Now* was first implemented in Vermont and targeted adults who were or who could become abusers (Henry & Tabachnick, 1997). The program is now run in many communities across several states. Another study developed a comprehensive neighborhood mapping (CNM) program in Scotland (Nelson & Baldwin, 2004). This feasibility study provided useful qualitative and exploratory information for engaging entire communities in preventing child sexual abuse. Although the study did not evaluate outcomes empirically, the researchers suggested that liaisons should be provided for individuals wanting to discuss a sexual crime who do not trust law enforcement. In addition, it was recommended that vulnerable youth should receive access to daytime facilities and agency interventions and that the physical environment should be modified to reduce abandoned buildings and dangerous areas. Finally, it was suggested that education should be increased through community campaigns, and that support services should be provided to adults (Nelson & Baldwin, 2004).

Overall, using professional channels may be a safer and more effective means of reducing child sexual abuse. All adults, particularly those in protective positions, may assist in reducing child sexual abuse by becoming involved actively in changing societal attitudes as noted earlier in the chapter and by becoming active in child sexual abuse prevention organizations. Such organizations include Stop It Now (www.stopitnow.com), Crimes Against Children Research Center (www.unh.edu/ccrc), the National Center for Prosecution of Child Abuse (www.ndaa-apri.org), the National Clearinghouse on Child Abuse and Neglect Information (www.calib.com/nccanch), and Prevent Child Abuse America (www.childabuse.org). In the long term, community awareness may increase in a cumulative manner as more and more children participate in prevention programs and grow up to become better informed adults (Bolen, 2003).

THE INTERNET AND OTHER SOURCES OF MEDIA

Within the past decade, the Internet has become a widely used resource. Given the extensive access that individuals in today's society have to the Internet and other sources of media, such mechanisms provide a ready means for providing information regarding prevention programs for child sexual abuse. Along with the many benefits of the Internet, however, there is a risk for potential harm to children. Children can become victims of child pornography on the Internet by either inadvertently viewing questionable material online or by becoming the subject of a film or photograph posted on the Internet (Calcetas-Santos, 2001). In addition, perpetrators use the Internet as a means to seduce or groom children (e.g., via online conversations that are sexually explicit, sending sexual pictures), to distribute or obtain child pornography productions, to arrange meetings or other communication with children, to reward potential child victims (e.g., offering Internet use as an incentive for children to visit the offender's home), and to advertise or sell children (Mitchell, Finkelhor, & Wolak,

2005a). Finally, the Internet provides an anonymous framework in which perpetrators can access information (Calcetas-Santos, 2001). Thus, in order to foster prevention of child sexual abuse, it is important for professionals, parents, and children to understand the risks associated with "going online."

In response to recognition of dangers such as these, countries worldwide have set up safeguards to help protect children from encountering harm when using the Internet. For example, the Hotline for Child Pornography on the Internet (based in the Netherlands) requests that any questionable material be reported. The hotline then asks the Web site administrator to remove the material from the noted Web site. If the information is not removed, the administrator of the noted Web site is turned over to the police (Aftab, 2001). Further, India has limited access to the Internet to those in the academic world, and Denmark's National Commissioner of Police has a Web page set up to report suspicious Web sites (Aftab, 2001). In addition to these worldwide efforts, however, families, schools, and communities must identify means of protecting children from the role that the Internet may play in child sexual abuse.

Parents are faced with limited options to protect their children from Internet harm, however. Filtering software, such as the Canadian-developed Nanny Net, can block potentially harmful sites or allow only a list of preapproved Web sites to be viewed. There is also software available that can monitor children's on- and offline activity through many Internet Service Providers (Aftab, 2001). Further, the Platform for Internet Content Selection allows Web sites to be rated (similar to the method used for television shows, movies, and video games) by the administrator of the Web site or by a third-party rating service. Web site ratings allow parents to determine whether the information presented on the site is appropriate for their children to view. Unfortunately, this method has not proven to be a comprehensive solution, as the rating companies are not able to keep up with the vast growth of new Internet Web sites (Aftab, 2001).

Search engine filters also have been developed to help counter the access of inappropriate sites by children. Examples of child-appropriate search engines are *Yahooligans!, Ask Jeeves for Kids,* and *DIG* (Disney's search engine; Aftab, 2001). *Yahooligans!* and *DIG* both use humans as reviewers for Web sites rather than filtering software

(Aftab, 2001). Obviously, the use of these child-appropriate search engines, as opposed to an adult search engine, limits the number of accessible sites and reduces the chances of children stumbling upon inappropriate material (Aftab, 2001). Further development in the area of filters and search engines is still necessary. As part of this work, Mitchell, Finkelhor, and Wolak (2005b) have suggested that evaluating filters in a real family environment and continuing to develop improved blocking software is necessary.

One of the most important ways professionals and parents can equip children for Internet safety, however, is simply through education (Aftab, 2001). Teaching children that the Internet can be a vital source of information is beneficial; however, they also must be aware of the potential harm that they can incur. For example, Wolak, Finkelhor, and Mitchell (2004) found that children and adolescents willingly agreed to meet with potential perpetrators after conversations online. In many cases, these potential perpetrators accurately portrayed themselves and presented as adults looking to engage in sexual relationships with children and adolescents. In addition, many of the surveyed children and adolescents indicated that they had strong feelings for these adults (e.g., they expressed feelings of love; Wolak et al., 2004). Mitchell, Finkelhor, and Wolak (2003) also found that only one-quarter of children in a recent study were distressed after viewing inappropriate material.

Thus, children and adolescents should be informed in a candid discussion (Wolak et al., 2004) that "going online" is similar to going outside, in that children should always be aware of strangers, never provide personal information to anyone, and alert their parents of any suspicious Web sites or interactions while on the Internet (Calcetas-Santos, 2001). Further, adolescents engaging in online conversations with a third party should be educated of the potential dangers and criminal nature of the relationship resulting from unsafe Internet practices (Wolak et al., 2004). It is also important to understand that, in light of recent research, family members and acquaintances may be using the Internet to target children close to them. Therefore, similar to other information provided to families about potential perpetrators, the definition of Internet victimization must be expanded (Mitchell et al., 2005a). In the end, child protection on the Internet requires increasing dissemination of information among researchers, involving parents' associations and other networks as educators, and designing research programs to help us further understand the problem (Aftab, 2001). Thus, professionals should investigate the aspect of Internet harm when working with child sexual abuse victims and design age-appropriate strategies geared toward intervention and prevention (Mitchell et al., 2005a).

In addition to the Internet, media coverage and prevention strategies that use mass media are important aspects of the prevention of child sexual abuse (Hoefnagels & Mudde, 2000). Examples of mass media approaches to child sexual abuse prevention have included educational videos (Burgess & Wurtele, 1998) and campaigns (Hoefnagels & Baartman, 1997). In contrast, media reports about child sexual abuse prevention often center on specific cases (Kitzinger & Skidmore, 1995), taking a reactive rather than a proactive stance. For example, a study in the United Kingdom found that media reports often sensationalized child abuse stories and failed to provide information on broader social issues and the prevention of child sexual abuse (Kitzinger & Skidmore, 1995). Thus, media reports after an incident of child sexual abuse should focus on creating community awareness about the possibility of abduction, educating children, providing therapy for abusers, and ensuring that professionals working with children are screened for past offenses (Kitzinger & Skidmore, 1995). Further, the media may overfocus on abuse from outside the home rather than on incidents of child sexual abuse within the family (Kitzinger & Skidmore, 1995; Russell, 1983).

Researchers have evaluated the efficacy of media coverage geared toward the prevention of child sexual abuse. When mass media communication is well implemented, professionals have identified an increase in victim discloser (Hoefnagels & Baartman, 1997), particularly when interventions were initially put in place and shortly thereafter (Hoefnagels & Mudde, 2000). Given these findings, media campaigns aimed at child sexual abuse prevention appear to have increased the utilization and availability of educational materials, increased the number of reported cases of child sexual abuse, and increased the public's willingness to discuss the issue of abuse (Hoefnagels & Mudde, 2000). As mentioned previously, it is more appropriate to target the perpetrators of child sexual abuse rather than children. Thus, an important strategy in the prevention of childhood sexual abuse is to ensure that adults take responsibility for the abuse. Certainly, media messages aimed at perpetrators have the ability to inform the public that any sexual contact with children is wrong (Hoefnagels & Mudde, 2000).

Owing to the societal focus and "wide-net" needed to reach potential perpetrators, the Internet and other sources of media have the potential to play an important role in preventing child sexual abuse and promoting health. Corporate responsibility and community demands may shift the tide of the media to more proactive, preventative information for its viewers and better socialization and deterrence for perpetrators. Before media prevention of child sexual abuse can be targeted accurately, however, researchers must develop further programs and determine their effectiveness (Kitzinger & Skidmore, 1995). Only then can mass media prevention efforts become a worthwhile endeavor in terms of protecting our children and a valuable adjunct to the family-, school-, and community-based programs that are already being used.

CONCLUSION

The good news about prevention is that it is possible and that many individuals feel that there is a need for prevention in different levels of the community (e.g., Abrahams et al., 1992; Chen & Chen, 2005; Wurtele et al., 1992). Further, there has been a 31 percent drop in the reports of child sexual abuse from 1992 to 1998 in the United States (Jones & Finkelhor, 2001). Considering the drop in female victimization during this same time period (Jones & Finkelhor, 2001) and the increased reporting of child sexual abuse as a result of child-focused programs (Araji et al., 1995; Bolen, 2003), it is likely that these numbers reflect actual decreases in child sexual abuse (Jones & Finkelhor, 2001). Researchers, community leaders, and institutions that allocate research funds now need to uncover the key components that have led to these potentially promising changes and provide support for the components of prevention programs that prove to have the greatest utility. Although the family-, school-, and community-based efforts that were discussed here are likely to have continued usefulness in future prevention efforts targeting child sexual abuse, other considerations should be made as well.

One such important area for prevention efforts is the way in which research funding is allocated. Increasing funding for community programs and research that target prevention efforts for potential perpetrators and for the improvement of health in interpersonal relationships may deter the development of sexually abusive behaviors (Renk et al., 2002; Trudell & Whatley, 1988). In particular, it appears that research benefiting children and adolescents is sorely lacking, with only 3 percent of federal research dollars being allocated to child and adolescent research (National Science and Technology Council, 1997). Further, research on children (including the effectiveness of prevention programs) receives less than 8 percent of its funding from the private sector and from foundations, as compared to 43 percent and 93 percent of nongovernment funding that is given to health and transportation research, respectively (National Science and Technology Council, 1997).

Much of the research that has already been completed and many of the suggestions for potential future work on the prevention of child sexual abuse relies on examinations of protective and risk factors. Thus, much of the research is correlational, and not causal, in design. As a result, more studies are needed to establish the efficacy, effectiveness, and causality of prevention efforts. Future research also needs to address the ways in which programs are implemented. For instance, programs may be most effective during times of community reorganization, when they are inexpensive and easy to implement (Kellam & Rebok, 1992; Reiss & Price, 1996), or when a certain level of community involvement is achieved. Finally, as prevention efforts continue to target child sexual abuse, the coordination of efforts across all settings serving children and their families should remain the focus of these efforts. It is only with this coordination that family-, school-, community-, and media-based efforts can serve children and their families in a synergistic and highly beneficial manner.

REFERENCES

Abrahams, N., Casey, K., & Daro, D. (1992). Teachers' knowledge, attitudes, and beliefs about child abuse and its prevention. *Child Abuse and Neglect, 16,* 229-238.

Aftab, P. (2001). The technical response: Blocking, filtering, and rating the Internet. In C. A. Arnaldo (Ed.), *Child abuse on the Internet: Ending the silence* (pp. 135-140). Paris: Berghahn Books.

American Academy of Pediatrics (n.d.). *Sexual abuse prevention.* Retrieved December 17, 2005 from http://www.aap.org/pubed/ZZZ7PP1YA7C.htm?&sub_cat=1.

American Psychological Association (2001). *Understanding child sexual abuse: Education, prevention, and recovery.* Retrieved December 17, 2005 from http://www.apa.org/releases/sexabuse.

Araji, S. K., Fenton, F., & Staugh, T. (1995). Child sexual abuse: Description and evaluation of a K-6 prevention curriculum. *Journal of Primary Prevention, 16,* 149-164.

Barnett, O., Miller-Perrin, C. L., & Perrin, R. D. (2005). *Family violence across the lifespan: An introduction.* Thousand Oaks, CA: Sage Publications.

Berrick, J. D., & Barth, R. P. (1992). Child sexual abuse prevention: Research review and recommendations. *Social Work Research and Abstracts, 28,* 6-15.

Bolen, R. M. (2003). Child sexual abuse: Prevention or promotion? *Social Work, 48,* 174-185.

Boswell, G., & Wedge, P. (2003). A pilot evaluation of a therapeutic community for adolescent male sexual abusers. *Therapeutic Communities: International Journal for Therapeutic and Supportive Organizations, 24,* 259-276.

Bowen, K. (2000). Child abuse and domestic violence in families of children seen for suspected sexual abuse. *Clinical Pediatric, 39,* 33-40.

Briggs, F., & Hawkins, R. M. F. (1994). Follow-up data on the effectiveness of New Zealand's national school based child protection program. *Child Abuse and Neglect, 18,* 635-643.

Bronfenbrenner, U. (1977). Toward an experimental ecology of human development. *American Psychologist, 52,* 513-531.

Burgess, E. S., & Wurtele, S. K. (1998). Enhancing parent-child communication about sexual abuse: A pilot study. *Child Abuse and Neglect, 22,* 1167-1175.

Calcetas-Santos, O. (2001). Child pornography on the Internet. In C. A. Arnaldo (Ed.), *Child abuse on the Internet: Ending the silence* (pp. 57-60). Paris: Berghahn Books.

Carlyon, P., Carlyon, W., & McCarthy, A. R. (1998). Family and community involvement in school health. In E. Marx & S. Wooley (Eds.), *Health is academic: A guide to coordinated school health programs* (pp. 67-95). New York: Teachers College Press.

Chen, J. Q., & Chen, D. G. (2005). Awareness of child sexual abuse prevention education among parents of grade 3 elementary school pupils in Fuxin City, China. *Health Education Research: Theory and Practice, 20,* 540-547.

Cohn, A., Finkelhor, D., & Holmes, C. (1985). *Preventing adults from becoming child sexual molesters.* Chicago: National Committee for Prevention of Child Abuse.

Committee for Children. (1996). *What do I say now? How to help protect your child from sexual abuse* (Video). Seattle, WA: Committee for Children.

Crosson-Tower, C. (2002). *Understanding child abuse and neglect* (5th ed.). Boston, MA: Allyn & Bacon.

Daro, D. (1993). Child maltreatment research: Implications for program design. In D. Cicchetti & S. L. Toth (Eds.), *Child abuse, child development, and social policy* (pp. 331-368). Norwood, NJ: Ablex Publishing Co.

Daro, D. (1994). Prevention of child sexual abuse. *The Future of Children, 4,* 198-223.

Daro, D., & McCurdy, K. (1994). Preventing child abuse and neglect: Programmatic interventions. *Child Welfare, 73,* 405-430.

Davis, M. K., & Gidycz, C. A. (2000). Child sexual abuse prevention programs: A meta-analysis. *Journal of Clinical Child Psychology, 29,* 257-265.

Deblinger, E., Hathaway, C., Lippmann, J., & Steer, R. (1993). Psychosocial characteristics and correlates of symptom distress in nonoffending mothers of sexually abused children. *Journal of Interpersonal Violence, 8,* 155-168.

DeLillo, D. (2001). Interpersonal functioning among women reporting child sexual abuse: Empirical findings and methodological issues. *Clinical Psychology Review, 21,* 553-576.

Elliott, M., Browne, K., & Kilcoyne, J. (1995). Child sexual abuse prevention: What perpetrators tell us. *Child Abuse and Neglect, 19,* 579-594.

Finkelhor, D. (1984). *Child sexual abuse: New theory and research.* New York: Free Press.

Finkelhor, D. (1990). New ideas for sexual abuse prevention. In R. K. Oates (Ed.), *Understanding and managing child sexual abuse* (pp. 385-396). Philadelphia: W. B. Saunders.

Finkelhor, D. (1993). Epidemiological factors in the clinical identification of child sexual abuse. *Child Abuse and Neglect, 17,* 67-70.

Finkelhor, D. (1994). Current information on the scope and nature of child sexual abuse. *Sexual Abuse of Children, 42,* 31-53.

Finkelhor, D., Asdigian, N., & Dziuba-Leatherman, J. (1995a). The effectiveness of victimization prevention instruction: An evaluation of children's responses to actual threats and assaults. *Child Abuse and Neglect, 19,* 141-153.

Finkelhor, D., Asdigian, N., & Dziuba-Leatherman, J. (1995b). Victimization prevention programs for children: A follow-up. *American Journal of Public Health, 85,* 1684-1689.

Finkelhor, D., & Dziuba-Leatherman, J. (1995). Victimization prevention programs: A national survey of children's exposure and reactions. *Child Abuse and Neglect, 19,* 129-139.

Fryer, G. E., Kraizer, S. K., & Miyoshi, T. (1987). Measuring actual reduction of risk to child abuse: A new approach. *Child Abuse and Neglect, 11,* 173-179.

Gibson, L. E., & Leitenberg, H. (2000). Child sexual abuse prevention programs: Do they decrease the occurrence of child sexual abuse? *Child Abuse and Neglect, 24,* 1115-1125.

Gilbert, N. (1989). Sexual abuse prevention training: Issues of state intervention. In J. Hudson & B. Galaway (Eds.), *The state as parent: International research perspectives on interventions with young persons.* Dordrecht, The Netherlands: Kluwer Academic.

Hazzard, A., Webb, C., Kleemeier, C., Angert, L., & Pohl, L. (1991). Child sexual abuse prevention: Evaluation and one-year follow-up. *Child Abuse and Neglect, 15,* 123-138.

Hébert, M., Lavoie, F., & Parent, N. (2002). An assessment of outcomes following parents' participation in a child abuse prevention program. *Victims and Violence, 17,* 355-372.

Hébert, M., & Tourigny, M. (2004). Child sexual abuse prevention: A review of evaluative studies and recommendation for program development. In S. P. Shohov (Ed.), *Advances in psychology research* (Vol. 29, pp. 123-155). New York: Nova Science Publishers, Inc.

Henry, F., & Tabachnick, J. (1997). *Stop It Now! Vermont: A new kind of public health campaign.* Retrieved from www.stopitnow.com/stopvt.html.

Hines, D. A., & Malley-Morrison, K. (2005). *Family violence in the United States: Defining, understanding, and combating abuse.* Thousand Oaks, CA: Sage Publications.

Hoefnagels, C., & Baartman, H. (1997). On the threshold of disclosure. The effects of a mass media field experiment. *Child Abuse and Neglect, 21,* 557-573.

Hoefnagels, C., & Mudde, A. (2000). Mass media and disclosures of child abuse in the perspective of secondary prevention: Putting ideas into practice. *Child Abuse and Neglect, 24,* 1091-1101.

Jones, L., & Finkelhor, D. (2001). *The decline in child sexual abuse cases.* Retrieved December 17, 2005 from Office of Justice Programs at http://www.ojp.usdoj. gov/pressreleases/2001/OJJ01037.html.

Kaufman, K., Barber, M., Mosher, H., & Carter, M. (2002). Reconceptualizing child sexual abuse as a public health concern. In P. A. Schewe (Ed.), *Preventing violence in relationships: Interventions across the life span* (pp. 163-196). Washington, DC: American Psychological Association.

Kaufman, K. L., Hilliker, D. R., & Daleiden, E. L. (1996). Subgroup differences in the modus operandi of adolescent sexual perpetrators. *Child Maltreatment, 1,* 17-24.

Kellam, S. G., & Rebok, G. W. (1992). Building developmental and etiological theory through epidemiologically based preventive intervention trials. In J. McCord & R. E. Tremblay (Eds.), *Preventing antisocial behavior: Interventions from birth through adolescence* (pp. 162-195). New York: Guilford.

Kellogg, N. D., & Menard, S. W. (2003). Violence among family members of children and adolescents evaluated for sexual abuse. *Child Abuse and Neglect, 27,* 1367-1376.

Kendall-Tackett, K., Williams, L., & Finkelhor, D. (1993). Impact of sexual abuse on children: A review and synthesis of recent empirical studies. *Psychological Bulletin, 113,* 164-180.

Kitzinger, J., & Skidmore, P. (1995). Playing safe: Media coverage of child sexual abuse prevention strategies. *Child Abuse Review, 4,* 47-56.

Ko, S. F., & Cosden, M. A. (2001). Do elementary school-based child abuse prevention programs work? A high school follow-up. *Psychology in the Schools, 38,* 57-66.

Kouyoumdjian, H., Perry, A. R., & Hansen, D. J. (2004). The role of adult expectations on the recovery of sexually abused children. *Aggression and Violent Behavior, 10,* 475-489.

Laforest, S. M., & Hébert, M. (Unpublished Manuscript). Étude exploratoire des besoins des meres d'enfants d'âge préscholaire en matiére de prevention d'agression sexuelle. UQAM.

Leifer, M., Kilbane, T., Jacobsen, T., & Grossman, G. (2004). A three-generational study of risk for sexual abuse. *Journal of Clinical Child and Adolescent Psychology, 33,* 662-672.

Levenson, J. S., & Morin, J. W. (2000). *Treating non-offending parents in child sexual abuse cases: Connections for family safety.* Thousand Oaks, CA: Sage Publications.

Lewin, L., & Bergin, C. (2001). Attachment behaviors, depression, and anxiety in nonoffending mothers of child sexual abuse victims. *Child Maltreatment, 6,* 365-375.

Maker, A., Kemmelmeir, M., & Peterson, C. (1999). Parental psychopathology as a predictor of childhood sexual abuse. *Journal of Family Violence, 14,* 47-59.

Marziano, V., Ward, T., Beech, A. R., & Pattison, P. (2006). Identification of five fundamental implicit theories underlying cognitive distortions in child abusers: A preliminary study. *Psychology, Crime, and Law, 12,* 97-105.

Massey-Stokes, M., & Lanning, B. (2004). Commentary: School health and family and community involvement: Making a difference in the prevention of child abuse and neglect. *Adolescent and Family Health, 3,* 154.

McCloskey, L., & Bailey, J. (2000). The intergenerational transmission of risk for sexual abuse. *Journal of Interpersonal Violence, 15,* 1019-1035.

McMahon, P. M. (2000). The public health approach to the prevention of sexual violence. *Sexual Abuse: A Journal of Research and Treatment, 12,* 27-36.

Melton, G. B. (1992). The improbability of prevention of sexual abuse. In D. J. Willis, W. E. Holden, & M. Rosenberg (Eds.), *Prevention of child maltreatment: Developmental and ecological perspectives* (pp. 168-189). New York: John Wiley.

Mitchell, K. J., Finkelhor, D., & Wolak, J. (2003). The exposure of youth to unwanted sexual material on the Internet: A national survey of risk, impact, and prevention. *Youth and Society, 34,* 330-358.

Mitchell, K. J., Finkelhor, D., & Wolak, J. (2005a). The Internet and family and acquaintance sexual abuse. *Child Maltreatment, 10,* 49-60.

Mitchell, K. J., Finkelhor, D., & Wolak, J. (2005b). Protecting youth online: Family use of filtering and blocking software. *Child Abuse and Neglect, 29,* 753-765.

Myers, J. E. B. (1996). Societal self-defense: New laws to protect children from sexual abuse. *Child Abuse and Neglect, 20,* 255-258.

National Science and Technology Council. (1997). *Investing in our future: A national research initiative for America's children for the 21st century.* Washington, DC: Executive Office of the President, Office of Science and Technology Policy.

Nelson, S., & Baldwin, N. (2004). The Craigmillar project: Neighbourhood mapping to improve children's safety from sexual crime [Special issue]. *Child Abuse Review, 13,* 415-425.

Parker, H., & Parker, S. (1986). Father-daughter sexual abuse: An emerging perspective. *American Journal of Orthopsychiatry, 56,* 531-549.

Pelcovitz, D., Adler, N., Kaplan, S., Packman, L., & Krieger, R. (1992). The failure of a school-based child sexual abuse prevention program. *Journal of the American Academy of Child and Adolescent Psychiatry, 31,* 887-892.

Pransky, J. (2001). *Prevention: The critical need.* Bloomington, IN: 1st Books Library Press.

Reiss, D., & Price, R. H. (1996). National research agenda for prevention research: The National Institute of Mental Health report. *American Psychologist, 51,* 1109-1115.

Renk, K., Liljequist, L., Steinberg, A., Bosco, G., & Phares, V. (2002). Prevention of child sexual abuse: Are we doing enough? *Trauma, Violence, and Abuse, 3,* 68-84.

Reppucci, N. D., Woolard, J. L., & Fried, C. S. (1999). Social, community, and preventive interventions. *Annual Review of Psychology, 50,* 387-418.

Rispens, J., Aleman, A., & Goudena, P. P. (1997). Prevention of child sexual abuse victimization: A meta-analysis of school programs. *Child Abuse and Neglect, 21,* 975-987.

Roberts, J. A., & Miltenberger, R. G. (1999). Emerging issues in the research on child sexual abuse prevention. *Education and Treatment of Children, 22,* 84-102.

Romano, N., Casey, K., & Daro, D. (1990). *Schools and child abuse: A national survey of principals' attitudes, beliefs, and practices.* Chicago: National Committee for the Prevention of Child Abuse.

Rumstein-McKean, O., & Hensley, J. (2001). Interpersonal and family functioning of female survivors of child sexual abuse. *Clinical Psychology Review, 21,* 471-490.

Russell, D. E. (1983). The incidence and prevalence of intrafamilial and extrafamilial sexual abuse of female children. *Child Abuse and Neglect, 7,* 133-146.

Russell, D. E. (1986). *The secret trauma: Incest in the lives of girls and women.* New York: Basic Books.

Tang, C. S., & Yan, E. C. (2004). Intention to participate in child sexual abuse prevention programs: A study of Chinese adults in Hong Kong. *Child Abuse and Neglect, 28,* 1187-1197.

Trudell, B., & Whatley, M. (1988). School sexual abuse prevention: Unintended consequences and dilemmas. *Child Abuse and Neglect, 12,* 103-113.

U.S. Department of Justice. (2005, December 19). *Citizen's guide to United States federal exploitation and obscenity laws.* Retrieved on December 27, 2005 from http://www.usdoj.gov/criminal/ceos/citizensguide_sexualabuse.html.

Wolak, J., Finkelhor, D., & Mitchell, K. (2004). Internet-initiated sex crimes against minors: Implications for prevention based on findings from a national study. *Journal of Adolescent Health, 35,* 424.e11-424.e20.

Wolfe, D. (1993). Child abuse intervention research: Implications for policy. In D. Cicchetti & S. L. Toth (Eds.), *Child abuse, child development, and social policy* (pp. 369-398). Norwood, NJ: Ablex Publishing Co.

Wurtele, S. K. (2002). School-based child sexual abuse prevention. In P. A. Schewe (Ed.), *Preventing violence in relationships: Interventions across the life span* (pp. 9-25). Washington, DC: American Psychological Association.

Wurtele, S. K., Kvaternick, M., & Franklin, C. F. (1992). Sexual abuse prevention for preschoolers: A survey of parents' behaviors, attitudes, and beliefs. *Journal of Child Sexual Abuse, 1,* 113-128.

Wurtele, S. K., Marrs, S. R., & Miller-Perrin, C. L. (1987). Practice makes perfect? The role of participant modeling in sexual abuse prevention programs. *Journal of Child Sexual Abuse, 1,* 113-128.

Wurtele, S. K., & Miller-Perrin, C. L. (1992). *Preventing child sexual abuse: Sharing the responsibility.* Lincoln, NE: University of Nebraska Press.

Chapter 11

Policy and Practice Implications

Rachel Evelyn Goldsmith
Sharon Shin Shin Tang
Jennifer J. Freyd

INTRODUCTION

Child sexual abuse (CSA) occurs at high rates in the United States and worldwide and it is associated with numerous negative consequences (Freyd et al., 2005). Yet, CSA is difficult to contemplate and discuss. Acknowledging the existence and the extent of CSA challenges many of the ways people attempt to understand individual and societal dynamics. CSA threatens people's belief in a just world (Janoff-Bulman, 1992), their trust in the benevolence of caregivers and other authority figures (see Freyd, 1996), and their conceptualizations of primarily genetic or biological models of psychological distress (Ross, 2000). Within some branches of the mental health profession, psychologists have long speculated and observed that both victims of CSA and larger societies may develop cognitive and emotional defenses to protect themselves from awareness of such abuse (Herman, 1992; Miller, 1984). Only recently have researchers begun to report empirical data that illuminate how such defenses operate (DePrince & Freyd, 1999).

Although inhibiting awareness for CSA can protect survivors and others from some degree of pain and discomfort, this response ultimately exacerbates abuse and its effects. Avoiding the topic of CSA may prevent the funding of relevant research and treatment ini-

Manuscript preparation was supported by the University of Oregon Foundation's Fund for Research on Trauma and Oppression.

Handbook of Social Work in Child and Adolescent Sexual Abuse
doi:10.1300/5804_11

tiatives, preclude public consciousness regarding the scope and severity of child maltreatment, underscore survivors' experiences of shame and isolation, and ultimately contribute to further instances of abuse. To reduce the occurrence of CSA and mitigate its effects, it is important to understand the phenomena involved in the impaired awareness for this form of trauma that is present on both individual and cultural levels. Other specific goals, including integrating current scientific efforts, increasing funding allocations, and incorporating trauma training into medical and psychological education, are also crucial for lowering the rates and impact of child sexual abuse.

PREVALENCE AND CONSEQUENCES OF CHILD SEXUAL ABUSE

Child sexual abuse is a relatively common phenomenon. Research indicates that in the United States, approximately 30 percent of women and 13 percent of men report having had sexual contact with adults as children (Bolen & Scannapieco, 1999; Finkelhor, 1994). Several factors are likely to contribute to underestimates of CSA prevalence, including victims' underreporting and memory failure (Fergusson, Horwood, & Woodward, 2000; Freyd, 1996). Most perpetrators of CSA are family members or others close to the child (Finkelhor, 1994). A 1996 report from the Department of Justice estimated rape and sexual abuse of children to cost $1.5 billion in medical expenses and $23 billion total annually to victims in the United States (Miller, Cohen, & Wiersema, 1996).

CSA is associated with serious emotional and behavioral consequences. Survivors of CSA may exhibit both internalizing symptoms and externalizing symptoms (Berliner & Elliott, 1996). Though some victims of CSA do not demonstrate increased levels of anxiety, depression, and lowered self-esteem as children (Mannarino, Cohen, & Gregor, 1989), difficulties in these areas may appear in adolescence (Gidycz & Koss, 1989). Many sexually abused children do demonstrate post-traumatic symptoms such as anxiety, fear, and trouble concentrating (Conte & Schuerman, 1987), as well as behavior problems (Berliner & Elliot, 1996). Other common psychological sequelae of CSA include post-traumatic stress disorder, depression, self-mutilation, and suicide (Kisiel & Lyons, 2001; Molnar, Berkman, &

Buka, 2001; Molnar, Buka, & Kesslaer, 2001). Because victims of trauma frequently simultaneously experience many psychological conditions usually conceptualized as discrete (for instance, personality disorders and depressive disorders), Ross (2000) proposes that interpersonal trauma accounts for much of the "comorbidity" evident in psychiatric diagnoses.

Beyond its relations to traditional psychological diagnoses, CSA may disrupt processes of attachment, emotional regulation, and stress response systems (De Bellis et al., 1994). In addition, survivors are at risk for revictimization (Messman-Moore & Long, 2003) and criminal behavior in adulthood (Fergusson, Horwood, & Lynskey, 1996; Putnam, 2003). In a review of sexual revictimization, Classen, Palesh, and Aggarwal (2005) noted that CSA is the most extensively documented predictor of revictimization, and determined that individuals who are repeated victims of sexual violence often demonstrate problems in interpersonal relationships, self-schemas, coping capacities, shame, and self-blame. McClanahan, McClelland, Abram, and Teplin (1999) investigated links between CSA and prostitution in 1,142 women in jail. They found that CSA almost doubled the probability of prostitution experiences.

CSA also produces deleterious health effects. Victims of CSA report a greater incidence of gastrointestinal, headache, gynecologic, and panic-related symptoms (Leserman, 2005), in addition to an increased risk for abusing alcohol and other substances (Kimerling & Goldsmith, 2000). In a study of 296 college women who completed an anonymous survey, De Von Figueroa-Moseley, Landrine, and Klonoff (2004) found that participants who reported CSA were 3.8 times more likely than nonabused participants to be current smokers and were 2.1 times more likely to have commenced smoking before the age of fourteen. CSA can lead directly or indirectly to HIV infection (Johnson, 2004; Kimerling & Goldsmith, 2000; Zurbriggen & Freyd, 2004). Among 409 adolescents, Voisin (2005) found that individuals exposed to CSA were nearly three times more likely to report increased numbers of HIV-risk behaviors than nonabused participants were.

Research reveals gender differences in victims' CSA experiences and reactions. Females report more sexual abuse by family members and close others, and abuse that begins at a younger age, in comparison to males, who report more sexual abuse by individuals outside of their family and abuse that commences at an older age (DePrince & Freyd, 2002; Goldberg & Freyd, 2006). In an anonymous survey of 733 college students, Ullman and Filipas (2005) found a greater prevalence and severity of CSA among female students, as well as higher levels of distress and self-blame immediately after the abuse. Females also reported an increased reliance on emotional withdrawal and intentional forgetting compared with male students.

Coping processes following CSA represent a confluence of internal and cultural attitudes regarding abuse. Though general conceptualizations of traumatic stress emphasize the fear and arousal conditioning that frequently accompanies trauma, CSA, like other forms of interpersonal trauma, usually involves additional emotional reactions such as shame, guilt, and betrayal (Freyd, 1996; Lee, Scragg, & Turner, 2001). These emotions may be compounded by a society that often ignores or denies abuse (Herman, 1992). deVries (1996) asserts that experiences of traumatic stress should be conceptualized as an interaction between the characteristics of the stressor and those of the victim's post-traumatic environment. Indeed, data indicate that support following disclosure of abuse improves psychosocial outcomes (Berliner & Elliott, 1996; Ullman, 2003). Conversely, negative reactions following disclosure or victim blame can lead to considerable distress (McFarlane & van der Kolk, 1996).

IMPAIRED AWARENESS FOR ABUSE

The motivation for both survivors of CSA and others to keep abuse outside of consciousness is likely to produce a spectrum of impaired awareness (for a review, see Goldsmith, Barlow, & Freyd, 2004). Dissociation refers to the fragmentation of experiences, whereby elements of a trauma are not integrated into a person's consciousness or sense of self (van der Kolk, van der Hart, & Marmar, 1996). Although everyone experiences dissociation to some degree, some individuals display extreme levels of dissociation, and may meet criteria for dissociative disorders. When individuals are the victims of abuse, they often dissociate during the abuse itself as a form of self-protection and exhibit post-traumatic dissociation to avoid the pain that accompanies this betrayal. Extensive research documents the connection between traumatic experiences and dissociation (Kisiel & Lyons, 2001;

Macfie, Cicchetti, & Toth, 2001; Ogawa, Sroufe, Weinfield, Carlson, & Egeland, 1997). Extreme dissociation is rare in the general population and, as such, may be viewed as pathognomonic for trauma exposure (Briere, 2006). Though it is very uncommon, some individuals develop dissociative identity disorder. Most individuals with this condition experienced severe childhood abuse (Foote, Smolin, Kaplan, Legatt, & Lipschitz, 2006).

Dissociative processes can inhibit the encoding and memory for trauma-related information (DePrince & Freyd, 1999), and memory impairment has been observed in survivors of traumatic events (Herman & Schatzow, 1987; Kardiner, 1941). The Diagnostic and Statistical Manual of Mental Disorders, Fourth Edition, Text Revision (DSM-IV-TR; APA, 2000) lists "inability to recall an important aspect of the trauma" (p. 468) as one possible symptom of post-traumatic stress disorder. Elliott (1997) mailed a questionnaire to a random sample of 724 individuals from across the United States that included questions regarding demographic information, traumatic experiences, and memory for the traumatic events. Of the 505 individuals who returned the survey, 72 percent reported some form of trauma, and 32 percent reported having experienced delayed recall of the event. Delayed recall occurred most frequently among individuals who witnessed the murder or suicide of a family member, sexual abuse victims, and combat veterans.

In addition to investigations regarding memory impairment for traumatic events in general, there is extensive research documenting impaired memory for CSA. Briere and Conte (1993) investigated memory for sexual abuse in 450 adults in a clinical sample. Two hundred sixty-seven individuals reported that there had been some period in their life before the age of eighteen when they had no memory of their abuse. In a prospective study of memory for CSA in women, Williams (1994) interviewed 136 women seventeen years after their visits to emergency rooms resulting from the abuse. Williams found that 38 percent of participants failed to report the abuse, even though they did reveal other personal information. Fergusson et al. (2000) conducted a longitudinal study of young adults that revealed that about 50 percent of those reporting histories of CSA or regular physical punishment at age eighteen did not report these events at age twenty-one. Couacaud (1999) investigated memory for abuse in

112 adult women who had been victims of CSA. Fifty-nine percent reported that there had been some period of time when they did not recall some or all of the abuse they experienced. Earlier age at onset, chronicity, severity, and abuse perpetrated by a parent all predicted delayed recall. Though females are more likely to report delayed recall for CSA than males, this difference may represent an artifact of the moderating variables of gender, age at onset of abuse, and relationship to the perpetrator on delayed recall (Goldsmith et al., 2004).

In cases in which children are abused by parents or caregivers, awareness of the abuse may be maladaptive. Freyd's (1996) "betrayal trauma theory" explains the ways that children isolate abuse experiences from memory and consciousness to preserve necessary attachment relationships with caregivers. If children's environments contain repeated and inescapable abuse, preventing awareness of the maltreatment they experience may allow them to function to some degree. Therefore, abuse by a caregiver is more likely to produce amnesic responses and other features of impaired awareness than abuse by a noncaregiver. Studies that investigate memory persistence for abuse demonstrate greater levels of memory impairment for trauma perpetrated by caregivers than for trauma perpetrated by other individuals or for noninterpersonal trauma (Freyd, 1996; Freyd, DePrince, & Zurbriggen, 2001). Although initially helpful, dissociation and memory impairment can come at a cost. The development of dissociative tendencies is linked to revictimization (Kimerling & Goldsmith, 2000) and transgenerational violence (Egeland & Susman-Stillman, 1996).

Despite considerable evidence for substantiated reports of delayed accurate recall for abuse (e.g., Burgess, Hartman, & Baker, 1995; Corwin & Olafson, 1997; Herman & Schatzow, 1987; Sheflin & Brown, 1996), its occurrence is often regarded with skepticism. Proponents of a "false memory syndrome" have supported their claims by research data that demonstrate the occurrence of errors in memory and cognition for nontraumatic experiences (for a review, see Pope, 1997). However, inquiries suggest that it is not appropriate to generalize such results to the processing of traumatic events. Individuals are vulnerable to suggestions of memories for events that do not deviate greatly from their actual experiences; however, it is very difficult for researchers to implant implausible memories (Pezdek, Finger, & Hodge, 1997; Pezdek & Hodge, 1999). In addition, research demonstrates that memory persistence is not related to memory accuracy (Dalenberg, 1996; Freyd, 1998; Williams, 1994). Researchers have begun to identify the cognitive and neurological mechanisms that are implicated in impaired memory for abuse (Anderson et al., 2004; DePrince & Freyd, 2004).

Though critics of delayed recall for abuse identify unethical or misguided psychotherapists and suggestible clients as mechanisms for "false memories" (McNally, 2003; Loftus and Ketchum, 1994), these explanations do not account well for the fact that many individuals report delayed recall for abuse using anonymous survey methodology (Goldsmith et al., 2004). Although the concept of a "false memory syndrome" has not received empirical support with external validity, it appears to have been successful in generating doubt regarding the veracity of victims' delayed recall for CSA. Brown, Scheflin, and Hammond (1998) speculate that one reason that some individuals question the phenomenon of delayed recall for abuse involves their motivations to retain statutes of limitations for prosecuting abuse. The American Psychological Association (1995) explained that the news media exaggerated the occurrence of false or repressed memories. Media sensationalism may result in public acceptance of this "syndrome," which in turn has the potential to discredit abuse survivors and turn attention away from the real problem of CSA.

Both discrediting victims of CSA and focusing attention on a few specific perpetrators may help individuals to maintain what feels like a safe and comfortable distance from CSA. Unfortunately, one result of this impulse is victim blame. Denying the occurrence of CSA and its effects or vilifying victims are examples of the DARVO phenomenon (Cheit & Freyd, 2005). DARVO is an acronym that represents a three-step process: deny the behavior; attack the accuser; and reverse the roles of victim and offender. These defenses may protect individuals from awareness of the extent of CSA and the possibility that they or those for whom they care may be affected by sexual maltreatment.

DISCLOSURE OF CSA

Hanson, Resnick, Saunders, Kilpatrick, and Best (1999) state that almost 90 percent of cases involving CSA do not result in reports to authorities. Most CSA victims do not disclose abuse immediately, and some report never disclosing the abuse until their participation in research studies. For example, Finkelhor, Hotaling, Lewis, and Smith (1990) found that only about 40 percent of men and women disclosed their abuse experiences immediately; 24 percent of women and 14 percent of men reported disclosing the abuse at a later time; and 33 percent of women and 42 percent of men did not disclose the abuse before their participation in the study. The closeness between the perpetrator and the child increases the likelihood of delayed disclosure (Foynes, Freyd, & DePrince, 2006; Smith et al., 2000). Others have observed the phenomenon that some children recant true claims of having been sexually abused (Elliott & Briere, 1994; Jones & McGraw, 1987). Somer and Szwarcberg (2001) reported that the severity of childhood traumatization contributed to delayed disclosure of the abuse. Other factors affecting delayed disclosure were victims' valuing obedience to grownups and fears of social rejection, people, and the criminal justice system. Because it appears uncommon for victims to disclose abuse spontaneously, it is important that health professionals ask their patients about abuse experiences (Read, McGregor, Coggan, & Thomas, 2005). Among both children and adults, being asked directly about abuse markedly increases the prevalence rates for CSA in clinical samples (Briere & Zaidi, 1989; Lanktree, Briere, & Zaidi, 1991).

It appears that the cultural context of trauma exerts considerable influence on the likelihood that victims will be believed and supported following disclosure. McFarlane and van der Kolk (1996) comment that although the phenomenon of delayed recall among some female survivors of CSA has been contested, it did not provoke controversy when Myers (1940) and Kardiner (1941) observed the same response in male combat veterans. Although some studies suggest that male victims of CSA disclose their abuse less often than females (Finkelhor et al., 1990) or take longer to disclose than females (Alaggia, 2004; Kendall-Tackett, Williams, & Finkelhor, 1993), others indicate that gender is not correlated with latency of disclosure (Goodman-Brown, Edelstein, Goodman, Jones, & Gordon, 2003). Furthermore, there may be outside factors influencing these findings, such as the relationship to the perpetrator. For instance, females tend to be at a greater risk of intrafamilial abuse (Goldberg & Freyd, 2006), which, in turn, has been associated with delayed disclosure (Goodman-Brown et al., 2003). Ethnocultural factors also appear to affect responses to abuse disclosure. For instance, research studies of maternal reactions following CSA include the finding that African-American mothers were more likely to believe their children than European-American or Hispanic mothers were (Kenny & McEachern, 2000).

PROFESSIONAL RESPONSES TO CSA

Mental health professionals vary in the extent to which they are cognizant of the prevalence and effects of childhood abuse. When victims of CSA elicit treatment for symptoms related to their victimization, they are likely to encounter many health professionals with little training for or awareness of the effects of CSA. Courtois (2002) notes that the topic of traumatic stress comprises only a small part of most therapists' training. Other mental health professionals (Ross, 2000) report being actively discouraged from attending to trauma and its effects during their training. A dearth of knowledge regarding CSA among mental health professionals may exacerbate the effects of victims' own impaired awareness for abuse experiences. When individuals understand their symptoms as understandable consequences of the maltreatment they endured, they may experience reductions in self-blame and other internalizing behaviors.

When conducting intakes and assessments, many mental health workers do not ask about childhood abuse (Read & Fraser, 1998; Young, Read, Barker-Collo, & Harrison, 2001), and exposure to childhood abuse is frequently not detected (Bolen & Scannapieco, 1999; Briere & Zaidi, 1989). Because abuse survivors themselves frequently lack insight regarding the etiology of their distress, health professionals' awareness of connections between abuse and mental health is especially important. Survivors of childhood abuse are likely to seek counseling or therapy not because of the abuse itself, but for depression (Berliner & Elliott, 1996), or negative feelings about themselves or their relationships (Briere, 2002). Read and Fraser's (1998) research identifies clinician discomfort, insufficient resources, and a lack of training regarding trauma as some of the reasons health-care professionals do not ask about trauma. McFarlane and van der Kolk (1996) state that distancing and victim blame may constitute coping strategies that professionals may employ to protect themselves from others' suffering.

Many different therapeutic approaches may assist victims of CSA. Abuse survivors may benefit from cognitive-focused therapy (Cohen, Mannarino, Berliner, & Deblinger, 2000) and from interpersonal psychotherapy (Talbot et al., 2005). Behavioral approaches, informed by models of classical and operant conditioning, can also inform treatment with survivors of trauma (van der Kolk, McFarlane, & van der Hart, 1996). Briere (2002) extends these approaches in a model of conditioned emotional responses (CERs) or relational schema that result from interactions with caregivers during childhood. When therapists respond to conditioned stimuli with care and empathy, clients reorganize links between traumatic memories and CERs. Briere (1996) describes the self-trauma model of psychotherapy, which emphasizes the development of self-skills that are compromised by relational experiences, including careful attention to the intensity, pace, and focus of therapy. The emotional regulation component of Linehan's (1993) dialectical behavior therapy (DBT) may be especially helpful for victims of CSA and other trauma. Follette, Ruzek, and Abueg (1998) describe a contextual-ecological perspective that evaluates clients' symptoms and problems in the past and present contexts in which these incidents commenced and the children perpetuated. This approach may be especially useful in terms of viewing deficits in awareness and disruptions in self-schemas as defenses that were once functional adaptations. It is currently not clear which approach is preferable when treating individuals affected by CSA. Martsolf and Draucker (2005) evaluated twenty-six outcome studies and two meta-analyses of abuse-focused psychotherapy for adults who experienced CSA. Abuse-focused psychotherapy ameliorated depression and post-traumatic symptoms, although no one therapeutic approach emerged as superior to others.

Although many psychologists have considered how traumatic stress perspectives may inform therapy with abuse victims, many individuals who experience CSA are unlikely to encounter therapists with expertise in this area. Read et al. (2005) found that often mental health professionals do not detect most cases of CSA. In a study by Agar and Read (2002), mental health professionals who were aware of their clients' abuse histories only referred to the abuse in 36 percent of their case summary formulations and 33 percent of their treatment plans. Abuse-focused therapy was provided to clients in only 22 percent of cases. Champion, Shipman, Bonner, Hensley, and Howe (2003) examined approaches to training in child abuse and neglect in doctoral programs in clinical counseling and school psychology accredited by the American Psychological Association. Based on data collected from programs' training directors, Champion and colleagues (2003) found that most programs addressed child maltreatment, but noted that training in this area did not meet the APA recommendations for competence in child abuse and neglect, and that it had not improved over the course of the previous decade. The data discussed earlier in the section indicate that professional training should increase both therapists' abilities to detect abuse and their understanding of the importance of its effects.

It is also crucial that medical professionals receive thorough training in responses to child maltreatment, including child sexual abuse. Patients' sexual abuse histories are often undetected by medical professionals (Leserman, 2005). Heger, Ticson, Velasquez, and Bernier (2002) examined data from 2,384 children. They found that only 4 percent of children referred for medical evaluations related to sexual abuse had medical examinations with abnormalities. Because abuse detection is greatly improved by questioning, and many victims of CSA do not present to mental health care agencies, medical care should include screening for potential maltreatment. In addition, both medical and mental health professionals should be aware that victims' cultural backgrounds might affect their willingness to seek treatment, their responses to the abuse, and the levels of care to which they have access (Cohen, Deblinger, Mannarino, & De Arellano, 2001).

Research demonstrates inconsistencies in responses to abuse, including reporting procedures and legal action. To illustrate, Delaronde, King, Bendel, and Reece (2000) determined that most mandated reporters were inconsistent in their reporting when they suspected the presence of child maltreatment. Vieth (2005) quoted Anna Salter, who has worked extensively with child molesters for more than twenty years, stating, "In the interviews I have done, they (the perpetrators) have admitted to roughly 10 to 1,250 victims. What was truly frightening was that all the offenders had been reported before by children, and the reports had been ignored" (p. 10). Both health and criminal justice professionals may be reluctant to believe children when they report CSA. Lanning (1996) asserts that children should neither be immediately believed nor be disbelieved and offers methods for corroborating claims of CSA. Cross, Walsh, Simone, and Jones (2003) conducted a meta-analysis that revealed that child abuse cases were less likely to lead to filing charges and incarceration when compared with most other felonies, but that when cases were filed they were more likely to be carried forward without dismissal. Menard and Ruback (2003) investigated proceedings of CSA cases in Pennsylvania and reported that differing financial allocations for CSA cases across counties resulted in divergent rates of reporting, verification, and sentencing. Additional investigations are necessary to evaluate the efficacy of mandated reporting of CSA and the ensuing legal action.

Professional and public awareness of CSA is likely to be influenced by patterns of media coverage. Media attention to CSA often does not accurately reflect its most common characteristics. In an analysis of media coverage of sexual abuse, Cheit (2003) determined that the media emphasizes "stranger danger" and does not report cases of intrafamilial abuse with a frequency appropriate to their occurrence. When CSA is covered in the media, stories may reflect consumers' predilection for specific narratives as opposed to descriptions of ongoing issues. In recent years, prominent stories have included sexual abuse in the Catholic church and subsequent attempts to hide the story, as well as allegations of sexual assault by Michael Jackson. Though these events have many components that are relevant to the processes described earlier, media emphasis on such salient cases may obscure the full scope of CSA. Attention to these celebrity cases may reinforce assumptions that CSA is rare and far removed from the experience of most individuals.

High levels of skepticism about CSA allegations likely has to do with certain *child abuse myths* that are pervasive in our culture and serve to deny the reality of child abuse. Tamarack (1986) identified fifty myths about CSA that were prevalent in contemporary literature. A theme common to many of these myths is the idea that CSA is rare and that children lie or are mistaken about their abuse history. Cromer and Freyd (2007) reported a gender bias (males believing abuse reports less) and personal history bias (people who have not experienced trauma being less likely to believe trauma reports). Gender and personal history interacted such that trauma history did not affect females' judgment nearly as much as it affected males' judgment.

CSA AND PUBLIC POLICY

The major federal legislation that addresses child abuse and neglect is the 1974 Child Abuse Prevention and Treatment Act (CAPTA). CAPTA serves states by providing funding for research, prevention, assessment, treatment, investigation, and prosecution efforts (National Clearinghouse on Child Abuse and Neglect Information, 2006). CAPTA also oversees the Office on Child Abuse and Neglect and the National Clearinghouse on Child Abuse and Neglect Information. Though CAPTA enables many children and families to receive needed services, it fails to protect a great number of children who are victims of a range of abuse experiences, including CSA (Gelles, 2001). Gelles (2001) notes that although the system has suffered from predictable limitations, including insufficient funding, staffing, training, and legal support, each of these areas has been addressed with little improvement. Solutions must address the limitations of each worker and could include specialized graduate training tracks in child welfare.

Since CAPTA was enacted, national organizations have been established to address trauma and its effects. In 1985, the International Society for Traumatic Stress Studies was founded to promote the research and dissemination regarding trauma phenomena, as well as intervention and treatment strategies. The Leadership Council on Child Abuse and Interpersonal Violence (formerly the Leadership Council on Mental Health, Justice, and the Media) was created in 1998 by psychological, legal, and policy professionals dedicated to serving victims of trauma (Leadership Council on Child Abuse and Interpersonal Violence, 2006). The Leadership Council identifies their mission as the ethical application of psychological science to human welfare. In 2001, the Donald J. Cohen National Child Traumatic Stress Initiative was established to ameliorate services for children and adolescents exposed to trauma and to facilitate multidisciplinary efforts in the field (National Child Traumatic Stress Network, 2006). The initiative provided a series of grants to the Center for Mental Health Services (CMHS), Substance Abuse Mental Health Services Administration (SAMHSA), and U.S. Department of Health and Human Services, to launch the National Child Traumatic Stress Network (NCTSN). The NCTSN comprises fifty-four agencies that offer community-based treatment to children and their families who have been affected by trauma.

Another recent development is the establishment of Child Advocacy Centers (CACs) to enhance community responses to child sexual abuse, including legal proceedings (National Children's Advocacy Center, 2006). CACs attempt to incorporate a multidisciplinary team, a medical examination of the child, child advocacy, case review, and a thorough interview of the child, mental health services, and tracking of case progress. CACs may increase the likelihood that victims of CSA will receive integrated care and may facilitate prosecutions of perpetrators. Jackson (2004) proposes a systematic evaluation of these centers in order to assess their effectiveness and ameliorate the ways communities address the CSA issue. There is evidence that child abuse assessment services can increase the probability that charges will be filed following CSA (Joa & Edelson, 2004). Schene (1996) recommends early prevention and intervention services to assist people before abuse occurs or post-traumatic issues worsen, and highlights the importance of integrated community systems that involve schools, social services, mental health, law enforcement, courts, and mental health care.

Although these developments represent increased visibility and action for CSA, responses to victims are still beset with challenges. In the United States, each state differs in their definition of child abuse and the legal age at which a person can consent to sexual activity with an adult (Berliner & Elliott, 1996). Child Protective Services (CPS) refers to the public structure of intervention for victims of child abuse and neglect and operates on county levels across the nation (Schene, 1996). Professionals who work with children are accountable for reporting CSA and other forms of abuse and neglect, and CPS employees investigate their reports. However, many CPS agencies cannot respond adequately to suspected cases of child maltreatment (Schene, 1996). Further research is necessary to identify additional reasons for gaps in services and to determine how the system can better prevent CSA and serve victims.

The statute of limitations laws comprise an important issue in legal proceedings for CSA. Because research indicates that victims of CSA may exhibit impaired memory of the abuse, such limitations could prevent the prosecution of their perpetrators. Federal legislation has abolished statutes of limitations for childhood sexual abuse and decreed that all cases of sexual abuse may be prosecuted during the lifetime of the victim. However, many states retain statutes of limitations concerning CSA that are often limited to a few years. For example, in South Dakota, cases must be prosecuted within three years from the time victims were abused or from the time they recall the abuse. Since most sexually abused children do not disclose until an average of ten years later, such a statute bars most cases from going to trial.

Largely due to the highly publicized cases of sexual abuse by Catholic priests in the past decade, states are increasingly enacting new legislation. Massachusetts, the center of much attention in the Catholic Church scandal, has recently proposed a bill to lift their statute of limitations on criminal child sex abuse cases. However, neither does the bill include cases of incest and sexual crimes against older teens nor does it eliminate the statute of limitations in civil cases.

RECOMMENDATIONS

Freyd et al. (2005) offer several recommendations to improve research and care pertaining to CSA. Both professionals and victims are most likely to benefit from interdisciplinary research efforts. These may be most effectively synthesized through ongoing international consensus panels that address scientific and treatment initiatives related to CSA. These panels should increase the inclusion of traumatic stress perspectives, including CSA education, in mental health and medical curricula. Another area for focus is more accurate and extensive education for health and legal professionals, the public, and the media. Professionals should work toward increased visibility and dissemination of CSA research. Services for potential and current victims of CSA will be enhanced by comprehensive cost-benefit analyses of prevention and intervention initiatives. These recommendations will require additional financial allocations to address CSA and improve treatment. Currently, cancer research receives $2 in funding for every $100 allocated for research, whereas child abuse research receives only $0.05 for every $100 dollars of research funding (Putnam, 2001). Freyd et al. (2005) also suggest that the National Child Traumatic Stress Network should be extended to address the overwhelming public health sequelae of child trauma and supported to create new methods of treatment. The substantial psychological and financial costs of CSA constitute sufficient reasons to create an Institute of Child Abuse and Interpersonal Violence within the National Institutes of Health (NIH) (Freyd et al., 2005).

In addition to improving integrated approaches among professionals who encounter CSA, individuals working in these areas must form liaisons with prominent figures who can advocate for victims of violence and agencies that provide research and treatment for trauma. Krugman (1999) notes that policy changes necessitate an "iron triangle" that includes effective lobbying organizations, members of congress who "champion" the issue, and internal assistance from a bureaucracy that supports the initiatives. Because of the current dearth of such connections, the child protection system is ineffective when contrasted with successful political efforts in other areas of health policy. Krugman (1999) adds that there are few prominent congressional advocates who focus on reducing the impact of child maltreatment and characterizes both the lobby and bureaucracy for these issues as weak. Another important issue for advocacy involves insurance costs for victims of CSA. It is disturbing to consider that these individuals may be penalized by insurance companies for preexisting psychological conditions related to the abuse they experienced. Finally, professionals working with CSA should advocate for the abolition of statutes of limitations for prosecuting CSA in all states.

Within mental health disciplines, professionals involved in training must increase attention within mainstream psychology to the role of interpersonal violence. CSA directly affects far more individuals than schizophrenia, obsessive-compulsive disorder, and bipolar disorder combined, yet it may be viewed as outside the canon—an interesting yet nonessential topic suitable for a guest lecture or a tangential consideration. Perhaps because of the lack of attention to trauma within their own training, or because of their own defenses against trauma, psychologists may regard perspectives that accurately address the impact of trauma with suspicion. Mental health training programs that do emphasize environmental components of psychological functioning such as violence and trauma often accomplish this feat by layering these considerations on top of a framework that views psychological conditions as distinct and offers scant attention to environmental etiologies of dysfunction.

It is important to address the extent to which training in mental health is governed by tradition. For instance, psychopathology courses are often structured to address psychological conditions individually, although psychological conditions usually co-occur (Kessler et al., 1994), especially among individuals who experience post-traumatic symptoms (Kessler, Sonnega, Bromet, Hughes, & Nelson, 1995). If only approaches to individual disorders are presented, mental health professionals may emerge from graduate programs with attitudes toward treatment that reflect a piecemeal attitude toward functioning, rather than a perspective that accurately accounts for environmental contributions on mental health. Such approaches are unlikely to encourage mental health workers in asking clients about abuse and detecting maltreatment when it occurs. If mental health professionals are to play an active role in reducing the occurrence and impact of CSA, the prevailing framework is not only undesirable, but also dangerous and unethical.

Reducing the prevalence and impact of CSA and its effects is likely to require creative solutions across several professional domains. For instance, Bolen (2003) questions the prevailing emphasis among child abuse prevention programs on providing services to potential victims and states that targeting potential offenders may improve prevention efforts. In particular, school-based interventions that instill healthy relationship patterns may reach and instruct many individuals before they pose risks to others. Such interventions could specifically redress the problem of widely accepted but inaccurate child abuse myths (Cromer & Freyd, 2007).

In order to improve child welfare, we must address the cognitive and emotional defenses against abuse that affect survivors, professionals, and the public. Additional research can clarify some of the ways that such defenses may prevent optimal responses to CSA. Despite the cultural components that may exacerbate victim blame, there are strengths of cultures and communities that can protect individuals from CSA and assuage its effects (deVries, 1996; Goldsmith, Hall, Garcia, George, & Wheeler, 2004). Improving our response to CSA and its consequences necessitates adopting a perspective that views the issue not as one of individual dysfunction, but one that influences the overall health of communities and cultures.

REFERENCES

Agar, K., & Read, J. (2002). What happens when people disclose sexual or physical abuse to staff at a community mental health centre? *International Journal of Mental Health Nursing, 11*(2), 70-79.

Alaggia, R. (2004). Many ways of telling: Expanding conceptualizations of child sexual abuse disclosure. *Child Abuse & Neglect, 28*(11), 1213-1227.

American Psychiatric Association. (2000). *Diagnostic and statistical manual of mental disorders* (4th ed., text revision). Washington, DC: American Psychiatric Association.

American Psychological Association. (1995). *Questions and answers about memories of childhood abuse.* Retrieved August 2003 from the American Psychological Association Web site: http://www.apa.org/pubinfo/mem.html.

Anderson, M. C., Ochsner, K. N., Kuhl, B., Cooper, J., Robertson, E., Gabrieli, S. W., et al. (2004). Neural systems underlying the suppression of unwanted memories. *Science, 303,* 232-235.

Berliner, L., & Elliott, D. M. (1996). Sexual abuse of children. In J. Briere, L. Berliner, J. A. Bulkley, C. Jenny & T. Reid (Eds.), *The American Professional Society on the Abuse of Children handbook on child maltreatment* (pp. 4-20). Thousand Oaks, CA: Sage Publications.

Bolen, R. M. (2003). Child sexual abuse: Prevention or promotion? *Social Work, 48*(2), 174-185.

Bolen, R. M., & Scannapieco, M. (1999). Prevalence of child sexual abuse: A corrective metanalysis. *Social Service Review, 73,* 281-313.

Briere, J. (1996). A self-trauma model for treating adult survivors of severe child abuse. In J. Briere, L. Berliner, J. A. Bulkley, C. Jenny & T. Reid, (Eds.), *The American Professional Society on the Abuse of Children handbook on child maltreatment* (pp. 140-157). Thousand Oaks, CA: Sage Publications.

Briere, J. (2002, June). *Not just PTSD: The complexity of posttraumatic states.* Paper presented at the 1st Annual Vancouver Trauma Conference on Trauma, Attachment, and Dissociation. British Columbia, Canada.

Briere, J. (2006). Dissociative symptoms and trauma exposure: Specificity, affect dysregulation, and posttraumatic stress. *Journal of Nervous and Mental Disease, 194,* 78-82.

Briere, J., & Conte, J. R. (1993). Self-reported amnesia for abuse in adults molested as children. *Journal of Traumatic Stress, 6*(1), 21-31.

Briere, J., & Zaidi, L. Y. (1989). Sexual abuse histories and sequelae in female psychiatric emergency room patients. *American Journal of Psychiatry, 146*(12), 1602-1606.

Brown, D., Scheflin, A. W., & Hammond, D. C. (1998). *Memory, trauma treatment, and the law.* New York: W. W. Norton & Company.

Burgess, A. W., Hartman, C. R., & Baker, T. (1995). Memory presentations of child sexual abuse. *Journal of Psychosocial Nursing, 33,* 9-16.

Champion, K. M., Shipman, K., Bonner, B. L., Hensley, L., & Howe, A. C. (2003). Child maltreatment training in doctoral programs in clinical, counseling, and school psychology: Where do we go from here? *Child Maltreatment, 8*(3), 211-217.

Cheit, R. E. (2003). What hysteria? A systematic study of newspaper coverage of accused child molesters. *Child Abuse and Neglect, 27*(6), 607-623.

Cheit, R. E., & Freyd, J. J. (2005). Let's have an honest fight against child sex abuse. *Brown University Child & Adolescent Behavior Letter, 21*(6), 8.

Classen, C. C., Palesh, O. G., & Aggarwal, R. (2005). Sexual revictimization: A review of the empirical literature. *Trauma, Violence, & Abuse, 6*(2), 103-129.

Cohen, J. A., Deblinger, E., Mannarino, A. P., & De Arellano, M. A. (2001). The importance of culture in treating abused and neglected children: An empirical review. *Child Maltreatment, 6*(2), 148-157.

Cohen, J. A., Mannarino, A. P., Berliner, L., & Deblinger, E. (2000). Trauma-focused cognitive therapy for children and adolescents: An empirical update. *Journal of Interpersonal Violence, 15*(11), 1202-1223.

Conte, J., & Schuerman, J. (1987). Factors associated with an increased impact of child sexual abuse. *Child Abuse and Neglect, 11,* 201-211.

Corwin, D. L., & Olafson, E. (1997). Videotaped discovery of a reportedly unrecallable memory of child sexual abuse: Comparison with a childhood interview videotaped 11 years before. *Child Maltreatment, 2*(2), 91-112.

Couacaud, K. L. (1999). Recall of childhood sexual abuse: Abuse characteristics and clarity of memory. *Dissertation Abstracts International: Section B: The Sciences & Engineering, 59*(7-B), #3686, USA: University Microfilms International.

Courtois, C. A. (2002). Traumatic stress studies: The need for curricula inclusion. *Journal of Trauma Practice, 1,* 33-58.

Cromer, L. D., & Freyd, J. J. (2007). What influences believing child sexual abuse disclosures?: The role of depicted memory persistence, participant gender, and trauma history. *Psychology of Women's Quarterly, 31*(1), 13-22.

Cross, T. P., Walsh, W. A., Simone, M., & Jones, L. M. (2003). Prosecution of child abuse: A meta-analysis of rates of criminal justice decisions. *Trauma, Violence & Abuse, 4*(4), 323-340.

Dalenberg, C. J. (1996). Accuracy, timing and circumstances of disclosure in therapy of recovered and continuous memories of abuse. *Journal of Psychiatry & Law, 24,* 229-275.

De Bellis, M. D., Chrousos, G. P., Dorn, L. D., Burke, L., Helmers, K., Kling, M. A., et al. (1994). Hypothalamic-pituitary-adrenal axis dysregulation in sexually abused girls. *Journal of Clinical Endocrinology & Metabolism, 78,* 249-255.

Delaronde, S., King, G., Bendel, R., & Reece, R. (2000). Opinions among mandated reporters toward child maltreatment reporting policies. *Child Abuse & Neglect, 24*(7), 901-910.

DePrince, A. P., & Freyd, J. J. (1999). Dissociative tendencies, attention, and memory. *Psychological Science, 10*(5), 449-452.

DePrince, A. P., & Freyd, J. J. (2002). The intersection of gender and betrayal in trauma. In R. Kimerling, P. Ouimette, & J. Wolfe (Eds.), *Gender and PTSD* (pp. 98-113). New York: The Guilford Press.

DePrince, A. P., & Freyd, J. J. (2004). Forgetting trauma stimuli. *Psychological Science, 15*, 488-492.

De Von Figueroa-Moseley, C., Landrine, H., & Klonoff, E. A. (2004). Sexual abuse and smoking among college student women. *Addictive Behaviors, 29*(2), 245-251.

deVries, M. W. (1996). Trauma in cultural perspective. In B. A. van der Kolk, A. C. McFarlane, & L. Weisaeth (Eds.), *Traumatic stress: The effects of overwhelming experience on mind, body, and society* (pp. 3-23). New York: Guilford Press.

Egeland, B., & Susman-Stillman, A. (1996). Dissociation as a mediator of child abuse across generations. *Child Abuse and Neglect, 20*(11), 1123-1132.

Elliott, D. M. (1997). Traumatic events: Prevalence and delayed recall in the general population. *Journal of Consulting & Clinical Psychology, 65*(5), 811-820.

Elliott, D. M., & Briere, J. (1994). Forensic sexual abuse evaluations of older children: Disclosures and symptomatology. *Behavioral Sciences and the Law, 12*, 261-277.

Fergusson, D. M., Horwood, L. J., & Lynskey, M. T. (1996). Childhood sexual abuse and psychiatric disorder in young adulthood. II: Psychiatric outcomes of childhood sexual abuse. *Journal of the American Academy of Child and Adolescent Psychiatry, 34*(10), 1365-1374.

Fergusson, D. M., Horwood, L. J., & Woodward, L. J. (2000). The stability of child abuse reports: A longitudinal study of the reporting behavior of young adults. *Psychological Medicine, 30*, 529-544.

Finkelhor, D. (1994). Current information on the scope and nature of child sexual abuse. *The Future of Children, 4*(2), 31-53.

Finkelhor, D., Hotaling, G., Lewis, I. A., & Smith, C. (1990). Sexual abuse in a national survey of adult men and women: Prevalence, characteristics, and risk factors. *Child Abuse and Neglect, 14*(1), 19-28.

Follette, V. M., Ruzek, J. I., & Abueg, F. R. (1998). A contextual analysis of trauma: Theoretical considerations. In V. M. Follette, J. I. Ruzek, & F. R. Abueg (Eds.), *Cognitive-behavioral therapies for trauma* (pp. 3-12). New York: Guilford Press.

Foote, B., Smolin, Y., Kaplan, M., Legatt, M. E., & Lipschitz, D. (2006). Prevalence of dissociative disorders in psychiatric outpatients. *American Journal of Psychiatry, 163*(4), 623-629.

Foynes, M. M, Freyd, J. J., & DePrince, A. P. (2006, November). *Child abuse, betrayal, and disclosure.* Presented at the 22nd Annual Meeting of the International Society for Traumatic Stress Studies, Hollywood, CA.

Freyd, J. J. (1996). *Betrayal trauma: The logic of forgetting abuse.* Cambridge, MA: Harvard University Press.

Freyd, J. J. (1998). Science in the memory debate. *Ethics & Behavior, 8*, 101-113.

Freyd, J. J., DePrince, A., & Zurbriggen, E. (2001). Self-reported memory for abuse depends on victim-perpetrator relationship. *Journal of Trauma and Dissociation, 2*, 5-16.

Freyd, J. J., Putnam, F. W., Lyon, T. D., Becker-Blease, K. A., Cheit, R. E., Siegel, N. B., et al. (2005). The science of child sexual abuse. *Science, 308*, 501.

Gelles, R. J. (2001, August). *CAPTA: Successes and failures at preventing child abuse and neglect.* Testimony prepared for United States House of Representatives Committee on Education and the Workforce Subcommittee on Select Education, Philadelphia, PA.

Gidycz, C. A., & Koss, M. P. (1989). The impact of adolescent sexual victimization: Standardized measures of anxiety, depression, and behavioral deviancy. *Violence and Victims, 4*(2), 139-149.

Goldberg, L. R., & Freyd, J. J. (2006). Self-reports of potentially traumatic experiences in an adult community sample: Gender differences and test-retest stabilities of the items in a Brief Betrayal-Trauma Survey. *Journal of Trauma & Dissociation, 7*(3), 39-63.

Goldsmith, R. E., Barlow, M. R., & Freyd, J. J. (2004). Knowing and not knowing about trauma: Implications for psychotherapy. *Psychotherapy: Theory, Research, Practice, Training, 41,* 448-463.

Goldsmith, R. E., Hall, G. C. N., Garcia, C., George, W., & Wheeler, J. (2004). Cultural aspects of sexual aggression. In K. Barrett & W. George (Eds.), *Race, culture, psychology, and the law* (pp. 403-418). Thousand Oaks, CA: Sage Publications.

Goodman-Brown, T. B., Edelstein, R. S., Goodman, G. S., Jones, D. P. H., & Gordon, D. S. (2003). Why children tell: A model of children's disclosure of sexual abuse. *Child Abuse and Neglect, 27*(5), 525-540.

Hanson, R. F., Resnick, H. S., Saunders, B. E., Kilpatrick, D. G., & Best, C. L. (1999). Factors related to the reporting of childhood rape. *Child Abuse and Neglect, 23*(6), 559-569.

Heger, A., Ticson, L.,Velasquez, O., & Bernier, R. (2002). Children referred for possible sexual abuse: medical findings in 2384 children. *Child Abuse and Neglect, 26,* 645-659.

Herman, J. L. (1992). *Trauma and recovery.* New York: Basic Books.

Herman, J. L., & Schatzow, E. (1987). Recovery and verification of memories of childhood sexual trauma. *Psychoanalytic Psychology, 4,* 1-14.

Jackson, S. L. (2004). A USA national survey of program services provided by child advocacy centers. *Child Abuse and Neglect, 28,* 411-421.

Janoff-Bulman, R. (1992). *Shattered assumptions: Towards a new psychology of trauma.* New York: Free Press.

Joa, D., & Edelson, M. G. (2004). Legal outcomes for children who have been sexually abused: The impact of child abuse assessment center evaluations. *Child Maltreatment, 9,* 263-276.

Johnson, C. F. (2004). Child sexual abuse. *Lancet, 364* (9432), 462-470.

Jones, D., & McGraw, E. M. (1987). Reliable and fictitious accounts of sexual abuse to children. *Journal of Interpersonal Violence, 2,* 27-45.

Kardiner, A. (1941). *The traumatic neurosis of war.* New York: Hoeber.

Kendall-Tackett, K. A., Williams, L. M., & Finkelhor, D. (1993). Impact of sexual abuse on children: A review and synthesis of recent empirical studies. *Psychological Bulletin, 113,* 164-180.

Kenny, M. C., & McEachern, A. G. (2000). Racial, ethnic, and cultural factors of childhood sexual abuse: A selected review of the literature. *Clinical Psychology Review, 20*(7), 905-922.

Kessler, R. C., McGonagle, K. A., Zhao, S., Nelson, C. B., Hughes, M., Eshleman, S., et al. (1994). Lifetime and 12-month prevalence of DSM-III-R psychiatric disorders in the United States: Results from the National Comorbidity Study. *Archives of General Psychiatry, 51*(1), 8-19.

Kessler, R. C., Sonnega, A., Bromet, E., Hughes, M., & Nelson, C. B. (1995). Posttraumatic stress disorder in the National Comorbidity Survey. *Archives of General Psychiatry, 52*(12), 1048-1060.

Kimerling, R., & Goldsmith, R. (2000). Links between exposure to violence and HIV-infection: Implications for substance abuse treatment with women. *Alcoholism Treatment Quarterly, 18*(3), 61-69.

Kisiel, C. L., & Lyons, J. S. (2001). Dissociation as a mediator of psychopathology among sexually abused children and adolescents. *American Journal of Psychiatry, 158*(7), 1034-1039.

Krugman, R. (1999). The politics. *Child Abuse and Neglect, 23*(10), 963-967.

Lanktree, C., Briere, J., & Zaidi, L. Y. (1991). Incidence and impacts of sexual abuse in a child outpatient sample: The role of direct inquiry. *Child Abuse & Neglect, 15*, 447-453.

Lanning, K. V. (1996). Criminal investigation of suspected child abuse. Section I: Criminal investigation of sexual victimization of children. In J. Briere, L. Berliner, J. A. Bulkley, C. Jenny, & T. Reid (Eds.), *The American Professional Society on the Abuse of Children Handbook on child maltreatment* (pp. 246-264). Thousand Oaks, CA: Sage Publications.

The Leadership Council on Child Abuse and Interpersonal Violence. (2006). *What is the leadership council?* Retrieved May 26, 2006 from http://www .leadershipcouncil.org/1/us/about.html.

Lee, D. A., Scragg, P., & Turner, S. (2001). The role of shame and guilt in traumatic events: A clinical model of shame-based and guilt-based PTSD. *British Journal of Medical Psychology, 74,* 451-466.

Leserman, J. (2005). Sexual abuse history: Prevalence, health effects, mediators, and psychological treatment. *Psychosomatic Medicine, 67*(6), 906-15.

Linehan, M. M. (1993). *Cognitive-behavioral treatment of borderline personality disorder.* New York: Guilford Press.

Loftus, E. F., & Ketcham, K. (1994). *The myth of repressed memory: False memories and allegations of sexual abuse.* New York: St. Martin's Press.

Macfie, J., Cicchetti, D., & Toth, S. L. (2001). The development of dissociation in maltreated preschool-aged children. *Development & Psychopathology, 13*(2), 233-254.

Mannarino, A. P., Cohen, J. A., & Gregor, M. (1989). Emotional and behavioral difficulties in sexually abused girls. *Journal of Interpersonal Violence, 4,* 437-451.

Martsolf, D. S., & Draucker, C. B. (2005). Psychotherapy approaches for adult survivors of childhood sexual abuse: An integrative review of outcomes research. *Issues in Mental Health Nursing, 26*(8), 801-25.

McClanahan, S. F., McClelland, G. M., Abram, K. M., & Teplin, L. A. (1999). Pathways into prostitution among female jail detainees and their implications for mental health services. *Psychiatric Services, 50*(12), 1606-13.

McFarlane, A. C., & van der Kolk, B. (1996). Trauma and its challenge to society. In B. A. van der Kolk, A. C. McFarlane, & L. Weisaeth (Eds.), *Traumatic stress: The effects of overwhelming experience on mind, body, and society* (pp. 417-440). New York: Guilford Press.

McNally, R. J. (2003). *Remembering trauma.* Cambridge, MA: Belknap Press/ Harvard University Press.

Menard, K. S., & Ruback, R. B. (2003). Prevalence and processing of child sexual abuse: a multi-data-set analysis of urban and rural counties. *Law and Human Behavior, 27*(4), 385-402.

Messman-Moore, T. L., & Long, P. J. (2003). The role of childhood sexual abuse sequelae in the sexual revictimization of women: An empirical review and theoretical reformulation. *Clinical Psychology Review, 23*(4), 537-571.

Miller, A. (1984). *Thou shalt not be aware.* New York: Farrar, Straus, and Giroux.

Miller, T. R., Cohen, M. A., & Wiersema, B. (1996). *Victim costs and consequences: A new look.* Washington, DC: United States Department of Justice.

Molnar, B. E., Berkman, L. F., & Buka, S. L. (2001). Psychopathology, child sexual abuse, and other childhood adversities: Relative links to subsequent suicidal behavior in the U.S. *Psychological Medicine, 31,* 965-977.

Molnar, B. E., Buka, S. L., & Kessler, R. C. (2001). Child sexual abuse and subsequent psychopathology: Results from the National Comorbidity Survey. *American Journal of Public Health, 91*(5), 753-760.

Myers, C. S. (1940). *Shell shock in France 1914-1918.* Cambridge, England: Cambridge University Press.

Ogawa, J. R., Sroufe, L. A., Weinfield, N. S., Carlson, E. A., & Egeland, B. (1997). Development of the fragmented self: Longitudinal study of dissociative symptomatology in a nonclinical sample. *Development & Psychopathology, 9*(4), 855-879.

Pezdek, K., Finger, K., & Hodge, D. (1997). Planting false childhood memories: The role of event plausibility. *Psychological Science, 8,* 437-441.

Pezdek, K., & Hodge, D. (1999). Planting false childhood memories in children: The role of event plausibility. *Child Development, 70,* 887-895.

Pope, K. S. (1997). Science as careful questioning: Are claims of a false memory syndrome epidemic based on empirical evidence? *American Psychologist, 52*(9), 997-1006.

Putnam, F. W. (2001). Why is it so difficult for the epidemic of child abuse to be taken seriously. In K. Franey, R. Geffner, & R. Falconer (Eds.), *The cost of child maltreatment: Who pays?* (pp. 185-198). San Diego, CA: Family Violence and Sexual Assault Institute.

Putnam, F. W. (2003). Ten-year research update review: Child sexual abuse. *Journal of the American Academy of Child and Adolescent Psychiatry, 42*(3), 269-278.

Read, J., & Fraser, A. (1998). Abuse histories of psychiatric inpatients: To ask or not to ask? *Psychiatric Services, 49,* 355-359.

Read, J., McGregor, K., Coggan, C., & Thomas, D. R. (2005). Mental health services and sexual abuse: The need for staff training. *Journal of Trauma & Dissociation, 7*(1), 33-50.

Ross, C. A. (2000). *The trauma model: A solution to the problem of comorbidity in psychiatry.* Richardson, TX: Manitou Communications, Inc.

Schene, P. (1996). Child abuse and neglect policy: History, models, and future directions. In J. Briere, L. Berliner, J. A. Bulkley, C. Jenny, & T. Reid (Eds.), *The American Professional Society on the Abuse of Children handbook on child maltreatment* (pp. 385-397). Thousand Oaks, CA: Sage Publications.

Sheflin, A. A., & Brown, D. (1996). Repressed memory or dissociative amnesia: What the science says. *Journal of Psychiatry and Law, 24,* 143-188.

Smith, D., Letourneau, E. J., Saunders, B. E., Kilpatrick, D. G., Resnick, H. S., & Best, C. L. (2000). Delay in disclosure of childhood rape: Results from a national survey. *Child Abuse and Neglect, 24,* 273-287.

Somer, E., & Szwarcberg S. (2001). Variables in delayed disclosure of childhood sexual abuse. *American Journal of Orthopsychiatry, 71*(3), 332-341.

Talbot, N. L., Conwell, Y., O'Hara, M. W., Stuart, S., Ward, E. A., Gamble S.A., et al. (2005). Interpersonal psychotherapy for depressed women with sexual abuse histories: A pilot study in a community mental health center. *Journal of Nervous and Mental Disorders, 193*(12), 847-850.

Tamarack, L. I. (1986). Fifty myths and facts about child sexual abuse. In E. Schlesinger (Ed.), *Sexual abuse of children in the 1980's* (pp. 3-15). Toronto: University of Toronto Press.

The National Child Traumatic Stress Network (2006). *The history of the NCTSN.* Retrieved May 23, 2006 from http://www.nctsnet.org/nccts/nav.do?pid=abt_hist.

The National Children's Advocacy Center (2006). *The CAC model.* Retrieved May 23, 2006 from http://www.nationalcac.org.

The National Clearinghouse on Child Abuse and Neglect Information (2004). *About CAPTA: A legislative history.* Retrieved May 25, 2006 from http://nccanch.acf.hhs.gov/pubs/factsheets/about.cfm.

Ullman, S. E. (2003). Social reactions to child sexual abuse disclosures: A critical review. *Journal of Child Sexual Abuse, 12*(1), 89-121.

Ullman, S. E., & Filipas, H. H. (2005). Gender differences in social reactions to abuse disclosures, post-abuse coping, and PTSD of child sexual abuse survivors. *Child Abuse and Neglect, 29*(7), 767-782.

van der Kolk, B. A., McFarlane, A.C., & van der Hart, O. (1996). A general approach to treatment of posttraumatic stress disorder. In B. A. van der Kolk, A. C. McFarlane, & L. Weisaeth (Eds.), *Traumatic stress: The effects of overwhelming experience on mind, body, and society* (pp. 417-440). New York: Guilford Press.

van der Kolk, B. A., van der Hart, O., & Marmar, C. R. (1996). Dissociation and information processing in posttraumatic stress disorder. In B. A. van der Kolk, A. C. McFarlane & L. Weisaeth (Eds.), *Traumatic stress: The effects of overwhelming experience on mind, body, and society* (pp. 303-327). New York: Guilford Press.

Vieth, V. I. (2005). Unto the third generation: A call to end child abuse in the United States within 120 years. *Journal of Aggression, Maltreatment, & Trauma, 12*(3/4), 5-54.

Voisin, D. R. (2005). The relationship between violence exposure and HIV sexual risk behavior: Does gender matter? *American Journal of Orthopsychiatry, 75*(4), 497-506.

Williams, L. M. (1994). Recall of childhood trauma: A prospective study of women's memories of child sexual abuse. *Journal of Consulting & Clinical Psychology, 62,* 1167-1176.

Young, M., Read, J., Barker-Collo, S., & Harrison, R. (2001). Evaluating and overcoming barriers to taking abuse histories. *Professional Psychology: Research & Practice, 32*(4), 407-414.

Zurbriggen, E. L., & Freyd, J. J. (2004). The link between childhood sexual abuse and risky sexual behavior: The role of dissociative tendencies, information-processing effects, and consensual sex decision mechanisms. In L. J. Koenig, L. S. Doll, A. O'Leary, & W. Pequenat (Eds.), *From child sexual abuse to adult sexual risk: Trauma, revictimization, and intervention.* (pp. 135-158). Washington, DC: American Psychological Association.

Index

Page numbers followed by the letter "t" indicate tables.

Handbook of Social Work in Child and Adolescent Sexual Abuse
© 2008 by The Haworth Press, Taylor & Francis Group. All rights reserved.
doi:10.1300/5804_12